# USING
# TECHNOLOGY
## *with* CLASSROOM
## INSTRUCTION
## *that* Works

### 2nd Edition

# HOWARD PITLER
# ELIZABETH R. HUBBELL  MATT KUHN

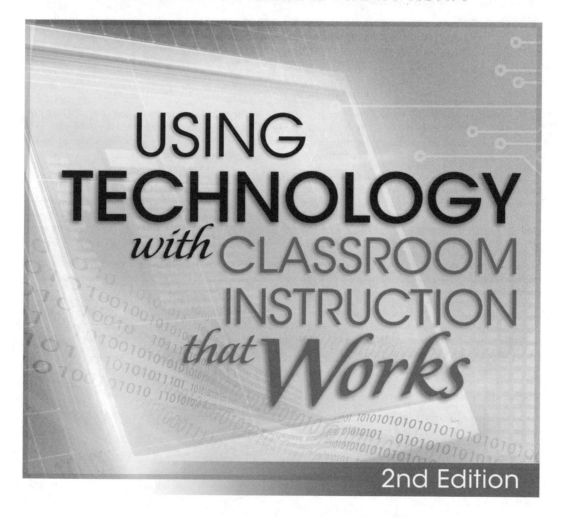

# USING TECHNOLOGY
*with* CLASSROOM
INSTRUCTION
*that* Works

## 2nd Edition

Foreword by Will Richardson

Alexandria, Virginia USA

Mid-continent Research for Education and Learning
Denver, Colorado USA

1703 N. Beauregard St. • Alexandria, VA 22311-1714 USA
Phone: 800-933-2723 or 703-578-9600 • Fax: 703-575-5400
Website: www.ascd.org • E-mail: member@ascd.org
Author guidelines: www.ascd.org/write

Mid-continent Research for Education and Learning
4601 DTC Boulevard, Suite 500 • Denver, CO 80237
Phone: 303-337-0990 • Fax: 303-337-3005
Website: www.mcrel.org • E-mail: info@mcrel.org

Gene R. Carter, *Executive Director*; Ed Milliken, *Interim Chief Program Development Officer*; Carole Hayward, *Interim Publisher*; Scott Willis and Laura Lawson, *Acquisitions Editors*; Julie Houtz, *Director, Book Editing & Production*; Ernesto Yermoli, *Editor*; Georgia Park, *Senior Graphic Designer*; Mike Kalyan, *Production Manager*; Valerie Younkin, *Desktop Publishing Specialist*

All web links in this book are correct as of the publication date below but may have become inactive or otherwise modified since that time. If you notice a deactivated or changed link, please e-mail books@ascd .org with the words "Link Update" in the subject line. In your message, please specify the web link, the book title, and the page number on which the link appears.

PAPERBACK ISBN: 978-1-4166-1430-2        ASCD product #112012        n8/12

Also available as an e-book (see Books in Print for the ISBNs).

Quantity discounts: 10–49 copies, 10%; 50+ copies, 15%; for 1,000 or more copies, call 800-933-2723, ext. 5634, or 703-575-5634. For desk copies: www.ascd.org/deskcopy

**Library of Congress Cataloging-in-Publication Data**
Pitler, Howard, 1952–
   Using technology with classroom instruction that works/Howard Pitler, Elizabeth Ross Hubbell, Matt Kuhn.—2nd ed.
      p. cm.
   Prev. ed. cataloged under title.
   Includes bibliographical references and index.
   ISBN 978-1-4166-1430-2 (pbk. : alk. paper)
   1. Educational technology. 2. Effective teaching. I. Hubbell, Elizabeth Rose. II. Kuhn, Matt. III. Using technology with classroom instruction that works. IV. Title.
   LB1028.3.U849 2013
   371.33—dc23
                                                                                2012011237

23 22 21 20 19 18 17 16 15                              7 8 9 10 11 12

# USING TECHNOLOGY with CLASSROOM INSTRUCTION that Works
## 2nd Edition

# List of Referenced Products

Adobe® Flash® and Adobe® Photoshop® are registered trademarks of Adobe Systems Incorporated.

AirMicroPad™ is a trademark of Scalar Corporation.

Android™, Google Apps for Education™, Google Calendar™, Google Chat™, Google Docs™, Google Earth™, Google Maps™, Google Sites™, Google SketchUp™, Google Sky™, and Google Videos™ are trademarks of Google Inc.

Angry Birds® is a registered trademark of Rovio Entertainment Ltd.

Animation Factory® is a registered trademark of Jupitermedia Corporation.

Artsonia's Kids' Art Museum™ is a trademark of Artsonia LLC.

AudioNote™ is a trademark of Luminant Software, Inc.

BBC Skillswise™ is a trademark of British Broadcasting Corporation.

Blackboard® is a registered trademark of Blackboard Inc.

Bluetooth® is a registered trademark of Bluetooth SIG, Inc.

BrainPOP® and BrainPOP Jr® are registered trademarks of FWD Media, Inc.

Bubbl.us™ is a trademark of LKCollab LLC.

Civiliation V™ is a trademark of Take-Two Interactive Software, Inc.

Common Core® is a registered trademark of Common Core, Inc.

Conflicthistory.com™ is a trademark of Conflicthistory.com.

Creative Commons® is a registered trademark of Creative Commons Corporation.

Cut the Knot™ is a trademark of Alexander Bogomolny.

Dance Dance Revolution® is a registered trademark of Konami Digital Entertainment Co. Ltd.

Delicious® is a registered trademark of AVOS Systems, Inc.

DigiTales® is a registered trademark of Bernajean Porter Consulting, LLC.

Diigo.com™ is a trademark of Diigo, Inc.

Discovery Education ® Streaming is a registered trademark of Discovery Communications, LLC.

DoodleToo™ is a trademark of DoodleToo.com.

DrawFree™ is a trademark of David Porter Apps, LLC.

Drawtree™ is a trademark of the University of Washington.

Dreamyard® is a registered trademark of The Dream Yard Drama Project, Inc.

eClicker™ is a trademark of Big Nerd Ranch, Inc.

Educational Testing Service® is a registered trademark of Educational Testing Service.

Eduware™ is a trademark of Eduware Inc.

eInstruction® is a registered trademark of eInstruction Corporation.

ePals® is a registered trademark of ePals, Inc.

Evernote® is a registered trademark of Evernote Corporation.

Excel®, Kinect®, PowerPoint®, SmartArt®, and Windows Media® are registered trademarks of Microsoft Corporation.

ExploreLearning™ is a trademark of ExploreLearning.

Facebook® is a registered trademark of Facebook, Inc.

FaceTime®, iMovie®, iPad®, iPhone®, iPod Touch®, Keynote®, and Quicktime® are registered trademarks of Apple Inc.

Flashcards Deluxe™ is a trademark of orangeorapple.com.

Flat Classroom™ Project is a trademark of Victoria Adams Davis & Julie Lindsay.

Flickr® is a registered trademark of Yahoo! Inc.

Gapminder® is a registered trademark of Gapminder Foundation.

Girls Inc. TeamUp!™ is a trademark of Girls Incorporated.

Global WRITeS™ is a trademark of Global Writes, Inc.

Glogster® is a registered trademark of Glogster, A.S.

Gmail® is a registered trademark of Google Inc.

Go! Animate™ is a trademark of GoAnimate.

Infinote™ is a trademark of Jeybee, LLC.

Inspiration®, InspireData®, and Kidspiration® are registered trademarks of Inspiration Software, Inc.

Intro to Math™ and Intro to Letters™ are trademarks of Montessorium.

Intuit® is a registered trademark of Intuit, Inc.

Isaac Newton's Gravity HD™ is a trademark of NAMCO BANDAI Games America Inc.

Jamendo® is a registered trademark of Jamendo S.A.

JASON Project™ is a trademark of The JASON Project.

Jigsaw Classroom™ is a trademark of Elliot Aronson.

Jing® is a registered trademark of TechSmith Corporation.

Ken-A-Vision® is a registered trademark of Ken-a-Vision Manufacturing Company, Inc.

Keynote Theme Park™ is a trademark of Wow You Design Inc.

Khan Academy™ is a trademark of Khan Academy, Inc.

Knowitall.org™ is a trademark of South Carolina ETV Commission.

Konus® is a registered trademark of KONUS Italia Group SRL.

LEGO®/Logo Robotics is a registered trademark of The LEGO Group.

Logger Lite® is a registered trademark of Vernier Software & Technology, LLC.

Make Beliefs Comix® is a registered trademark of Bill Zimmerman.

Maplesoft® is a registered trademark of Waterloo Maple Inc.

MathBoard™ is a trademark of palasoftware Inc.

Math Playground® is a registered trademark of Coleen King.

Micropoll™ is a trademark of Survey Analytics LLC.

MindMeister® is a registered trademark of MeisterLabs GmbH.

Moodle® is a registered trademark of the Moodle Trust.

Tech4Learning® is a registered trademark of Tech4Learning, Inc.

Text Compactor™ is a trademark of Knowledge by Design, Inc.

The Differentiator™ is a trademark of Ian Byrd.

The Edublogger™ is a trademark of Edublog

The Internet Archive™ is a trademark of Internet Archive.

The National Gallery of Writing™ is a trademark of The National Council of Teachers of English.

The Sims® is a registered trademark of Electronic Arts Inc.

ThinkFree® is a registered trademark of Hancom Inc.

Tiny Tower™ is a trademark of Nimblebit LLC.

TitanPad™ is a trademark of TitanPad.

Twitter® is a registered trademark of Twitter, Inc.

Ultimate Research Assistant™ is a trademark of Andy Hoskinson, LLC.

Vantage Learning™ is a trademark of Vantage Learning USA, LLC.

Vernier® is a registered trademark of Vernier Software & Technology LLC.

Vimeo® is a registered trademark of Connected Ventures, LLC.

Visual Dictionary Online™ is a trademark of QA International.

Visual Thesaurus® is a registered trademark of Thinkmap, Inc.

Visuwords™ is a trademark of The Logical Octopus.

VoiceThread™ is a trademark of VoiceThread,LLC.

Vtech® is a registered trademark of VTech Electronics North America, LLC.

Watch Know™ is a trademark of Community Foundation of Northwest Mississippi.

Web20Badges.com™ is a trademark of Sardan.

Webspiration™ is a trademark of Inspiration Software, Inc.

Wii® is a registered trademark of Nintendo, Nintendo of America Inc.

Wikipedia® is a registered trademark of Wikimedia Foundation, Inc.

Wikispaces® is a registered trademark of Tangient LLC.

WolframAlpha® is a registered trademark of Wolfram Alpha LLC – A Wolfram Research Company.

Wordle™ is a trademark of Johnathan D. Feinberg.

Writeboard™ is a trademark of  37signals, LLC.

Zooburst® is a registered trademark of Zooburst, LLC.

Zunal WebQuest Maker™ is a trademark of Zunal.com.

# List of Figures

## Chapter 6

## Chapter 7

## Chapter 8

## Chapter 9

# Foreword

Two billion people in this world currently have access to the web. By the end of this decade, five billion will be connected through smart phones, tablets, laptops, and who knows what other devices we'll have dreamed up by then. Those connections will be ubiquitous, and we've only just begun to imagine the ways in which our lives and our children's lives will change because of them.

For our kids to make the most out of this amazing, enormous change in the way we learn and live, we're going to have to step up our game as educators and fundamentally change our own practice, both professionally and personally. Regardless of our own comfort level with technology as a tool to help us learn or teach, we have to move the conversation from "if" to "how"—and we need to do that sooner rather than later.

This shift hasn't been easy in the two decades since computers began making inroads into schools. And for the systems in which we teach, it won't be easy moving forward. As author Clay Shirky writes, "Institutions will try to preserve the problem to which they are the solution." Schools are no exception. But here's the challenge: the problem itself has fundamentally changed: It's no longer about a lack of access to information or teachers, but rather about overabundant access, no matter where we are or when we need it. In no small way, this shift is going to require us to rethink and redefine the roles of schools and classrooms—and our roles as teachers—in students' lives. And at the center of that rethink will be technology.

This second edition of *Using Technology with Classroom Instruction That Works* is a great place to start that redefinition. As in the first edition, it's filled with specific examples of how teachers can begin to integrate a variety of technologies to enhance instruction and engage students more fully in the classroom. But more, it captures nicely the huge shift in the last half decade from using tools and applications on a local computer to using the myriad of new social technologies that reside "in the cloud" online. More and more, we will have to learn to learn effectively and efficiently in that space as the world grows increasingly connected by the day.

More important, this book supports the reality that technology in all of its forms is no longer an add-on to the work that we as educators do. It is now a fundamental part of the way we live and learn and teach. In every subject, in every grade, we need to be able to offer our students a variety of learning experiences that are steeped in the rich potential that these tools now offer, not just in terms of productivity but in terms of the creative and inquiry-based learning that we know works best for students.

Right now, our students (and we) have the chance not only to connect with the world, but to change it by sharing and resharing contributions online. This presents an enormous opportunity and an enormous challenge. In order to fully understand the potentials and pitfalls, we must begin to embrace this moment and these changes and help our students to make sense of them.

The shift from the local, time-and-place learning of the analog world to the globally connected, anytime, anywhere learning of the digital world will no doubt be the most important work we as educators do over the next decade. This book is a great place to begin that work.

—Will Richardson

# Introduction

What a different world we live in now than when we were writing the first edition of this book in the summer of 2006. Consider that, at that time,

- Karl Fisch had not yet released the now-seminal "Did You Know?/Shift Happens" (2006) presentation.
- You had likely never heard of the Android mobile technology platform or the iPhone, iPod Touch, or iPad mobile digital devices.
- We knew that Google was in the process of creating the Google Docs program, but it had not yet been released.
- The Google Sites program would not emerge for several years.
- The Gmail webmail service was still by invitation only.
- Twitter would first launch in July, but would not be widely used until the following year.
- Facebook had fewer than 8 million users (Vogelstein, 2007). By April of 2012, it had over 900 million (Facebook, n.d.).

Our students must learn not only how to use current technologies, but also how to evaluate which ones work best for particular tasks or projects. To that end, it is with great enthusiasm that we bring you the second edition of *Using Technology with Classroom Instruction That Works*. Technology books have a notoriously short shelf life due to the constant evolution of hardware, software, concepts, and ideas. Even when we were writing the first edition of this book, we knew that the book's content was likely to be short-lived—and yet, that first edition is still in the top-40 rankings on Amazon.com in the category of Education & Reference > Schools & Teaching > Computers & Technology.

We think we know the reason for this staying power: Although the technologies we discussed in the first edition may have evolved or even been replaced, the purpose driving their use has remained the same. For instance, in the first edition, we gave an example of a teacher who used the SurveyMonkey online questionnaire tool to gather data on his students' current knowledge and understanding of the Battle of Leyte Gulf. The need to gather data from students remains, but the tools for doing so have multiplied: Although SurveyMonkey remains a powerful and popular tool, it now has competition in the form of such programs as eClicker, Socrative, and Poll Everywhere that offer greater mobility for users.

Our intent is not to write a book about technology, but rather a book about using technology as one among several tools for providing good instruction. This way of thinking about technology is helpful for educators overwhelmed by the constant onslaught of the latest gadgets and applications. We have highlighted some of our favorites in this book, but educators should by no means feel limited by or obligated to choose any of the tools that we mention; instead, they should identify what they want a tool to do, then explore a few of the applications that do so, each with its own unique features. The advent of tablet devices and the slew of apps available for them can motivate educators to try out a variety of tools with students, and in so doing help them learn how to transfer their knowledge of existing technologies to ever newer inventions.

## ⏻ Why Technology?

Many exciting developments and findings have emerged since we last summarized the research on the effects of technology on student learning. For example, as multimedia tools have become cheaper to produce and more accessible to users, they have been shown to have a positive effect on student understanding and to help students fill in missing information and make better inferences (Chambers, Cheung, Madden, Slavin, & Gifford, 2006; So & Kong, 2007; Kendeou, Bohn-Gettler, White, & van den Broek, 2008). These findings are reflected in the growing popularity of the "flipped classroom" concept, in which teachers record lectures as video broadcasts (or "vodcasts") and assign them to students as homework, saving class time for high-level discussions and activities (Schaffhauser, 2009). Even long-established technologies have proven beneficial to student learning: The use of databases, for example, has been found to increase students' cognitive loads by helping them to classify and interpret data and communicate findings (Li & Liu, 2007).

Research indicates that the use of technology can best affect student learning when learning goals are clearly articulated beforehand (Ringstaff & Kelley, 2002; Schacter, 1999). Applied effectively, technology not only increases student learning, understanding, and achievement but also motivates students to learn, encourages collaborative learning, and helps develop critical thinking and problem-solving skills (Schacter & Fagnano, 1999). Of course, computers have long been used to help students improve their performance on tests of basic skills, but the application of technology in schools has progressed beyond this narrow purpose. As Russell and Sorge (1999) assert,

> The new technologies allow students to have more control over their own learning, to think analytically and critically, and to work collaboratively. This "constructivist" approach is one effort at educational reform made easier by technology.... Since this type of instructional approach, and the technologies involved with it, are recent developments, it is hard to gauge their educational effects. (pp. 1–2)

We would add that student achievement outcomes are also difficult to measure because many existing assessments do not adequately capture the higher-order thinking skills that new technologies have the potential to affect.

Research shows that integrating technology into instruction tends to move classrooms from teacher-dominated to student-centered learning environments. In such "constructivist" classrooms, students tend to work cooperatively, have more opportunities to make choices, and play a more active role in their learning (Mize & Gibbons, 2000; Page, 2002; Waxman, Connell, & Gray, 2002). Technology allows teachers to differentiate instruction more efficiently by providing a wider variety of avenues for learning that reach all learning styles.

Some of the differences in how learning occurs in technology-rich classrooms as compared to traditional ones may account for consistent findings that technology can be especially effective with at-risk and special needs students (Barley et al., 2002; Page, 2002). A research synthesis conducted by McREL suggests that the following characteristics of computer-assisted instruction (CAI) contribute to the learning of at-risk students (Barley et al., 2002):

- CAI is nonjudgmental and motivational.
- CAI gives frequent and immediate feedback.
- CAI can individualize learning through designs to meet students' needs.
- CAI allows for more student autonomy.
- CAI provides a multisensory learning environment (images, sounds, and symbols). (p. 97)

As we know, Benjamin Bloom created a taxonomy of learning activities that ranges from simple, factual recall of material to the application and evaluation of concepts (see Figure 1). Technology can certainly be used to provide immediate feedback for drill and practice, but it can also be used as a tool for the analysis, synthesis, and evaluation of information.

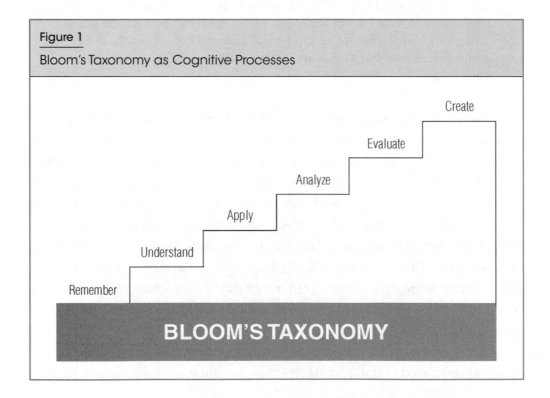

**Figure 1**

Bloom's Taxonomy as Cognitive Processes

Create

Evaluate

Analyze

Apply

Understand

Remember

BLOOM'S TAXONOMY

Dr. Rae Niles, director of curriculum and technology for Sedgwick Public Schools in Kansas, tells the following story about one of her students to exemplify the impact that technology can have upon student learning:

> Educators from more than 45 different school districts came to visit our high school during the first year of our one-to-one laptop computer initiative. Most came thinking they were going to see the technology and left realizing it wasn't really about the technology at all. It was about the teaching and the learning and how the technology had transformed what was occurring within the school walls.
>
> Typically, when visitors arrive at our school we conduct a 25- to 30-minute impromptu tour of the facilities, allowing for spontaneous conversations with faculty and students. Following the tour, the visitors then dialogue with a "panel of experts." The panel of experts consists of ten 16-, 17-, and 18-year-old students with a range of abilities and socio-economic status who have been asked that morning to serve as experts for our guests.
>
> There are two simple ground rules for the types of questions the guests can ask the students: 1) there is nothing off limits that can be asked, and 2) there is nothing the students should be afraid to answer if what they are answering is the truth. During one visit, immediately after outlining the process for the next 45 minutes, the superintendent from a neighboring school district, in a very accusatory tone, turned to one of the students and said, "So, how is this [the one-to-one laptop computer access] really making a difference for you?"
>
> The young man, Casey, looked at the superintendent then looked back at me, obviously struggling with his response and stunned at how to answer. There was turmoil clearly written across Casey's face. He didn't know how to answer, or even if he *should* answer the man's question. Clearly struggling with how to articulate his response, Casey looked the superintendent squarely in the eyes and said, "Sir, sir, I'm special ed. and I've been special ed. all my life. But with this thing here"—he pointed to his laptop computer—"I am just as smart as the next kid."
>
> To say you could hear a pin drop would be an understatement. Those in the room sat in stunned silence. The superintendent recoiled and immediately asked, "No, *really* how is it making a difference for you?"
>
> Casey responded, "I don't read so well and learning through my eyes is hard. With the laptop what I do is write what I am going to turn in, like an essay or answers to the questions the teacher has on the assignment, and then I go up to the menu bar and pull down to 'speak it.' Then I put on my headphones, close my eyes, and listen as the computer reads back

to me what I have written. If what I have written makes sense, then I know what I have written is OK to hand in. If not, then I can go back and make my corrections."

Casey was a senior, and for the first time since his placement in special education as a 1st grader he had been allowed to learn the way he learned best, not the way his teachers *assumed* he learned best. For almost 12 years, his learning style had been controlled by his teachers. Technology had allowed Casey to use his strengths to learn in the way he learned best.

Casey went on to graduate from high school and to successfully complete a two-year fire science degree from a nearby community college. He now works as a firefighter/EMT, and was married this past spring. The effect of technology on his success beyond high school may never be fully measured, but there is no doubt that technology allowed him to use his strengths to learn how he learned best and to help him believe he could be successful. (R. Niles, personal communication, 2006)

## ⏻ New Instructional Planning Framework

It is our intention, with this book, to show teachers how to effectively use the dynamic tools available to them to enrich their students' learning experiences, encourage project-based instruction, and give their students the skills they need to become lifelong learners and critical thinkers as they define the first half of the 21st century. This book is ideally a companion to *Classroom Instruction That Works, 2nd Edition* (Dean, Hubbell, Pitler, & Stone, 2012), and not a substitute; that book will provide a solid grounding for using the technologies discussed in this book.

Since 2007, McREL has updated the research behind *Classroom Instruction That Works,* as reflected in the second edition of that book. While the categories of strategies (see Figure 2) have not changed, the second edition analyzes more recent studies and modifies classroom recommendations accordingly. Most important, our thinking about the strategies and how to use them in the planning process has evolved since the first edition of *Classroom Instruction That Works.* The strategies are now organized in a framework for planning instruction (see Figure 3) to help teachers use them more purposefully and with greater intentionality.

The strategies in the first component of the framework, Creating the Environment for Learning, serve as the backdrop for every lesson. When teachers

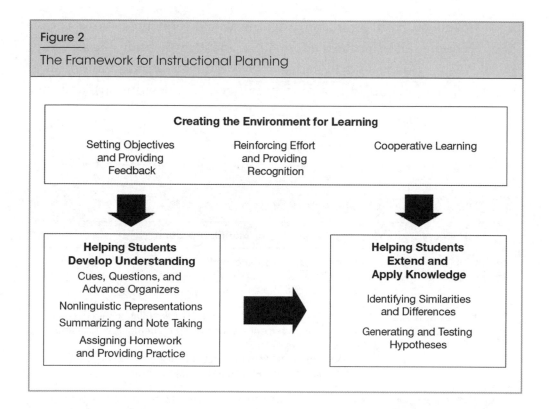

**Figure 2**

The Framework for Instructional Planning

**Creating the Environment for Learning**

Setting Objectives and Providing Feedback

Reinforcing Effort and Providing Recognition

Cooperative Learning

**Helping Students Develop Understanding**

Cues, Questions, and Advance Organizers

Nonlinguistic Representations

Summarizing and Note Taking

Assigning Homework and Providing Practice

**Helping Students Extend and Apply Knowledge**

Identifying Similarities and Differences

Generating and Testing Hypotheses

create an environment for learning, they motivate and focus student learning by helping students know what is expected of them, providing them with opportunities for regular feedback on their progress, and assuring them that they are capable of learning challenging content and skills. They encourage students to actively engage in and "own" their learning, providing opportunities for students to share and discuss their ideas, develop collaboration skills, and learn how to monitor and reflect on their learning.

The second component of the framework, Helping Students Develop Understanding, includes strategies predicated on the fact that students come to the classroom with prior knowledge and must integrate new learning with what they already know. The strategies included in this component help teachers use students' prior knowledge as scaffolding for new learning. Acquiring and integrating new informational knowledge requires students to construct meaning from, organize, and store the information. Constructing meaning is an active process: Students recall prior knowledge, make and verify predictions, correct misconceptions, fill in unstated information, and identify confusing aspects of the knowledge (Marzano & Pickering, 1997). Students organize information by recognizing patterns (e.g., a sequence of events, a description), and they

## Figure 3
### The Nine Categories of Instructional Strategies

| Category | McREL Definition |
|---|---|
| **Setting Objectives and Providing Feedback** | • Provide students a direction for learning and information about how well they are performing relative to a particular learning goal so that they can improve their performance. |
| **Reinforcing Effort and Providing Recognition** | • Enhance students' understanding of the relationship between effort and achievement by addressing students' attitudes and beliefs about learning.<br>• Provide students with rewards or praise for their accomplishments related to the attainment of a goal. |
| **Cooperative Learning** | • Provide students with opportunities to interact with each other in groups in ways that enhance their learning. |
| **Cues, Questions, and Advance Organizers** | • Enhance students' ability to retrieve, use, and organize what they already know about a topic. |
| **Nonlinguistic Representations** | • Enhance students' ability to represent and elaborate on knowledge using mental images. |
| **Summarizing and Note Taking** | • Enhance students' ability to synthesize information and organize it in a way that captures the main ideas and supporting details. |
| **Assigning Homework and Providing Practice** | • Extend the learning opportunities for students to practice, review, and apply knowledge.<br>• Enhance students' ability to reach the expected level of proficiency for a skill or process. |
| **Identifying Similarities and Differences** | • Enhance students' understanding of and ability to use knowledge by engaging them in mental processes that involve identifying ways items are alike and different. |
| **Generating and Testing Hypotheses** | • Enhance students' understanding of and ability to use knowledge by engaging them in mental processes that involve making and testing hypotheses. |

store information most effectively by creating a mental image of it. Acquiring and integrating procedural knowledge involves constructing a model of the steps of the process, developing a conceptual understanding of the process and understanding and practicing its variations, and using the process fluently or without much conscious thought (Marzano & Pickering, 1997).

Strategies in the third component of the framework, Helping Students Extend and Apply Knowledge, emphasize the importance of helping students move beyond "right-answer" learning to expanded understanding and use of concepts and skills in real-world contexts. These strategies help students become more efficient and flexible in using what they have learned. They involve the use of complex reasoning processes, which are necessary for students to use knowledge meaningfully (Marzano & Pickering, 1997).

## ⏻ New Categories of Technology

In the first edition of this book, we identified seven categories of technology that helped us think about how we use various 21st century tools. It is indicative of the ever-changing nature of technology that, when we revisited our work for this second edition, we found those seven categories to be no longer adequate. For example, the category of web resources now makes little sense, as the advent of cloud computing has effectively turned nearly every tool into a possible "web resource." Similarly, we have integrated the category of spreadsheet software into the larger category of data collection and analysis now that we have multiple tools that allow users to easily aggregate data from many sources and filter them in multiple ways to reveal trends and patterns. You can see our new and expanded list of nine categories of technology in Figure 4.

We have often been asked by readers or workshop participants why we did not include a category for display tools such as interactive whiteboards, LCD projectors, and document cameras. Our answer is that display tools without appropriate software are little more than overhead projectors; it is the marriage of hardware and software that enables us to modify our environment to learn or teach. We believe that instructional technology at its best allows the learner to do things that would be impossible, unsafe, impractical, or uninspiring to do otherwise. Although display tools are certainly necessary to have in the classroom, we feel that referring to them as "instructional technologies" is

**Figure 4**

The Nine Categories of Technology

| Category | Definition | Examples |
|---|---|---|
| Word Processing Applications | Applications that create documents in which the text can be displayed in linear or visual modes. | Google Docs, Microsoft Word, Wordle |
| Organizing and Brainstorming Software | Software that helps users to organize thinking, connect and categorize ideas, and show processes. | Webspiration, Inspiration, SmartTools |
| Data Collection and Analysis Tools | Tools that allow users to gather and analyze data. | SurveyMonkey, Microsoft Excel, eClicker, Poll Everywhere |
| Communication and Collaboration Software | Software that replaces or enhances traditional forms of communication with video, audio, text, or any combination of the three; allows users to share and discuss ideas, pictures, web links, etc.; and enables parties to work together even when geographically separated. | Skype, FaceTime, TypeWith.me, Diigo, Facebook, Twitter |
| Instructional Media (learner as consumer) | Technologies that provide or facilitate the creation of videos or recordings that are intended for use in learning. | BrainPOP, Discovery Education Streaming, and Khan Academy |
| Multimedia Creation (learner as producer) | Technologies that allow users to combine audio, video, music, pictures, drawings, or any combination into a final product. | PowerPoint, Keynote, Photoshop, iPhoto, Glogster, VoiceThread, iMovie |
| Instructional Interactives | Technologies that are manipulated by the learner to enhance understanding of a skill or concept, including games, manipulatives, and software that assesses the learner and differentiates the activity or curriculum based on the learner's needs. | MathBoard, Intro to Math, Star Chart |
| Database and Reference Resources | Resources that provide users with information and data. | RubiStar, Visual Thesaurus, Wikipedia, WolframAlpha, GapMinder |
| Kinesthetic Technology | Technologies that interact with the user's geographical or physical location and movements. (We have not included many examples from this category in this book due to its currently limited availability in the classroom; however, we expect the category to grow exponentially over the next five to ten years.) | Nintendo Wii, Xbox Kinect, GPS devices |

misleading; these are simply necessary utilities for the day-to-day business of learning.

The software that is included with many interactive whiteboards can fall into different categories of technology depending on how it is used. For example, if a teacher is using concept-mapping software to help students brainstorm, that would be classified as Organizing and Brainstorming Software, but if the class is playing an interactive learning game on the whiteboard, the software would be classified under Instructional Interactives.

## ⏻ How to Get the Most from This Book

The chapters within this book's planning sections follow a similar structure. We begin with a short overview of the selected strategy, followed by classroom recommendations and specific examples of technologies that support the strategy. All chapters include teacher- and student-created examples, many of which reflect actual lesson plans, projects, and products. Throughout, we also provide specific directions for when to use the tools, how they help students implement the strategies, and which tools work best for which tasks. We have kept our directions for skill-based use of the hardware or software minimal, as we truly want this book to be a practical guide rather than a procedural manual—and besides, the wide availability of free tutorials on the Internet makes providing detailed procedures unnecessary. The directions we do provide reflect the most current iterations of these products at the time of this book's publication.

The book concludes with a focus on how to plan for technology in the classroom. We include lessons we have learned from our work and discuss how technology is one among several important components in a rich 21st century learning environment.

Technology can transform the environment and procedures for communication, teaching, and learning. Collected in this book are a number of truly useful educational tools and examples, aligned to research-based instructional strategies (see Figure 5). We hope that this book will give educators the power to see technology being used as the "verb" of what students are doing, rather than limiting themselves to the "noun" of the content they are learning.

**Figure 5**

## Matrix of Strategies and Technologies

| | Word Processing Applications | Organizing and Brainstorming Software | Data Collection and Analysis Tools | Communication and Collaboration Software |
|---|---|---|---|---|
| Setting Objectives | X | X | X | X |
| Providing Feedback | X | | X | X |
| Reinforcing Effort | | | X | |
| Providing Recognition | | | X | X |
| Cooperative Learning | | | | X |
| Cues, Questions, and Advanced Organizers | X | X | X | |
| Nonlinguistic Representations | X | X | X | |
| Summarizing and Note Taking | X | X | | X |
| Assigning Homework and Providing Practice | X | | X | X |
| Identifying Similarities and Differences | X | X | X | |
| Generating and Testing Hypotheses | | X | X | |

## Figure 5

### Matrix of Strategies and Technologies—(*continued*)

| | Instructional Media | Multimedia Creation | Instructional Interactives | Database and Reference Resources |
|---|---|---|---|---|
| Setting Objectives | | | | X |
| Providing Feedback | X | | X | X |
| Reinforcing Effort | | | | |
| Providing Recognition | | X | X | |
| Cooperative Learning | | X | | |
| Cues, Questions, and Advanced Organizers | X | | X | |
| Nonlinguistic Representations | X | X | X | X |
| Summarizing and Note Taking | | X | | |
| Assigning Homework and Providing Practice | X | X | X | |
| Identifying Similarities and Differences | | | | X |
| Generating and Testing Hypotheses | | | X | |

# Creating the Environment for Learning

# 1

# Setting Objectives
# and Providing Feedback

In the first edition of *Classroom Instruction That Works* (Marzano, Pickering, & Pollock, 2001), the strategies of *setting objectives* and *providing feedback* were categorized together, as they are here. In the first edition of *Using Technology with Classroom Instruction That Works*, however, we separated the two strategies and accorded a discrete set of planning questions to each. These planning questions eventually morphed into the three-part framework reflected in the organization of this book, allowing us to recombine the strategies. Combining the two strategies reflects our thinking that setting objectives and providing feedback work together to help students know what their learning goals are and how they are progressing toward them.

## ⏻ Setting Objectives

Setting objectives is the process of establishing a direction to guide learning (Marzano, Pickering, & Pollock, 2001; Pintrich & Schunk, 2002). When teachers communicate objectives for student learning, students can see more easily the connections between what they are doing in class and what they are supposed to learn. By gauging their starting point in relation to the learning objectives and determining what they need to pay attention to and where they might need help from the teacher or others, students can minimize their anxiety about their ability to succeed (Dean, Hubbell, Pitler, & Stone, 2012). We have four recommendations for classroom practice related to setting objectives:

## RECOMMENDATIONS

- Set learning objectives that are specific but not restrictive.
- Communicate learning objectives to students and parents.
- Connect learning objectives to previous and future learning.
- Engage students in setting personal learning objectives.

Research shows that allowing students to set some of their own learning goals increases their motivation to learn (Hom & Murphy, 1983). Technology enhances this process by helping students to organize, clarify, and communicate learning objectives. Technology also provides teachers with access to resources that can help them to identify and refine standards and objectives. In this chapter, we will show you how to use the following technology tools to set objectives: *word processing applications, organizing and brainstorming software, data collection and analysis tools, database and reference resources, instructional media, instructional interactives,* and *communication and collaboration software.*

## Word Processing Applications

Word processors—be they traditional, stand-alone applications or collaborative, cloud-based ones—provide a simple way of creating tools and protocols for setting objectives. One such tool is a KWL chart, where students write down what they *k*now about a topic, what they *w*ant to learn about the topic, and what they have *l*earned at the end of the unit or activity covering the topic. This is a great way to activate prior knowledge and have students personalize their learning goals. KWL charts are simple to create using the draw tools in a word processor. In Microsoft Word, such a simple chart would be easy to make by clicking **Insert > Table** on the toolbar and selecting a three-by-two table. Though Microsoft Word makes creating such KWL charts easy, it does not have the advantages of a cloud-based program such as Google Docs, which allows for shared templates, digital feedback, and an online inbox. As Figure 1.1 shows, creating a KWL chart in Google Docs is simply a matter of inserting three vertical columns or drawing three vertical rectangles and then putting the appropriate headings in each column.

Why go through the effort to create an electronic chart when it would be easier to just draw one on a piece of paper? Recall that our second classroom recommendation is to communicate learning objectives to students and parents. If the KWL chart is electronic, you can include it in an e-newsletter, post it to your class website, or—best of all—share it on the cloud for student-centered use.

| Figure 1.1 | | |
| KWL Chart Created in Google Docs | | |
| What I/We **K**now | What I/We **W**ant to Know | What I/We **L**earned |
| | | |

To use Google Docs, you will first need a Google account. Your students will also need accounts in order to access the document. Google accounts can be created for free at https://www.google.com/accounts/NewAccount. (If your students are under 13 years of age, consider establishing a Google Apps for Education domain for your school, which allows you to assign accounts to each student.) To create a KWL table in Google Docs, you must first log on to your Google account, click the **More** tab on the toolbar, and select **Documents**. Then choose **Create > Document**. In the new document, click on **Table > Insert Table > 3 x 2**. Write the headings in the first row and save. It's a good idea to save the table as a template so others cannot overwrite it and so that students can easily access it. To submit a template to your domain template gallery, just follow these steps:

1. Go to https://docs.google.com and select the checkbox next to the document that you wish to save as a template.

2. Select **More > Submit to template gallery**.

3. Enter a short description, pick one or two categories for the template, and select a language.

4. Choose **Submit a Template**.

5. Your new template is now available at https://docs.google.com/templates under the My Templates menu.

Figure 1.2 shows an example of a Google Docs template filled in by a student at the beginning of a high school language arts unit analyzing dilemmas in the book *The Hunger Games*. This digital document could become part of a digital portfolio and is easily shared online; it also can serve as a student feedback loop and formative assessment. The "Learned" section would be filled out as the unit progresses and would serve as a check for understanding for students and teacher.

---

**Figure 1.2**

KWL Chart on *The Hunger Games*

| What I/We **K**now | What I/We **W**ant to Know | What I/We **L**earned |
|---|---|---|
| Dilemmas are difficult problems to solve with few right answers.<br><br>It is important to develop problem-solving skills. | How would I decide in dealing with the dilemmas in *The Hunger Games*, and how does this compare to the decisions of the main characters? | |

---

## Organizing and Brainstorming Software

This family of software includes the well-known titles Kidspiration (for grades preK–5) and Inspiration/Webspiration (for intermediate and older students). These useful tools provide an easy way for students to plan and organize their thoughts at the beginning of a unit, during instruction, and after a unit. One advantage to using software rather than traditional chart paper is that the graphic organizers can be saved, edited, shared, and stored as a part of a student's digital portfolio.

Allowing students to personalize their learning goals helps ensure that they understand what they are learning and why. It has the added motivating benefit of allowing students some control and voice in their learning. A very simple but effective way to help students personalize their learning goals is to create a template using Kidspiration, Inspiration/Webspiration, or similar organizing and brainstorming software.

As you present your broad learning objective, standard, or benchmark to your students, have them use a template such as the one shown in Figure 1.3, created by an Oregon high school teacher, to consider what they would most like to learn and what they might focus on to meet the learning objective. With teacher and student learning goals in place, the lesson's purpose is clear from the outset, and the instruction that follows becomes more meaningful. End the class period by reviewing what was accomplished toward meeting the objectives.

**Figure 1.3**

Organizing Template Created in Inspiration

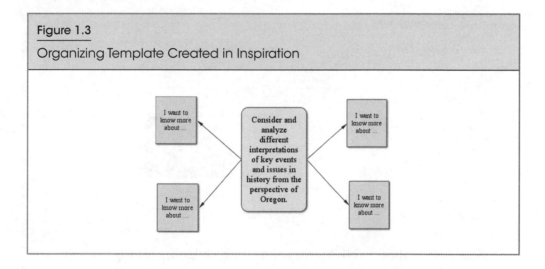

Another way to encourage students to personalize and track progress toward their learning objectives is with a KWHL chart (similar to the KWL chart mentioned earlier). Figure 1.4 shows a web created by Mr. Fua, a 4th grade math intervention teacher, using the MindMeister program. Mr. Fua begins a unit on fractions by asking his students the KWHL questions: What do you *know*? What do you *want* to learn? *How* will you find out? What do you *learn*?

Mr. Fua creates the KWHL template on his computer and then shares it with each of his students, who are able to open the template on their own school-provided iPads. As they complete the chart, the students create a clear visual of their current knowledge, which will help them make decisions about what else they would like to know. The "What do you know?" section gives Mr. Fua a clearer picture of his students' understanding and gaps about fractions; the "How will you find out?" box prompts students to plan their learning steps and to decide where and how to learn what they want to know.

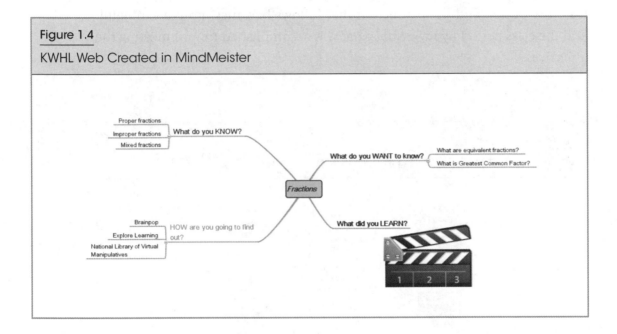

**Figure 1.4**

**KWHL Web Created in MindMeister**

Students without well-developed writing skills, including younger students, those with special needs, and second language learners, can often represent their knowledge best using graphics and symbols. In Kidspiration, students can draw the symbols they need using the Symbol Maker tool, which allows them to design practically any graphic using a variety of lines, shapes, brushes, and colors on a "canvas." And teachers can customize the symbol library in both Kidspiration and Inspiration by inserting, deleting, or creating a new symbol library of their choosing. This is exactly what one elementary teacher did as she was preparing her class to read the book *Knots on a Counting Rope* by Bill Martin Jr. She found graphics depicting the book cover, setting, and characters and made a custom symbol library for her students to use. They used Kidspiration to create webs showing what they knew about the book before and after reading the story.

To install a custom graphic into a symbol library, take these steps:

1. Place the graphic on your Inspiration document by going to **Edit > Insert Graphic** and selecting the graphic. (In Kidspiration, go to **Teacher > Enable teacher menu**, then click on **Edit Symbol Libraries** and **Import Graphic**.)

2. Open the Symbol palette and display the library to which you want to install the graphic.

3. Choose **Utility > Add Symbol to Library**.

4. Select **Standard Symbol Size** or **Actual Size**, and then click **OK**.

5. When your symbol is installed, it appears at the bottom of the Symbol palette entries and can be used just like any other symbol.

Students of all ages can also use their voices to record thoughts and ideas about their new learning. Recording a sound in Inspiration is easy. Simply select the symbol or topic with which you want the sound associated. Choose **Tools > Insert Video or Sound > Record Sound**. When you are ready to record the sound or voice, click the **Record** button on the display. You can record up to one minute of sound at one time. Be sure to hit **Save** when you are finished.

Because the technology allows users to modify information, edit plans, and easily add new learning, students can work on their KWHL charts throughout a unit.

Inspiration includes two templates that are worth exploring as you work with students to personalize their learning objectives. The first is the Assignment Completion Plan, which comes with Inspiration version 9.0 and higher and is located in the Thinking and Planning folder. Mrs. Maxfield, a high school family and consumer sciences teacher, uses the template shown in Figure 1.5 to help her students organize a "Build a Better Cereal" project. Her students will work in small groups to develop a new breakfast cereal that is both nutritious and appealing to consumers. The project requires multiple steps and due dates. The Assignment Completion Plan template serves as both an aid in the planning process, making clear the expectations and due dates, and as an advance organizer. Mrs. Maxfield's students can see at a glance the entire scope of the project and plan to accomplish each phase of the project by the due date. Because all students in a group share a common Inspiration document, they can each check on their interim progress and make sure the group stays on track.

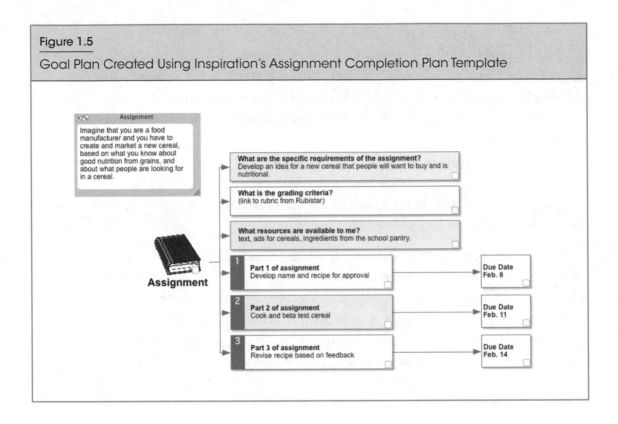

**Figure 1.5**

Goal Plan Created Using Inspiration's Assignment Completion Plan Template

This is a wonderful step-by-step approach that provides a great way for students to organize their learning and set goals. It's worth noting the benefits once again: Naming and dating the steps involved in meeting a goal lends concreteness to the process and increases the likelihood of accomplishing tasks.

The second Inspiration template that's useful for helping students personalize learning objectives and plan how to accomplish their work is called Personal Goal and is also located in the Thinking and Planning folder of version 9.0 and higher. In the example of the template shown in Figure 1.6, notice how a chemistry student has set goals for her personal learning and identified steps she needs to take.

One of the potential barriers to using organizing and brainstorming software is that it is not readily available on many home computers; if you were to try to e-mail a web created in this software to parents as part of efforts to further the communication of classroom learning goals, few would be able to open the file. Fortunately, there is a way around this. Both Kidspiration and Inspiration allow users to export a web as a graphic image, such as a JPEG or PNG.

To export an Inspiration document as an image, simply choose **File > Export**, then choose the **Graphics File** tab. This will bring up a screen asking

**Figure 1.6**

Inspiration's Personal Goal Template

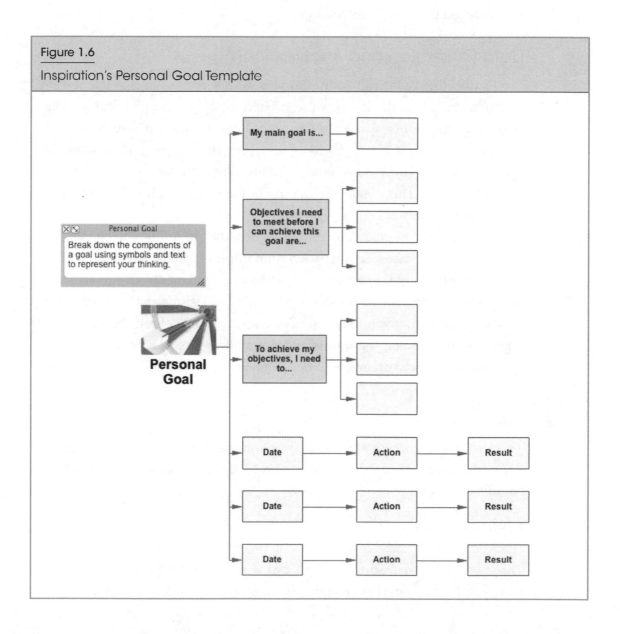

you to choose the format in which you would like to export your Inspiration file. Your choices are GIF, JPEG, and PNG. After you click next to the type of graphic you would like, just hit **Save** and your Inspiration diagram will be converted. This exported graphic is a snapshot of the Inspiration file. It can be inserted into a word processing program and e-mailed to parents, providing you with another way to keep them abreast of your objectives and their child's personalized objectives and learning.

## Data Collection and Analysis Tools

Collecting data with online surveys allows you to engage learners and gather and analyze the information needed to set meaningful and personalized objectives. Once you learn the procedures, setting up a survey is quick and easy. Most sites allow you to archive your surveys so you can revise and use them over again. What's more, you can collect the same survey data from multiple classes. This makes the sharing of the results with individual classes all the more powerful.

There are a few guidelines for putting together an online survey. First, consider including some engaging background information on the topic. This way, you can use the survey to activate and assess your students' prior subject knowledge. Second, be sure to include open-ended questions that will reveal any misconceptions that you might need to address. Finally, keep the survey short enough to ensure a large response and give students credit for completing it.

Here are some examples of free or inexpensive online survey websites:

▸ SurveyMonkey
www.surveymonkey.com

This survey site enables anyone to create online surveys quickly and easily. It has a free basic service that provides most of the features a teacher would need to survey students.

▸ Poll Everywhere
www.PollEverywhere.com

This site allows for real-time display of survey results. Participants can vote using either computers or cell phones.

▶ Socrative
www.socrative.com

This program allows teachers to create surveys, quizzes, and polls.

▶ eClicker
www.bignerdranch.com/software/mobile/eclicker

Available in the iTunes store, this app allows teachers to create quizzes and surveys and lets students vote using their own iOS devices and a free participant app.

▶ Google Forms
www.google.com/google-d-s/forms

This free tool from Google, available in the Google Docs program, allows users to create surveys or questionnaires and send the link to participants. The resulting data fill in a Google Spreadsheet. The user can then view a summary of the responses in graphic form.

What does the use of data collection tools to inform goal setting look like in the classroom? Consider the example of Mr. Solomon, a 7th grade social studies teacher whose curriculum standards include many learning objectives about World War II. Mr. Solomon wants to focus his World War II unit on the decisions of important civilian and military leaders and the major turning points in the war. One of these turning points was the Battle of Leyte Gulf, one of the last major battleship engagements in world history. This sea battle's outcome left the Japanese islands and mainland coast unprotected by any significant Japanese naval or air power.

There are many paths this lesson might take. Mr. Solomon decides to use SurveyMonkey to create a survey that will engage his students and help him to assess their prior knowledge, identify their misconceptions, and focus the class objectives based on their preferences. His survey lists five possible class objectives based on his curriculum standards and features an introduction he wrote based on research from The Naval History and Heritage Command (www.history.navy.mil/special%20highlights/wwiipacific/wwiipac-index.html). Mr. Solomon e-mails the survey to students to complete as a homework assignment and arranges for students who do not have Internet access at home to complete the survey in the library before school. (If most of his students had not had access to e-mail accounts, he could have arranged for them to complete the survey in the school computer lab.) Mr. Solomon's survey is shown in Figures 1.7 and 1.8.

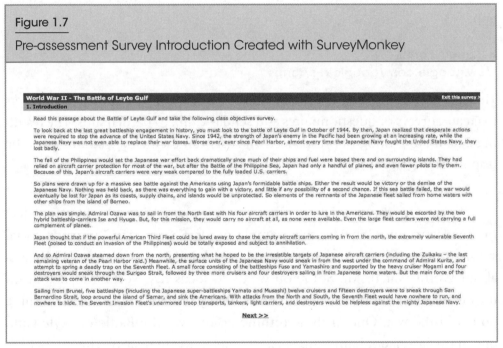

### Figure 1.7

### Pre-assessment Survey Introduction Created with SurveyMonkey

*Reproduced courtesy of SurveyMonkey.com.*

Mr. Solomon accesses the survey results online and tracks the answers as they are recorded. He then saves the data for use next year. Back in class, he shares the survey results with his students and chooses the two most popular objectives as the focus of the week's lessons on the Battle of Leyte Gulf. He also allows his students to personalize some of their goals to reflect what aspects of the content are most important to them. As you can see from the results in Figure 1.9, the survey helps Mr. Solomon narrow the class objectives to "explain how the Japanese battle plan progressed and how the Americans reacted" and "explain why the Battle of Leyte Gulf was a major turning point in World War II." He'll address the other objectives in relation to these two main objectives.

The survey also helps Mr. Solomon identify student misconceptions to address before the class focuses on the main objectives. When he shares the survey results with the class, it elicits a vibrant discussion and debate about which objectives were the most important. The survey results guide his lessons and assessments for the rest of the week.

---

**Figure 1.8**

**Pre-assessment Survey Created with SurveyMonkey**

**World War II - The Battle of Leyte Gulf**                                    Exit this survey >>
**2. The Battle of Leyte Gulf**

1. What do you know about the results of the Battle of Leyte Gulf?

* 2. Which of the following learning objectives is most important to you?
  - Understand how the Battle of Leyte Gulf fit into the overall Japanese strategy in the Pacific.
  - Describe the major leaders and the effects of their decisions in the Battle of Leyte Gulf.
  - Explain how the Japanese battle plan progressed and how the Americans reacted.
  - Explain why the Battle of Leyte Gulf was a major turning point in World War II.
  - Describe the significance of the Battle of Leyte Gulf in relation to the American invasion of the Japanese held Philippine Islands.
  - Other (please specify)

3. How important do you think the Battle of Leyte Gulf was to each nation's effort to win the war?

|                | Very Important | Important | Somewhat Important | Not Important |
| -------------- | -------------- | --------- | ------------------ | ------------- |
| United States? | ○              | ○         | ○                  | ○             |
| Japan?         | ○              | ○         | ○                  | ○             |

<< Prev          Done >>

*Reproduced courtesy of SurveyMonkey.com.*

## Database and Reference Resources

Information that was once only available by purchasing expensive books and materials is now easily accessible and searchable on the Internet. You can use the vast number of standards and curriculum resources online as a guide when setting objectives during the planning process. One way of applying online resources to this end is to access standards online, transform them into objectives, and incorporate these objectives into a rubric that students can personalize.

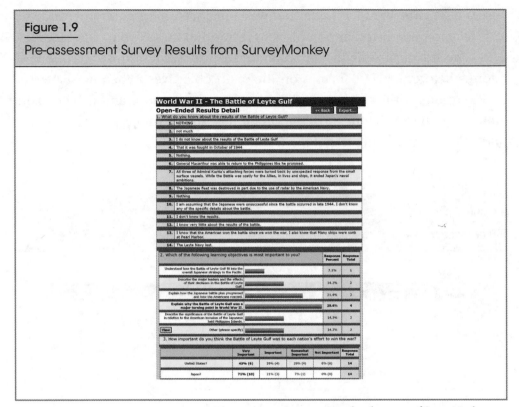

**Figure 1.9**

**Pre-assessment Survey Results from SurveyMonkey**

*Reproduced courtesy of SurveyMonkey.com.*

What are the steps you can follow to translate broad standards and benchmarks into rubrics to guide student learning? Start by looking up your school, district, or state standards, or by using those found in the Common Core. Here are two online sources that may help you:

▶ **McREL's Compendium of Standards: Content Knowledge**
www.mcrel.org/standards-benchmarks

McREL is well-known for its work in standards development. Its database of K–12 content standards and other valuable standards tools is used by district- and state-level educators across the nation. Recently, McREL has added links to standards from the Common Core.

▶ **Common Core**
www.corestandards.org

This site provides access to the Common Core standards as well as resources with more information about Common Core.

## Creating Standards-based Objectives

Let's say you are a middle school science teacher and that one of the standards in your curriculum is "Understands atmospheric processes and the water cycle." You might begin by going online to access McREL's Content Knowledge and finding the relevant benchmarks and indicators you will use to set the class and individual objectives (Figure 1.10).

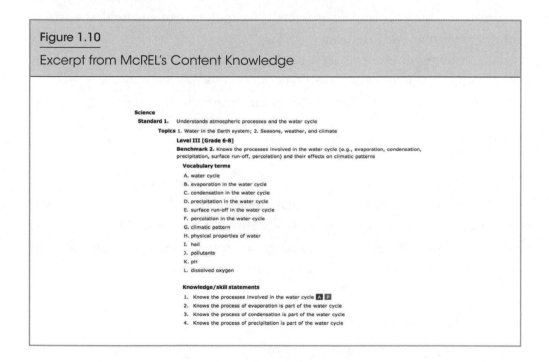

**Figure 1.10**

## Excerpt from McREL's Content Knowledge

You decide that for this student project you will group some of the indicators into three objectives:

• *Objective 1:* Depict all of the water cycle patterns and processes in a clearly understandable and related fashion by researching the water cycle and creating a digital poster suitable for printing.

• *Objective 2:* Accurately describe five major processes in the water cycle and how they act as an interdependent cycle, using your poster as a visual aid.

• *Objective 3:* Correctly explain how the five major processes from Objective 2 affect climatic patterns, using your poster as a visual aid.

## Creating Rubrics

Now that you have set your objectives, how do you communicate them to your students? One answer: Create a rubric. Specific, criterion-referenced rubrics let students know exactly what is expected of them. However, rubrics like these are not always easy to design and can eat up precious lesson planning time in a teacher's busy schedule. Fortunately, technology can ensure that effective rubrics are just a few clicks away.

A number of resources are available that help teachers and even students create rubrics. The following are a few of the websites dedicated to providing and designing rubrics. Explore these sites to create a multitude of rubric types.

▶ RubiStar
http://rubistar.4teachers.org

This is a tool to help the teacher who wants to use rubrics but does not have the time to develop them from scratch. RubiStar provides generic rubrics that you can print and use for many typical lessons. It also provides these generic rubrics in a format that can be customized. You can change almost all suggested text in the rubric to make it fit your own objectives.

▶ Tech4Learning
http://myt4l.com/index.php

This site has a number of predesigned rubrics on a variety of topics as well as a rubric generator you can use to create your own.

Ready to build a rubric from your learning objectives? Remember, the project objectives require the students to create and use a digital poster. For this example, go to RubiStar (http://rubistar.4teachers.org/), scroll down to the Create a Rubric section, and choose **Products**. Then choose **Making a Poster** to create a new rubric based on a template. Revise the Making a Poster rubric for a middle school project to research and create an accurate digital poster of the water cycle. Choose the criteria to fit the needs of your lesson, based on the objectives you created with your students. Notice that as you choose criteria, the rubric is automatically filled in for you. You can customize the text and add categories as you wish. Finally, choose **Submit** when you are ready to generate your rubric. The rubric maker will look something like Figure 1.11.

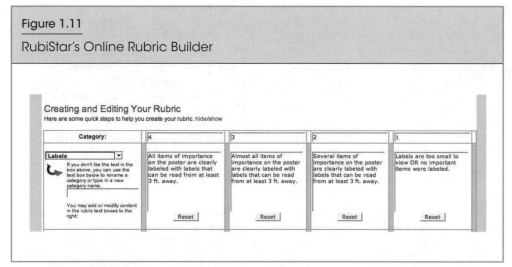

**Figure 1.11**

**RubiStar's Online Rubric Builder**

Note: Development of this educational resource was supported, in part, by the U.S. Department of Education awards to ALTEC [Advanced Learning Technologies in Education Consortia] at the University of Kansas Center for Research on Learning, which included Regional Technology in Education Consortium 1995–2005. Copyright 1995–2006 ALTEC at the University of Kansas.

When you have completed all of the steps and have created your rubric, choose among saving the rubric online, printing it, or downloading it. The finished rubric will look something like the one in Figure 1.12. You might also guide students through this process so that they can customize the rubric for their own goals, based on the overall class objectives.

Now that you know how to create a standards-based rubric, go back to RubiStar and look at the library of rubrics already available for you to use or modify. Click **Find a Rubric** on the menu across the top of the screen and enter up to three keywords. You will be amazed at the number of rubrics available for you to use or modify.

**Figure 1.12**

**Presentation Rubric Built with RubiStar**

| CATEGORY | 4 | 3 | 2 | 1 |
|---|---|---|---|---|
| Overall Concept and Pattern Description | Depicts all five of the major water cycle patterns and processes in a clearly under-standable and related fashion | Depicts most of the major water cycle patterns and processes in an understandable and related fashion | Depicts some of the major water cycle patterns and processes in a somewhat under-standable and related fashion | Depicts a few of the major water cycle patterns and processes in a confusing and unrelated fashion |
| Process and Cycle Description | Accurately describes all five major processes in the water cycle and how they act as an interdepen-dent cycle, using the poster as a visual aid | Describes all five major processes in the water cycle and how they act as an interdepen-dent cycle, using the poster as a visual aid | Describes most major processes in the water cycle, with some use of the poster as a visual aid | Describes few of the major pro-cesses in the water cycle, with little use of the poster as a visual aid |
| Explanation of Climatic Effects | Correctly explains how the five major processes in the water cycle affect climatic patterns, using the poster as a visual aid | Correctly explains how most of the five major pro-cesses in the water cycle affect climatic patterns, using the poster as a visual aid | Explains how some of the five major processes in the water cycle affect climatic pat-terns, with some use of the poster as a visual aid | Explains how a few of the five major processes in the water cycle affect climatic patterns, with little use of the poster as a visual aid |
| Graphics: Originality | Several of the graphics reflect an exceptional degree of student creativ-ity in design and display | One or two of the graphics reflect an exceptional degree of student creativ-ity in design and display | The student made the graphics, but the designs are based on the designs or ideas of others | There are no student-made graphics |
| Graphics: Relevance | All graphics relate to the topic and add to the presen-tation's impact; all borrowed graphics are accompa-nied by a source citation | All graphics relate to the topic; all borrowed graph-ics are accompa-nied by a source citation | Most graphics relate to the topic although some are superfluous; most borrowed graph-ics are accompa-nied by a source citation | Graphics do not relate to the topic OR several bor-rowed graphics are not accompa-nied by a source citation |

## Communication and Collaboration Software

Communication and collaboration software, such as blogs (short for "web logs") and e-mail applications, provide another way for you and your students to set and communicate goals and objectives.

### E-mail

E-mail, though relatively "old school" by now, is still a simple and effective way to set objectives in or out of school time. One aspect of setting objectives through e-mail is the ease with which messages can be stored and recorded for future use in assessment and conferencing with students and parents. An e-mail newsletter is a second application of the technology that can be used for setting objectives. For example, you might collaborate with teachers in your grade level, subject, or team and create a group newsletter to send to all parents on an e-mail distribution list. (For those parents who do not have an e-mail address, simply print out the e-mail and ask students to hand-deliver it to their parents.) Your newsletter might include a standard section that outlines the upcoming curricular topics and learning objectives for the class. Keeping parents informed about class learning objectives is one way to recognize them as the important team players that they are. It also helps parents keep their children focused on the right learning goals at home.

Here is an example of how one elementary grade-level team uses e-mail and newsletters to set objectives. At the beginning of the year, the 1st grade team collected all e-mail addresses available from parents. The team found that about 92 percent of parents had an e-mail address they could access at home, work, or both. Now, the members of the team take turns editing a monthly 1st grade newsletter. The newsletter includes a message from the principal covering general school news and concerns, and it reports on events in special curriculum areas (music, art, physical education), along with news about clubs, sports, or other special subjects and activities.

The 1st grade teachers also post the electronic newsletter on their individual classroom blogs, and they print and post a hard copy on the classroom wall. They go over it with their students once a month on the day it is sent out to parents so that families can discuss it at home. The 1st grade team makes sure that all newsletters start out with the topics and a summary of the learning objectives for the upcoming month. The team has found that this has cut down on parent complaints and misinformation. In addition, they have noticed increased parental involvement since the team went to the e-mail newsletter system. The 8 percent of parents who do not use e-mail still rely on their children to deliver a hard copy to them, but each month, more and more parents are sending in their e-mail addresses to become part of the e-mail distribution system.

Before the 1st grade team started collaborating and sending newsletters by e-mail, parents often complained that they were confused by the multiple hard-copy newsletters coming home at different times from the music teacher, principal, teachers, and various committees. Furthermore, many students damaged or lost newsletters or forgot to give the newsletters to their parents. One teacher commented that she used to be very frustrated to discover at teacher/parent conferences how little her students' parents knew about the learning objectives in her class. How could she ask parents to supervise homework, projects, and studying if they didn't even know what students were trying to learn? Now, more parents indicate that they receive and read the newsletter because it has all the information they need in one communication. They know when to expect the newsletter each month, and they no longer have to worry about students losing or damaging the newsletter before they see it. The class objectives are now easy to access. And as a final bonus, the time and money once invested in buying paper and arranging for bulk printing can be funneled into other activities.

## Blogs

A blog is a web-based publication of periodic journal entries ("posts"), usually presented in reverse chronological order with the most current post appearing first. One way to think of a blog is as an online journal with one or many contributors. Because a blog is a personalized, dynamic web page, it is much easier to maintain and design than a traditional, static web page. Using a blog is similar to facilitating a focus group online.

Here's an example. Mrs. Birnbaum, a language arts teacher, wants to encourage reading during the upcoming winter break. She sets up a classroom blog and posts the titles and short, teaser-style descriptions of 10 short stories, along with possible learning objectives for each. Then she assigns the students to visit the blog site, read the posts, and choose three short stories to read over the break. After they read their three stories, they must comment on them, using one of the given learning objectives and another objective of their own. These posted comments show up as a threaded (chronological) discussion with other students who chose the same story. By the end of the winter break, Mrs. Birnbaum returns with information on each student's reading choices, objectives, and discussions. As you can see, this is not only a great tool for setting student objectives, it also is a wonderful way to differentiate student learning. Finally, when students return to the classroom, Mrs. Birnbaum facilitates the discussions of each story by first bringing up the online discussions from the blog. This gives students interesting information about the stories they did not read and makes it possible for them to post comments to the discussions of other stories.

There are many free online services available to guide you through the basic steps required to set up a blog. Most blog sites do not require you to download any software; they work through your Internet browser. Here is a list of the common features and capabilities that free blog services include:

- A variety of color and style templates to choose from
- Facilitator biography and information page link
- Response/read level settings (e.g. public, class list, facilitator only)
- Comment type settings (anonymous or by user name only)
- Comment on posts or reply directly to other comments
- Delay, delete, or screen comments from users
- Facilitator and user pictures next to postings
- No banners or pop-up ads

If you are willing or able to pay a small fee, you will have access to more features, such as surveys and storage space; however, the free services are usually sufficient for classroom use.

Finally, the best way for you to understand how to use blogs to set objectives is to look at how other teachers use blogs with their classes. Below are some blog examples for you to browse. Many of the teachers who created them are just beginning to explore the full potential of using blogs with their students. As you delve into these example sites, think about ways you might use a blog with your own students.

▶ Mr. Mackey's Science Blog
http://mrmackeyscience.blogspot.com

This science class blog is linked to a comprehensive website used for all aspects of teaching 8th grade science. The blog is used to post current events, news, commentary, and useful links.

▶ The Edublogger: Check Out These Class Blogs!
http://theedublogger.com/check-out-these-class-blogs/

This collection of exemplary class blogs is regularly updated.

▶ Learning Is Messy
http://learningismessy.com/blog

The teacher who runs this site, Brian Crosby, shows how he uses blogs to provide students with feedback and help them create digital portfolios.

## ⏻ Providing Feedback

Providing students with feedback that is corrective, timely, and focused on criteria, along with involving students in the process, creates a classroom environment that supports learning. The classroom practices featured in this chapter emphasize that the goal of providing feedback is to give students information about how well they are performing relative to a particular learning objective so that they can improve their performance.

We have four recommendations for classroom practice with regard to providing feedback:

### RECOMMENDATIONS

- Provide feedback that addresses what is correct and elaborates on what students need to do next.
- Provide feedback appropriately in time to meet students' needs.
- Provide feedback that is criterion referenced.
- Engage students in the feedback process.

Research shows that the more immediate the feedback is in classroom settings, the greater its impact on student behavior (Kulik & Kulik, 1988). Technology is especially effective when it comes to providing this kind of feedback. Games and simulations, for example, allow teachers and students to get near-instantaneous feedback *during* the learning process, allowing for immediate redirection or correction of misconceptions. Contrast this with holding feedback until the end of the lesson, unit, or school year. Technology also makes it easier to complete multiple reviewers' feedback and allows the feedback process to happen ubiquitously.

In this section, we address the technology resources that facilitate and enhance the process of providing feedback for students and teachers: *word processing applications, data collection and analysis tools, database and reference resources,* and *communication and collaboration software.*

## Word Processing Applications

While many teachers and students use word processors as tools for writing, these programs also have features that support robust and timely feedback. In Microsoft Word, for instance, teachers and students can use the Track Changes and Insert Comments features to give and gather feedback from multiple reviewers.

The example in Figure 1.13 shows the feedback that Karen, a student writer, received from two different peer reviewers; the software displays each reviewer's comments in a different color. These comments can serve as the starting point for editorial decisions. Karen, for example, might accept some of the suggestions and reject others.

To track changes in Microsoft Word, be sure to select **Review > Track Changes** from the toolbar. (The Track Changes icon looks like a piece of paper with red lines and a pencil.) To insert a comment, click **New Comment**. The changes will show as seen in Figure 1.13. Saving documents in a group-shared folder provides a way for an entire classroom of students to quickly access one another's work, and give and receive feedback from their teacher and their peers.

Another useful tool available in Microsoft Word is the Flesch-Kincaid Readability Scale, which calculates the complexity of a piece of writing in terms of sentence length and the number of syllables in the words used. When the tool is activated, every time a student runs a spell check, the software will display summary information and assign "reading ease" and grade-level ratings to the text. Although initially students who take advantage of this tool might be interested mostly in their ratings, they can learn to use it to gather feedback on the sophistication of their writing. Figure 1.14 shows the Flesch-Kincaid readability assessment of Karen's essay.

### Figure 1.13

### Microsoft Word Document Showing Tracked Changes and Inserted Comments

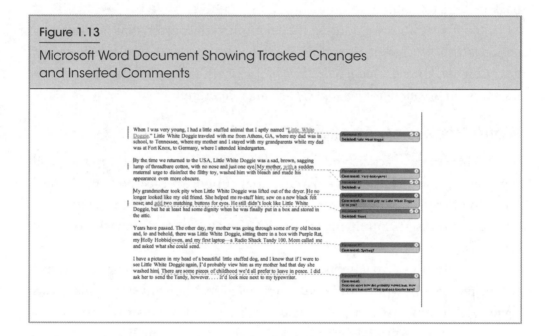

To use this feature, go to the **File** menu and select **Options**, then select **Proofing**. Click on the checkboxes for **Check grammar with spelling** and **Show readability statistics**.

Once students know the readability scale level of a piece of writing, they can revise it before turning it in, paying close attention to word choice and variation. (You might also encourage students to use the built-in thesaurus in Word or at www.visualthesaurus.com to refine their word usage.) After Karen addressed some of the peer- and teacher-suggested changes and comments in her original essay (which, as the figure shows, rated an 8.5 on the Flesch-

Kincaid Grade Level scale), the final version's score rose to 10.2. It's easy to see how this feature might help students approach the feedback and revision process as an engaging, game-like challenge.

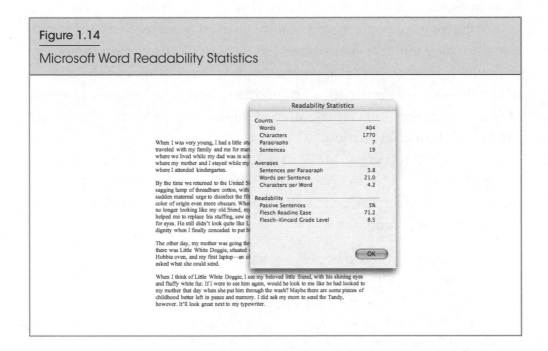

**Figure 1.14**

Microsoft Word Readability Statistics

## Data Collection and Analysis Tools

A frustration of being one teacher responsible for the learning of many students is that it can be tremendously difficult to provide each of them with specific and immediate feedback. Data collection and analysis tools are a wonderful help here.

### Classroom Response Systems

Teachers use classroom response systems—also known as *student response systems*—to instantly gather and disseminate specific feedback. To collect data, some systems use sets of hardware remotes, while others take advantage of any device with a web browser; in either case, the system generates an immediate analysis of student responses. Manufacturers of popular classroom response systems include eClicker, eInstruction, Eduware, Promethean, and Renaissance Learning. The screen shots included in this section are from the eClicker application, as used on multiple device types and hosted by an iPad. Although other technologies may offer more options, such as constructed response and gradebook integration, eClicker is very inexpensive and easy to use.

Classroom response systems can be used to assess all levels of understanding using multiple-choice questions. Although it's common to think of multiple-choice questions as appropriate only when evaluating students' grasp of simple facts and vocabulary, when multiple-choice questions are appropriately designed, they can evaluate all levels of skill within Bloom's taxonomy, from recall through evaluation.

Consider this example: Mr. Faulk, a 3rd grade teacher, is using the eClicker application on his iPad to create a formative assessment that will check his students' understanding of animal classification. He enters the following questions into the application:

1. Animals with backbones are called _____.
2. Animals without backbones are called _____.
3. Which of these animals is a vertebrate?
4. Which of these animals is an invertebrate?
5. Which of these is *not* a class of vertebrates?
6. Members of this class of vertebrates breathe with gills their entire life and lay eggs.
7. Members of this class of vertebrates spend part of their lives in water and part on land. They lay eggs.
8. Members of this class of vertebrates spend most of their time on land. Almost all lay eggs, but a few give live birth. They breathe with lungs. They are cold-blooded.
9. Members of this class of vertebrates are warm-blooded. They lay eggs, breathe with lungs, and are covered with feathers.
10. Which of these is not a characteristic of mammals?
11. A mouse is an example of _____.
12. A gecko is an example of _____.
13. A whale is an example of _____.

Notice that the numbered questions progress from basic, recall-level tasks to those requiring more comprehension and analysis of the basic facts and vocabulary regarding vertebrate classification. For each of these questions, Mr. Faulk is able to insert a range of answer options. He also has the option to insert pictures for each question. Figure 1.15 shows the question view of eClicker that he uses to create and edit questions on the iPad.

**Figure 1.15**

Question View of eClicker Session

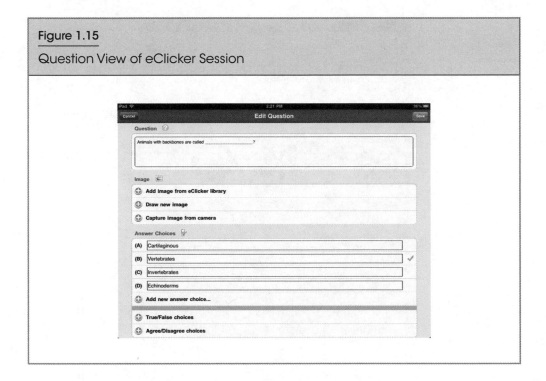

Before he administers the assessment, Mr. Faulk provides the class with a URL from eClicker. Each student uses an iPod Touch to connect to the application. Mr. Faulk then explains that the students will respond to each question within a set amount of time and launches the session. The student view of one of the questions is shown in Figure 1.16. Mr. Faulk has used pictures in this question to help his emerging readers.

During the assessment, students receive immediate feedback and are able to see from question to question whether or not they are answering correctly. At the end of the assessment, the teacher has a graphical assessment summary available of the answers for each question. Figure 1.17 shows such a summary for the question "Which of these animals is an invertebrate?"

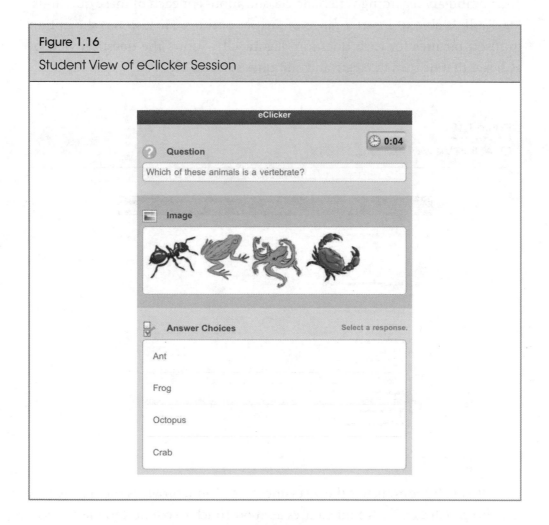

**Figure 1.16**

Student View of eClicker Session

As you can see from the figure, a large number of students responded that they thought a snake (B), rather than a starfish (D), was an example of an invertebrate. Such data are excellent feedback for the teacher, indicating that he needs to revisit this section of the lesson and address misconceptions. Mr. Faulk might direct students to online resources such as those found at www.brainpopjr.com/science/animals or www.sheppardsoftware.com for further instruction, and perhaps have certain students retake the assessment.

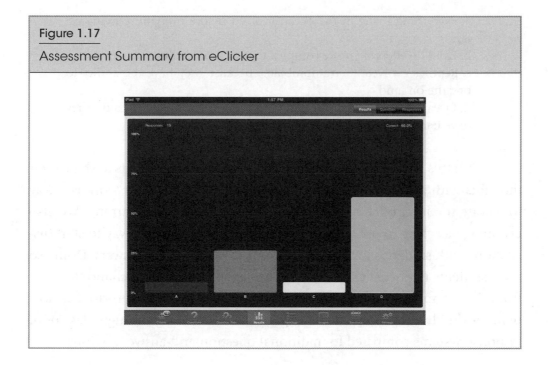

**Figure 1.17**

Assessment Summary from eClicker

Later in their study of animal classification, Mr. Faulk will pose more in-depth questions in order to assess whether his students are able to synthesize or evaluate the information. Examples of higher-order questions include the following:

1. Imagine that, during a walk through a desert climate, you come across an animal sitting under a rock that you have never seen before. You know from its body shape, eyes that sit high on its head, and its skin texture that it is either a reptile or an amphibian, but you're not sure which. Without endangering yourself or the animal, how would you go about finding out which it is?

   a. Ask a local if there are any nearby streams or lakes, now or at some time during the year.

   b. Touch the animal to see if the skin is moist and smooth or dry and scaly or bumpy.

   c. Watch to see what it eats.

   d. Observe how it reacts to water.

2. The scientific theory of evolution claims that life evolved on Earth as simple organisms living in oceans and ponds. Based upon this theory, which of these claims is reasonable?

a. Everything living in the ocean evolved before everything living on land.

b. Land dwellers are more complex than ocean dwellers.

c. Reptiles evolved after amphibians, because they have the ability to breathe on land.

d. Ocean dwellers are more suited to their environment because they have had more time to evolve compared to land dwellers.

With this batch of questions, Mr. Faulk will ask his students to share their thoughts with a partner before choosing the answer; this pair work is a way to elevate the level of classroom discussion and synergy of learning. We also encourage teachers to use classroom response systems in this way to start discussions with students, inviting individuals to defend their answers. Doing so gives students the benefit of answering anonymously and the chance to learn from debate and discussion in the classroom. You might be surprised at how many formerly reserved students engage in the learning through classroom response systems compared to traditional question-and-answer sessions.

## Grading Software

Manufacturers continue to develop more and more sophisticated grading software for use at all grade levels. In universities, some of the newest tools are capable of grading student essays and other larger projects, a process once believed to be something only humans could do. Makers of this type of software include Vantage Learning, Maplesoft, Educational Testing Service, and SAGrader. Such software has shown great success in providing assessment and useful feedback (Aleven, Ashley, Lynch, & Pinkwart, 2008). Indeed, studies show a strong correlation between computer-generated scores and those of human experts (Adam, 2001). In one documented case, teachers found that using Vantage Learning's MY Access! software in their classes led to an improvement in student writing and an increase in how much time students devoted to the writing process (High Schools Plug into Online Writing Program, 2003).

Grading software can also help shift learning beyond the traditional classroom setting. Automated essay scoring, for instance, is well-suited to distance learning environments: Because the essay feedback is returned in seconds and can indicate which sections should be rewritten, students can make significant revisions before submitting their final product. If computer-assisted testing becomes the norm in universities, one can only expect K–12 classrooms to eventually adopt this practice.

## Database and Reference Resources

Because we covered rubrics extensively in our discussion on setting objectives, we will not go into as much detail here, but we cannot emphasize enough the wisdom of using rubrics to set objectives and to provide feedback. Because rubrics provide detailed descriptions, they help teachers to meet the classroom recommendation of giving feedback that's specific to a criterion as opposed to giving a simple grade or score. We also encourage the use of rubrics for peer evaluation. As students learn to work collaboratively, they need scaffolding in how to provide feedback in a specific, constructive, and supportive manner.

### Instructional Media

Instructional media allow students multiple venues in which to review a concept, practice a skill, or dive into new content of special interest. Students can receive valuable feedback by posting their projects, ideas, reports, and other work online in a multimedia format for others to view and comment upon. Feedback can come from any combination of students, teachers, parents, or outside experts. Popular instructional media platforms include schooltube .com, vimeo.com/videoschool, facebook.com, and voicethread.com.

One of our classroom recommendations for providing feedback is to encourage students to reflect upon their own learning and to give and receive feedback from peers. Technology can allow for feedback, group conversations, and comments to be collected and shared in one place, and can facilitate interaction among students in a classroom or even around the world. One example of such technology is voicethread.com, an online media album that can hold many types of media (images, documents, and videos) and allows people to comment on the media in four different ways: using voice (via microphone or telephone), text, audio files, or videos (via webcam). Video can even be exported for offline use on a DVD or video-enabled MP3 player. Ms. Weeks, a 5th grade teacher, wants her students to reflect upon their own learning objectives and elicit feedback from their parents. She is also looking for ways to get parents more involved with the education of her students. To this end, she convinces her principal to allow her to use VoiceThread as an alternative to traditional teacher-parent conferences. (Any parent who still wishes to meet face-to-face with the teacher is encouraged to do so.)

Kaitlyn is in Ms. Weeks's class. As Ms. Weeks facilitates, she searches www .voicethread.com for "How to create a voice thread." A number of teacher-created examples come up, and Ms. Weeks recommends a particular one that she has researched in advance. Kaitlyn creates a presentation for her parents that showcases her accomplishments in each subject and asks for their digital feedback. Throughout the presentation, she narrates her work and reflects upon her progress and continuing challenges. Kaitlyn's presentation can be found at voicethread.com/share/346039. Figure 1.18 shows the slide view of her presentation without the comments.

Kaitlyn's example shows just one of many ways that VoiceThread can be used to garner feedback. It can also be used for one-to-one assessment between the teacher and each student, as a brainstorming platform for a collaborative learning group, and as a project presentation tool.

### Figure 1.18
### Kaitlyn's Student-Parent Conference Presentation

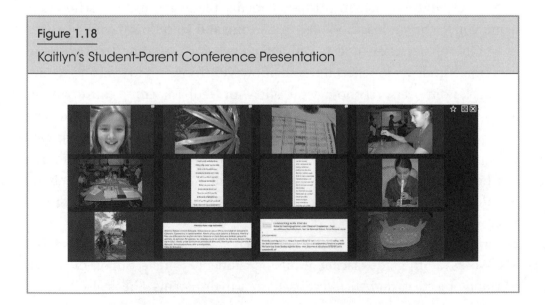

**Instructional Interactives**

In this section, we focus on web resources and applications that present quizzes and games to provide immediate feedback. Educators and parents sometimes express concern about the role that games have in education, but we suspect they do so because they have an erroneous sense that "games in the classroom" means students zoned out in front of a computer or TV screen. If the games and simulations are carefully chosen, they can be both educational and entertaining—anything but mindless. Remember that doctors, soldiers, pilots, and even customer-service agents use simulations and games for training. In fact, a number of research studies suggest that bringing games and simulations into the K–12 classroom positively affects student motivation, retention, transfer, and skill level (Halverson, 2005; Klopfer, 2005; Prensky, 2000; Squire, 2001). And many educational and entertainment games encourage 21st century skills such as solving problems, collaborating with other players, and planning (Klopfer, 2005). Another great characteristic of computers as "instructors" is that they are nonjudgmental entities. A struggling student can practice a skill as many times as necessary to achieve mastery, and the computer, unlike a human instructor, will never grow frustrated.

The plethora of apps available in the iTunes store provides ever-expanding options for students to access games for learning. For example, palasoftware Inc.'s MathBoard provides students with a series of math problems and a "chalkboard" practice area in which to work them out. If students get a problem wrong, the "Problem Solver" feature can walk them through the steps of solving the equation. In this way, students practice basic skills while also getting feedback on difficult concepts. Here are just a few of hundreds of popular apps for the iPhone or iPad that provide feedback to students:

▶ Intro to Math and Intro to Letters by Montessorium
http://montessorium.com/

These apps replicate several didactic materials that are commonly found in Montessori classrooms to help students learn letters and numbers.

▶ Flashcards Deluxe by OrangeorApple.com
http://orangeorapple.com/Flashcards/

This app allows students to create their own virtual flashcards for any subject. When students use the flashcards, the app provides them with feedback on whether they answer correctly immediately, hesitate before answering correctly, or answer incorrectly.

In addition to apps for the iPhone and iPad, there are many online games that provide feedback to students on basic skills and concepts. Here is a sampling:

▶ Math Playground
www.mathplayground.com/index.html

This action-packed site for K–6 students provides engaging games that encourage students to challenge themselves.

▶ ExploreLearning
www.explorelearning.com

This web resource is for 3–12 grade students and teachers. ExploreLearning allows students to use "gizmos"—virtual manipulatives—to experiment in science and mathematics. After going through a guided tutorial using the gizmos, the students take a short quiz. Their answers are assessed and they receive detailed feedback. Although ExploreLearning is a subscription site, a free 30-day pass is available upon sign-up. ExploreLearning's research shows that computer-based simulations are the ideal medium for conveying information in math and science (Cholmsky, 2003).

▶ Cut The Knot
www.cut-the-knot.org/games.shtml

This site is for teachers, parents, and students who seek engaging mathematics. It's a repository of nearly 700 applets that illustrate mathematical concepts. An applet is a software component that runs in the context of another program—a web browser, for example. An applet usually performs a very narrow function, and it will run on any computer's browser.

Other web resources provide information in a multimedia format and then quiz students on basic comprehension of the material. Although we discuss these types of resources in more detail in other sections of this book, there are two that warrant mention here due to the rich and immediate feedback that they provide students:

▶ BrainPOP
www.brainpop.com

This subscription-based resource has short Flash movies on a wide variety of topics in science, social studies, mathematics, English, health, and technology. The movies use clear animation to demonstrate concepts and highlight new vocabulary. After watching a movie, students can take a brief quiz and e-mail the results to their teacher, or they can rewatch the movie and retake the quiz as many times as they need to do so. BrainPOP also features some free movies and a free trial.

▶ BBC Skillswise
www.bbc.co.uk/skillswise

This website provides fact sheets, interactive applets, games, and quizzes in mathematics and language skills for grades K–6. Each quiz is broken into three levels so that students can advance as they learn the skill. This is especially helpful for teachers looking to provide differentiated instruction and assessment.

## Communication and Collaboration Software

Communication and collaboration tools, such as blogs, wikis, e-mail, videoconferencing, and social networks, can provide timely, interactive, and criterion-based feedback to students. Each of these types of software has distinct classroom applications. For example, classroom blogs are inexpensive and easy to maintain and manage without the need for web development skills. Wikis are similar to blogs but more versatile: a way for groups to collaborate by contributing and easily accessing information on a given topic. Because a wiki allows all users to easily add and edit content, it's especially suited for collaborative writing and project-based learning. The constant feedback mechanism of a wiki is what makes it a uniquely powerful learning tool. And because it is web based, contributors do not necessarily need to be in the same geographical area, nor do they need to be working synchronously. Next, there's e-mail, which provides a written record of two-way communication that is easy to archive. Finally, while videoconferencing has been used mostly for distance learning and teacher professional development, its use in K–12 education is growing. Because videoconferences allow two or more locations to interact via two-way video and audio transmissions simultaneously, they serve to connect rural communities, distant classrooms, and experts with learning sources and classes from around the world.

Let's take a closer look at each of these types of communication software.

## Blogs and Wikis

A blog (short for "web log") is a website in which items are posted on a regular basis and displayed in reverse chronological order. Like other media, blogs often focus on a particular subject, such as education, technology, or politics. However, blogs differ from other types of websites in that moderators frame the discussions and then invite readers to reply to posts. This works best in a written format, although blogs have the additional capability to display graphics and even video. The manager or facilitator of a blog can decide if others will be allowed to comment on postings to the blog.

If you want your classroom blog to be interactive with students, you will need to enable this comments feature. You can do this by allowing only certain registered users to post (your students) while blocking out all others. Alternatively, you may set up your classroom blog to be open to postings from anyone. Remember, though, that blogs open to public postings sometimes receive inappropriate comments from unaccountable sources (online vandalism).

We recommend teachers decide which students can post to the classroom blog and make sure students understand the acceptable use policy in your school or district. Often, losing the privilege to comment to the class blog is consequence enough to keep students from posting inappropriate or offensive comments. Furthermore, as the manager of the blog, you can screen certain student postings before you allow them to be posted. Inappropriate blog comments are not as big a problem as you might think as long as students are only able to comment to the blog by using their actual names as their user name; most students do not want their name on an offensive posting for all the school and their parents to see.

One example of providing feedback with a blog is a poetry journal blog. Ms. Jeargen, a middle school English teacher, posts a prompt on the class blog for students to write and contribute poems. The students reply to the post with their poems. As a follow-up, Ms. Jeargen posts a poetry rubric to the blog, reviews the rubric in class, and directs the students to review their classmates' poems and use the rubric to provide criterion-based feedback on three poems. In this way, students are exposed to other poems and both give and receive timely and meaningful feedback. Ms. Jeargen then closes the assignment thread from further student comments and provides her own criterion-based feedback as the last comment for each poem. Next, she starts a separate discussion that prompts the students to write their final draft of the poem. This thread is closed to comments. It will be used as the final product and can be viewed by other classes, parents, and the community. The various steps in the assignment are depicted in the project flow chart in Figure 1.19.

Wikis are similar to blogs, but more versatile. They allow all users to easily add and edit content, and are especially well suited for collaborative writing and project-based learning. The constant feedback mechanism of wikis is what makes them uniquely powerful learning tools. And because wikis are web-based, contributors do not necessarily need to be in the same geographical area or working synchronously to participate.

**Figure 1.19**

**Project Flow Chart for a Class Poetry Blog**

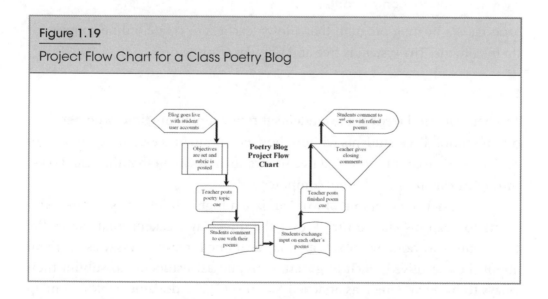

Here are some recommended resources for blogs and wikis:

▶ Google Sites
http://sites.google.com

Google makes creating a free classroom website a simple and intuitive experience. Once at the site, just click **Create**, select from among the templates offered, and fill out the necessary fields.

▶ Wikispaces
www.wikispaces.com

Wikispaces is a place for people to easily build web pages together. Anyone can join the site for free, create a space, and begin contributing within a matter of minutes.

▶ PBworks
http://pbworks.com

This is a user-friendly wiki service site. Once at the site, click **Education** for information regarding classroom use. Free sites allow for up to 2 gigabytes of storage and 100 users. More storage space is available for a fee.

▶ Moodle
www.keytoschool.com/moodle/

Moodle is a hosting program that allows teachers to create online courses for their students. The system is free and popular worldwide.

### E-mail

Teachers can send feedback to students through e-mail anytime, whether in or out of school. Even students without home computer access can set up a web-based e-mail account through a free service such as Gmail that they can access through a classroom or library computer.

Consider the example of Mr. Dunlap, a high school civics teacher who wants to keep his class on track over the three-day weekend that marks the Presidents' Day holiday. He sets a Friday deadline for a short essay assignment about the executive branch of government and asks students to submit their essays to him via e-mail, as attached Microsoft Word documents. Mr. Dunlap grades the essays he receives at his leisure, then e-mails the graded essays back to the students on Sunday afternoon. Students receive this feedback in the form of the tracked changes and also in comments that he makes about the essays in his e-mail message. If a particular student's essay suggests that the student doesn't fully understand the assignment, Mr. Dunlap attaches the rubric for the essay. He can easily copy parents in this correspondence, and the e-mail software maintains a record of these exchanges along with essay submission and return dates. In addition, all the files are electronic, meaning there are no stacks of papers to shuffle through. It's easy to see that using e-mail to provide feedback has the additional benefits of being efficient, timely, and specific.

## Videoconferencing

Sometimes videoconferencing is the ideal way to gain access to unique expertise, cultures, and locations. For example, Mrs. Valenza, a Spanish teacher, wants to give her students conversational experiences. She arranges a videoconference using Skype software (www.skype.com) with an English language class at the sister school in Spain. The students perform skits in Spanish and English during the videoconference. Afterward, the teachers exchange feedback about the skits and the language usage for each class. They encourage their students to ask questions: the U.S. students in Spanish, and the Spanish students in English. Both groups of students also use a blog to give feedback to one another, again using the other group's native language to create their posts. The U.S. students receive valuable feedback from the teacher in Spain via videoconference and from the students via the project blog.

Garnering feedback from authentic audiences like these is a powerful motivator. Other types of authentic audiences students can access through educational technology include poetry clubs, research scientists, and historical societies. Teachers can find a number of free programs available online to help them set up a videoconference. These include Skype (www.skype.com), iChat (Macintosh only; www.apple.com/macosx/apps/all.html#ichat), and Google Video Chat (www.google.com/chat/video).

## Social Networks

Social networking is one of the primary ways our students communicate with each other outside of the classroom. Sites like Facebook and Twitter are to students what the telephone was to older generations—simply what they use to communicate. Yet many schools tend to view these sites as dangerous and block student access to them.

There are clear educational advantages to social networks. These include the presence of an authentic, worldwide audience, the ability to give and receive feedback in a timely manner, and the ability to engage in in-depth conversations. In a traditional classroom, a world history teacher might give his students a prompt to write to as homework. The students would then write a paragraph or two and be done with it. By contrast, if the teacher instead posts the prompt as a tweet via Twitter, students might post their responses, knowing that they will be seen by their classmates. Rather than forgetting about the assignment until the next day, students are likely to return to the Twitter discussion several times over the course of the afternoon and evening to see how their classmates answered the prompt and to see if any classmates commented on their responses.

Many educators have expressed frustration that their schools or districts prohibit the use of many of the tools discussed in this chapter. Rather than an outright ban on social networks and other online tools, policymakers should consider how the technology could be used to enhance education and teach the appropriate, legal, and ethical use of media that are clearly many of our students' preferred methods of communication.

# 2

# Reinforcing Effort and Providing Recognition

In the first edition of *Using Technology with Classroom Instruction That Works*, we categorized the strategies of *reinforcing effort* and *providing recognition* separately. Upon further consideration, however, we came to the conclusion that our research focuses on providing recognition *for* effort and hard work and have therefore recombined the strategies here.

## ⏻ Reinforcing Effort

People attribute success to different sources: to their own innate abilities, to the assistance of others, to luck, and to effort. Of these, the fourth, *effort,* is the most useful attribution. Have you ever heard the saying that "Success comes in cans; failure in can'ts"? The person who said it first recognized that effort is the most important factor in achievement. Research shows that the level of belief in self-efficacy plays a strong role in motivation for learning and achievement (Schunk, 2003). The instructional strategy of *reinforcing effort* enhances students' understanding of the relationship between effort and achievement by addressing their attitudes and beliefs about learning.

To use the strategy of reinforcing effort effectively, teachers must understand the relationship between effort and achievement and the importance of consistently exposing students to information related to effort. They also must know that students can be taught the importance of effort and what it means to expend effort productively. In this chapter, we will discuss practices for reinforcing effort that reflect the following recommendations for classroom practice:

## RECOMMENDATIONS

- Teach students about the relationship between effort and achievement.
- Provide students with explicit guidance about exactly what it means to expend effort.
- Ask students to keep track of their effort and achievement.

Technology helps students and teachers to better track the effects of effort and provide more immediate feedback to students. In this section, we will show you how *data collection and analysis tools* can support the instructional strategy of reinforcing effort.

## Data Collection and Analysis Tools

The research tells us that not all students realize the importance of effort. Many attribute their success or failure to external factors. Many of us have heard a struggling mathematics student say something like, "I'm just not good at math. My mom wasn't good at math either." When a student makes a connection between academic successes and factors outside of his or her control—things like heredity, gender, or race—it's easy to develop a defeatist attitude. After all, why bother if you know that you just aren't capable because of your genes?

Some students also see friends who are successful and attribute their success to outside factors. They might even have the misconception that people of a certain background excel in a particular curricular area. By relying on a stereotype, these students ignore the effort other students put into doing well. The research indicates, however, that students can change their beliefs and make a connection between effort and achievement.

One easy way to help students make the connection between effort and achievement is by using a spreadsheet. The first step in the process is to create a rubric that gives students a clear idea of what effort looks like. Figure 2.1 shows an effort rubric created by Ms. Parker, a 4th grade teacher, using Google Docs.

**Figure 2.1**

**Effort Rubric Created in a Google Docs Spreadsheet**

| | A | B | C | D | E |
|---|---|---|---|---|---|
| 1 | CATEGORY | 4 Exemplary | 3 Proficient | 2 Emerging | 1 Not Acceptable |
| 2 | Attitude - I feel positive about working on my math facts. | I always have a positive attitude about learning my math facts. | I often have a positive attitude about learning my math facts. | I usually have a positive attitude about learning my math facts. | I often have a negative attitude about learning my math facts. |
| 3 | Commitment - I think working hard will pay off. | I practice math facts at home 5 or more times a week. | I practice math facts at home 3 - 4 times a week. | I practice math facts at home 2 times a week. | I practice math facts at home 0 - 1 time a week. |
| 4 | Pride - I feel satisfied when I improve on my math facts. | I try my hardest all of the time when practicing my math facts and my weekly score improves 5 points or more. | I try my hardest most of the time when practicing my math facts and my weekly score improves 3 points or more. | I try my hardest some of the time when practicing my math facts and my weekly score stays the same. | I do not try very hard when practicing my math facts and my weekly score goes down. |

After Ms. Parker reviews the rubric with her students and is sure they all have an understanding of each category, she asks them to log on to the class network and open a blank spreadsheet that she created ahead of time (see Figure 2.2).

**Figure 2.2**

**Effort and Achievement Spreadsheet**

| | A | B | C | D | E |
|---|---|---|---|---|---|
| 1 | Category | Week 1 | Week 2 | Week 3 | Week 4 |
| 2 | Attitude | | | | |
| 3 | Commitment | | | | |
| 4 | Pride | | | | |
| 5 | Total Effort Score | | | | |
| 6 | Quiz Score | | | | |

To set up a spreadsheet like the one in Figure 2.2, follow these steps:

1. Open your browser and go to http:/docs.google.com.
2. Select **Create > Spreadsheet**.

3. In the first row, label the cells as follows: Category, Week 1, Week 2, Week 3, and Week 4.

4. In the first column, below the Category label, add the category names to the first three cells. Then add the following two cells: one labeled Total Effort Score, and one labeled Quiz Score.

5. Format the spreadsheet to perform automatic calculations by clicking on the Total Effort Score cell for week one and typing =sum(b2:b4). This command tells the spreadsheet to add all of the numbers from cell B2 through B4.

6. Copy the command and paste it into the Total Effort Score cells for Week 2, Week 3, and Week 4.

As Ms. Parker's students begin their four-week unit on math facts, they also begin a project on effort and achievement, using the effort rubric to assess themselves honestly on their preparation for their weekly mathematics quiz. Each Friday, right before they take the quiz, students open their spreadsheets and enter their rubric scores for that week. The following Monday, when they get their quizzes back, they enter their quiz scores.

At the end of the four-week unit, the students follow Ms. Parker's instructions to highlight the rows for Total Effort Score and Quiz Score on their spreadsheets and to go to **Insert > Chart > Charts > Line > Insert** to reveal a chart that clearly shows the relation between the students' effort and scores they earned on their quizzes (see Figure 2.3 for an example).

Of course, this exercise alone won't change all of Ms. Parker's students' thinking about effort and achievement. Students need consistent and systematic exposure to teaching strategies like this one in order to really grasp the impact that effort can have on their achievement.

A powerful way of convincing students that effort is truly tied to achievement is to show them combined data on groups that students associate themselves with; for example, 5th grade students, social studies students, and incoming freshmen. When students see that others have faced many of the same difficulties they face and have overcome these obstacles and achieved goals with strong effort and good attitude, they too can see the connection between effort and achievement. When students have well-known or personal stories from which to learn, effort is reinforced and students begin to take more responsibility for their own success.

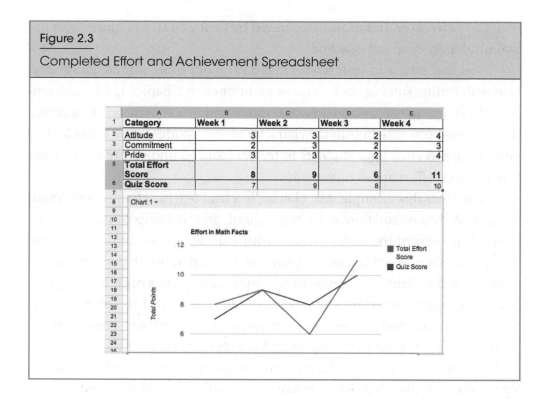

**Figure 2.3**

**Completed Effort and Achievement Spreadsheet**

| | A | B | C | D | E |
|---|---|---|---|---|---|
| 1 | Category | Week 1 | Week 2 | Week 3 | Week 4 |
| 2 | Attitude | 3 | 3 | 2 | 4 |
| 3 | Commitment | 2 | 3 | 2 | 3 |
| 4 | Pride | 3 | 3 | 2 | 4 |
| 5 | Total Effort Score | 8 | 9 | 6 | 11 |
| 6 | Quiz Score | 7 | 9 | 8 | 10 |

Without the enhancement of technology, reinforcing effort in schools often is done by individual teacher comments or by collecting and sharing vignettes, testimonials, and observations from the learning community. For example, one elementary school uses a bulletin board near the main office. The title of the bulletin board is "Caught in the Act of Trying Hard," and on it are the collected stories of students putting forth a strong effort to achieve. Maintaining this bulletin board not only reinforces effort but also provides recognition.

Now let's look at how technology could enhance this initiative. The faculty and staff observational data, which were the basis for the bulletin board, could be collected online, through the school's website. The school might dedicate a section of its website to showing these examples: reinforcing effort and reassuring students that they too can succeed if they keep trying. Student success stories like these are more meaningful, more relatable, than stories of larger-than-life heroes. This is particularly important for high school students who can grow more and more discouraged by their perceived failures, give up, and ultimately drop out of school.

You and others in your school might carry out more formal data collection with online surveys, such as those mentioned in Chapter 1. This technology allows you to use a standard effort rubric and incorporate it into a survey that will give you insight into the character of your students and provide data you can use to encourage students to try hard and to underscore the connection between effort and achievement.

Consider this example: Mr. Ekuban is a lead teacher charged with managing freshmen orientation at his high school, and he wants to make sure he instills members of the freshmen class with a strong appreciation for the role that effort plays in achievement. Using an original rubric based on one he located on the RubiStar website (http://rubistar.4teachers.org), he designs a free survey with SurveyMonkey (www.surveymonkey.com) to collect anonymous effort data and stories from the successful juniors and seniors in the high school's National Honor Society. Mr. Ekuban then shares the survey data with the incoming freshmen during their orientation to show them the ways in which students like them have overcome difficulties and achieved with strong effort and good attitude. His survey and the resulting data are shown in Figures 2.4 and 2.5.

As you might suspect, these data also alerted Mr. Ekuban to common success factors unique to his school. This awareness helped him show his students the relationship between effort and achievement.

A survey like this is good for more than just collecting overall effort data. You might also use it with specific projects, such as science fairs, research papers, or other class projects, to show students what it takes to do that project well.

## ⏻ Providing Recognition

Some teachers wonder if providing recognition, particularly in the form of praise, is the right thing to do. They are right to wonder: some research on praise and recognition has shown negative effects on intrinsic motivation (Henderlong & Lepper, 2002; Kamins & Dweck, 1999). Praise that is person- or ability-oriented rather than task- or process-oriented can have unintentional negative effects on intrinsic motivation: when students have setbacks in the domain that was praised, they may think they have lost their ability and may react afterward with helplessness. Still, other research indicates that when teachers use a mastery-oriented approach to provide recognition and praise, praise can be used to promote student engagement and decrease behavioral problems (Moore-Partin, Robertson, Maggin, Oliver, & Wehby, 2010; Simonson, Fairbanks, Briesch, Myers, & Sugai, 2008). Further, if students perceive the praise to be sincere, and if it promotes self-determination, encourages students to attribute their performance to causes that they can control, and establishes attainable goals and standards, then praise can actually influence intrinsic motivation (Henderlong & Lepper, 2002). Teachers therefore must use praise with caution.

### Figure 2.4

### Survey on Effort Created with SurveyMonkey

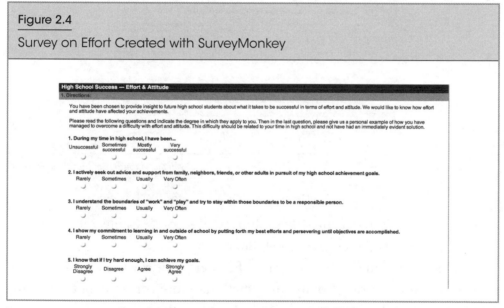

*Reproduced courtesy of SurveyMonkey.com.*

Recognition and praise may have a more direct impact on socio-emotional indicators such as self-efficacy, effort, persistence, and motivation than on learning. As a result, teachers may not see immediate academic improvements from the effective use of recognition and praise; however, the link between positive socio-emotional indicators and learning suggests that fostering the former will have positive effects on the latter over time (Bouffard,

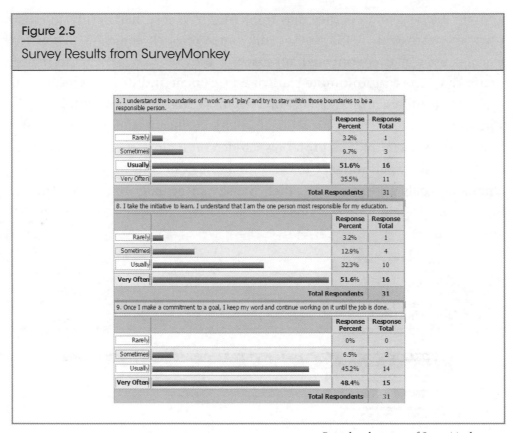

**Figure 2.5**

**Survey Results from SurveyMonkey**

*Reproduced courtesy of SurveyMonkey.com.*

Boisvert, Vezeau, & Larouche, 1995; Elliot, McGregor, & Gable, 1999; Greene, Miller, Crowson, Duke, & Akey, 2004; Phan, 2009).

Most people like to be recognized for their efforts, whether the recognition comes in the form of praise or something more concrete. But providing recognition must be done appropriately. Based on the research, we have three recommendations for classroom practice:

## RECOMMENDATIONS

- Promote a mastery-goal orientation.
- Provide praise that is specific and aligned with expected performance and behaviors.
- Use concrete symbols of recognition.

One of the most powerful ways that technology facilitates the use of this strategy is that it gives teachers a way to expand recognition beyond giving a student an *A+* on an assignment or posting it on the classroom bulletin board. With technology, teachers can easily make exemplary work available for the appreciation of peers, parents, and professionals across the world. In *The Wisdom of Crowds*, James Surowiecki (2004) makes the similar argument that a large and diverse group is able to collectively make better decisions and recognize what's "best" better than a single individual. Websites such as blogs and Facebook operate by this principle, allowing visitors to recognize which news items or web clippings are most useful. In this section, we show how a teacher can use the following resources to provide recognition: *data collection and analysis tools, multimedia,* and *communication and collaboration software.*

## Data Collection and Analysis Tools

We have already described the use and capabilities of web-based surveys and student response systems. Here, we offer two ways to use the same tools to provide recognition.

Because web-based surveys and classroom response systems allow students to receive feedback from both teachers and peers, you can use these tools to recognize those students who earn the highest-scoring feedback. When doing so, always remember to base recognition on a clear standard of performance. This is especially crucial with student recognition of their peers' work. Teacher-set parameters are the best way to ensure that the recognition reflects the standards-based criteria and not student popularity or another outside factor.

Here's an example of how a teacher might use data collection tools to provide recognition. Having just concluded a unit on the Great Depression, middle school students post original movies, essays, digital images of artwork, or other products to a designated website. On or before the assignment's due date, all students make their blog posts anonymously, using a teacher-assigned code instead of their actual names. Then the students use a web-based survey, such as Micropoll (http://micropoll.com), to review a project rubric, view the posted products, and give rubric-based feedback, including a "grade." The program tallies the scores, after which the teacher reveals the names of the students whose products receive the highest scores, and they are formally recognized as completing high-quality work that meets the criteria described in the project rubric. An example of one of the rubric rating questions is found in Figure 2.6.

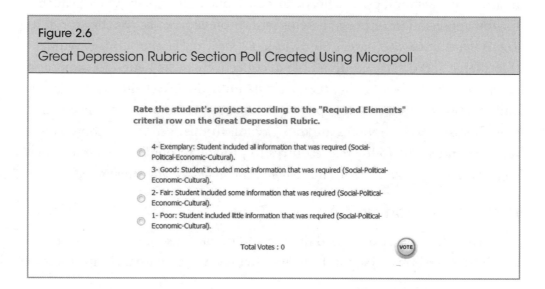

Figure 2.6

Great Depression Rubric Section Poll Created Using Micropoll

In another example, a mathematics teacher might give a pop quiz using a classroom response system, with the expectation that if the students' collective responses achieve an agreed-upon proficiency level, such as 90 percent accuracy, they will all earn bonus points to redeem later in the year. When the quiz is complete, the classroom response system returns an immediate verdict on the students' performance: They've earned their bonus points! The teacher gives the students verbal praise and distributes "bonus point coupons," following the classroom recommendation to provide concrete symbols of recognition. Note that in this example the teacher rewards the entire class, encouraging students to help each other achieve. At other times, it might be appropriate to look at individual student response records and reward students individually.

## Multimedia

Handing a student a personalized certificate to celebrate high-quality work is a surefire way to make that student feel appreciated and motivate further success. There are several resources that make it easy for teachers to provide this kind of recognition. For example, at http://www.billybear4kids.com/show/ awards/certificates.html, you can easily create and print out certificates.

Another way to provide students with concrete recognition is to hand out badges for achievement. Teachers can either print out badges or provide them in virtual form on classroom blogs or wikis. The badges shown in Figure 2.7 were created using the free online badge generator at www.web20badges.com.

**Figure 2.7**

Example of Badges Created at Web20Badges.com

## Web Showcases and Picture Galleries

When a student brings home an example of outstanding schoolwork to show his or her parents, the parents often praise the child and post work on the household refrigerator for everyone in the home to see and admire. This is a good example of informally recognizing a student based on individual achievement. Technology provides a way to take this recognition to the next level. Posting exceptional student work on the Internet opens up possibilities for recognition from friends, peers, professionals, and relatives across the globe. Many of these websites stay up for years, providing examples to other students and becoming a lasting source of pride and confidence for the recognized students.

For instance, Reagan, a struggling 5th grade student, sets a goal with her teacher to write a three-page story about her favorite time of the year. She agrees to include proper writing conventions and to produce a paper that is free of grammatical errors. After working hard at drafting, revising, and editing, she accomplishes her goal. The teacher posts the story to the class's "Student Work

Showcase" on the school's website and includes an annotation that recognizes the story as an accomplishment compared to the student's learning objectives. After the posting, Reagan telephones her grandparents in another state so they can see her work on their home computer.

Physical education and art teachers often use online picture galleries as a means of recognition because exhibitions are natural extensions of those content areas, but picture galleries are a fantastic way of motivating students and recognizing their efforts in any content area. Of course, always check your district's policy on the posting of student work. And also take care to post a diverse sampling of student work and not just products from the best and brightest students. When selecting work to post, assess how well a student has achieved his or her own goals for improvement rather than comparing the work to that of other students.

One example of a photo gallery service is the popular www.flickr.com. Setting up a free account is simply a matter of providing a user name and a password. Once you have an account, you can upload pictures, enter comments, and send a link to the account web page to students, parents, and colleagues. You can also restrict the page to only certain viewers or choose to make it available to the general public. If you add a few key word tags in your account profile, anyone will be able to find the page by searching Flickr.

Additional examples of providing recognition through web showcases and picture galleries are available at the following websites:

▶ Artsonia Kids' Art Museum
www.artsonia.com

Here you'll find an excellent example of an art showcase where students can share their artwork. At the time of this writing, the site hosts over 13 million pieces by children from all over the world. Teachers are welcome to submit student artwork or lesson plans.

▶ The National Gallery of Writing
http://galleryofwriting.org/galleries/gallery_of_ncte

Run by the National Council of Teachers of English, this website showcases a vast assortment of writing samples—letters, memoirs, lists, poems, podcasts, essays, short stories, instructions, reports, editorials, biographical sketches, speeches, and other types of texts—with the stated aim of providing a mosaic of writing in the United States.

▶ Writing Lesson of the Month Network
http://writinglesson.ning.com/group/publishingstudentwriting

This website offers peer-reviewed K–12 writing lessons matched with examples of student work.

▶ Kennedy High School Art Gallery
http://www.kenn.cr.k12.ia.us/gallery/artgallery/index.asp

This fantastic collection of high school student art is from Cedar Rapids, Iowa, and includes animations, sculpture, photography, drawings, paintings, and digital art.

▶ Mr. Riggs Art Showcase
http://web.me.com/art911/artist911/welcome.html

Colorado art instructor Mr. Riggs created this site to showcase the work of his K–8 students.

▶ PS22 Chorus
http://ps22chorus.blogspot.com/

This Webby award–winning website showcases video clips of performances by the 5th grade chorus at PS22 in Staten Island, New York.

▶ New Technology High School Student Portfolios
www.newtechhigh.org

All students at New Technology High School in Napa, California, are required to post student work portfolios. Click the **Student Work** tab to find exemplars from many past and current portfolios.

▶ Exemplars K–12
www.exemplars.com

This site features teacher assignments alongside benchmarked student work samples, classroom-tested standards-based assessment materials keyed to national standards, and rubrics for mathematics, science, and language arts.

## Communication and Collaboration Software

Today's communication software capitalizes on individuals' natural desire to socialize, to connect with one another, and to express their opinions. In the modern classroom, audio recordings and videoconferencing present new ways for teachers to provide recognition to all learners.

### Audio Recordings

Audio recordings can be an unexpected and exciting way for students to receive recognition. Hearing the congratulatory tone and enthusiasm in a teacher's voice often leaves a lasting impression. Many computer operating systems, including Windows and Mac OS, include a simple sound recorder program. You might also use many simple audio recording applications available for download, such as AudioNote or Jing.

Here's an example of how a teacher might incorporate audio e-mail recognition. Mr. Webster, a high school geometry teacher, is grading a set of mathematics quizzes and finds that one of his students has made significant improvement in the ability to calculate and graph the slope of a linear equation. For a week, he has worked closely with this student, trying to ensure that she grasps the key concepts. He is so happy with her progress that he decides to send the student a simple audio recording praising her for meeting her goal to improve this skill. He simply opens his audio recording program on his computer, vocalizes his praise, saves the file, and sends her an e-mail greeting with the direction to open the attached audio file. She receives the audio message and is delighted to get the timely recognition.

### Instant Messaging

Instant messaging can be a quick and easy way to recognize student effort on a project. Sending an IM along the lines of "Just graded your quiz. WOW!!! Your hard work really paid off! You nailed it J" can motivate a student to continue working his or her hardest on the next goal.

### Videoconferencing

Videoconferencing allows two-way or multipoint communication in more personable, meaningful, and relevant ways than e-mail or telephone can provide.

Through videoconferencing, students can communicate with peers and have contact with professionals who can serve as authentic audiences for student work.

A thriving example of using videoconferencing to provide recognition is the Global WRITeS project. (WRITeS is an acronym for Writers and Readers Incorporating Technology in Society.) This nonprofit organization's mission is to promote literacy through performing arts using technology resources such as videoconferencing and digital media. This project, based in the Bronx, New York, brings together performance poets, classroom teachers, and students to create integrated poetry units. As students write their poems, they practice performing them for students in other classrooms connected via room-based videoconferencing. After the performances, they revise their writing, incorporating the feedback they receive from their peers.

Technology plays a diverse and significant role in this example and models how effective videoconferencing can be as a tool for providing recognition. Initially, students use blogs to publish and share written work with each other. Then they use videoconferencing to engage in real conversations about their poetry, particularly during the writing and practice phase where they give and receive feedback on performances. In a school district that is geographically spread out, such as the Bronx, it is costly and difficult to bring students to the same physical location for this kind of regular collaboration. Videoconferencing drastically reduces travel time, allowing more time for other subjects. All students get to see all performers, as well as the judges, during the slam sessions, and older students who have previously experienced the slam sessions mentor younger students. Perhaps most important, the students receive personalized feedback from peers and published performance poets. Through videoconferencing, student writing is validated in face-to-face exchanges.

For additional resources related to the Global WRITeS project, visit one of the following websites:

▶ Global WRITeS
www.globalwrites.org

This is the official website for the Global WRITeS project. Users can find more information about the project, examples of student work, and research data.

▶ DreamYard
www.dreamyard.com

DreamYard is an innovative arts-in-education organization that integrates the arts into the curricula of elementary, middle, and high school students. On this website, users can find out more information about DreamYard and about lesson plans and student artifacts.

## ⏻ Instructional Interactives

Almost all educational games online provide some sort of recognition for achieving a certain level. These games are often fun, motivating ways to help students practice basic skills and learn key concepts. The IXL website (www .ixl.com/awards), for instance, offers a variety of games for helping preK–8 students learn mathematics concepts. Every time students achieve a preset goal in one of the games, they receive a virtual award.

# 3

# Cooperative Learning

The instructional strategy of *cooperative learning* focuses on having students interact with each other in groups in ways that enhance their learning. This strategy is grounded in the theory that learning can be maximized through well-designed, intentional social interaction with others (Gerlach, 1994; Vygotsky, 1978). Cooperative learning provides an environment where students can reflect upon newly acquired knowledge, process what they are learning by talking with and actively listening to their peers, and develop common understanding about topics. As students talk through material, they deepen their understanding of it and become more conscious of the strategies necessary for arriving at an answer (Bandura, 2000). This process helps them to retain what they are learning.

Cooperative learning can also increase motivation for learning by establishing a strong kinship and sense of obligation to one another among students, which can lead to greater buy-in and increased achievement (Roseth, Johnson, & Johnson, 2008). In well-designed cooperative learning activities, participants develop a sense of positive interdependence—a "sink or swim together" attitude where success on the part of one promotes success among the others. In addition, cooperative learning has been shown to increase academic engagement and self-esteem, improve student attitudes toward school, and decrease social segregation and loneliness (Johnson & Johnson, 2003; Johnson & Johnson, 2005; Morgan, Whorton, & Gunsalus, 2000).

It is helpful to use informal groups for short, impromptu activities that take no longer than a few minutes. There are a variety of structures teachers might use, and many are as simple as announcing, "Numbered heads together" or "Turn to someone sitting next to you." For formal groups, however, teachers should intentionally design assignments to include these two basic components: *positive interdependence* (sink or swim together) and *individual and group accountability* (each of us has to contribute to the group achieving its goal).

We have three recommendations for classroom practice based on the research on cooperative learning:

## RECOMMENDATIONS

- Include elements of both positive interdependence and individual accountability.
- Keep group size small.
- Use cooperative learning consistently and systematically.

As Thomas Friedman notes in *The World Is Flat* (2005), we are living in a time when learning and innovation are increasingly global. To prepare for the fast-paced, virtual workplace that they will someday inherit, students need to be able to learn and produce cooperatively—both in person and online. A 2009 report by World at Work estimated that close to 35 million U.S. workers telecommute at least one day per month—a figure that appears to be rising rapidly, as there were 20 million U.S. teleworkers in 2001. In these working situations, employees very often must communicate with other members of a project team remotely. To prepare students to be successful in this type of environment, we need to provide them with opportunities to connect and collaborate with peers, some of whom they may never meet face-to-face, on projects that require multiple skills and talents.

Technology can play a unique and vital role in cooperative learning by facilitating group collaboration, providing structure for group tasks, and allowing members of groups to communicate even if they are not working face to face. It can help us realize the hope of schools as places that serve students anytime, anywhere and facilitate their growth into lifelong learners. Studies show that there is a modest increase in effect size when students use technology collaboratively, or work together with computers (Urquhart & McIver, 2005). In this chapter, we will show you how *multimedia* and *communication and collaboration software* can facilitate cooperative learning.

## ⏻ Multimedia

Student-generated multimedia is a natural environment for cooperative learning. Creating even a short video or animation is a complex task that requires many roles and responsibilities. By nature, both multimedia projects and cooperative learning groups require attention to detail in the planning process. When these types of activities go astray in the classroom, it is often due to inadequate up-front preparation. Rubrics help students understand what is expected of them and how their participation will be evaluated. While this is important in any learning activity, it is especially important in cooperative learning activities. Figure 3.1 shows a rubric that Ms. Ortiz, a middle school teacher, distributes to her students at the beginning of a two-week movie project about the lives of famous mathematicians. She used RubiStar (http://rubistar.4teachers.org) to create the rubric.

After introducing the project and providing the students with a project rubric, Ms. Ortiz turns her attention to student roles and responsibilities. The class works in small groups of three or four to create short movies focused on curricular topics. She creates a chart like the one shown in Figure 3.2 as an advance organizer to guide students in the process and assigns each student two or three of the responsibilities. Some of the tasks require one student, while other roles, such as researchers, journalists, or actors, require multiple students. The students are allowed to work on the project every other class period for two weeks, with homework assigned for their basic computation work.

At the end of the two weeks, the students view each others' movies and take notes as necessary. Together, they learn about Pythagoras, Euclid, Fibonacci, Pascal, Archimedes, and Banneker, and about how the work that these men did relates to our use of mathematics today. In this way, the students are not only working together in cooperative groups to create the movies, but are actually participating in cooperative teaching.

### Website Creation

Students can collaborate on showing their learning by building a webpage or website using such online tools as Facebook, Google Sites, SchoolFusion, or wikis. For example, Mrs. Williams, a 6th grade science teacher in Colorado, has

**Figure 3.1**

Rubric for a Cooperative Multimedia Project

Multimedia Project: Curriculum Movie
Teacher: Ms. Ortiz
Student Name:

| CATEGORY | 4 | 3 | 2 | 1 |
|---|---|---|---|---|
| Content | Covers topic in depth with details and examples. Subject knowledge is excellent. | Includes essential knowledge about the topic. Subject knowledge appears to be good. | Includes essential information about the topic, but there are 1–2 factual errors. | Content is minimal OR there are several factual errors. |
| Rough Draft | Rough draft is ready for review on due date. Student shares draft with a peer and makes edits based on feedback. | Rough draft is ready for review on due date. Student shares draft with a peer and peer makes edits. | Rough draft not ready for review on due date. Student provides feedback and/or edits for peer. | Rough draft not ready for review on due date. Student does not participate in reviewing draft of peer. |
| Organization | Content is well organized; headings or bulleted lists group related material. | Content is logically organized for the most part. | Headings or bulleted lists group material, but the overall organization of topics appears flawed. | There is no clear or logical organizational structure, just lots of facts. |
| Storyboard | Storyboard includes all required elements as well as a few additional elements. | Storyboard includes all required elements and one additional element. | Storyboard includes all required elements. | One or more required elements are missing from the storyboard. |
| Originality | Product shows a large amount of original thought. Ideas are creative and inventive. | Product shows some original thought. Work shows new ideas and insights. | Product uses other people's ideas (giving credit), but there is little evidence of original thinking. | Product uses other people's ideas but does not give them credit. |
| Attractiveness | Student makes excellent use of video, graphics, sounds, and effects to enhance the presentation. | Student makes good use of video, graphics, sounds, and effects to enhance the presentation. | Student uses video, graphics, sounds, and effects, but occasionally these detract from the presentation content. | Student uses video, graphics, sounds, and effects, but these often distract from the presentation content. |

| | Figure 3.2 Group Roles in a Cooperative Multimedia Project | |
|---|---|---|
| **Role** | **Role or Task Description** | **Student Name(s)** |
| Researcher (2) | Will research the topic and meet with a teacher in that content area to be sure information is accurate. | |
| Scriptwriter (2) | Will take the research provided by the researchers and write a script for the movie. (The teacher must approve a storyboard before the script is finalized. A content area teacher will review the final draft of the script for accuracy.) The script will be in play format and will indicate all resources needed and the settings where the action takes place. | |
| Journalist (1 or 2) | Will provide any on-camera interviews with experts. Journalists will use the provided research to write interview questions that will get additional information needed for the movie. | |
| Tech Expert (1 or 2) | Will provide help with all technology (e.g., iMovie, GarageBand, and GraphicConverter). | |
| Project Coordinator (1) | Will work with the team to build a project timeline and then will monitor all project activities. Responsible for coordinating resources with other teams. (Remember that other teams will be using the video cameras.) | |
| Camera Operator (1 or 2) | Will be responsible for checking out, using, and properly returning video cameras and tripods. | |
| Actor (as needed) | Will use the provided script to bring the movie to life. Actors should be expressive and show appropriate excitement but stay within the script. | |

her students create multimedia web pages using Glogster (www.glogster.com) to demonstrate their understanding of various classroom projects throughout the year. At the beginning of the year, she introduces the students to a Glogster Project rubric (Figure 3.3). As the year progresses, her students' learning becomes less teacher-directed and more student-centered. Examples of Glogster projects can be found at www.glogster.com/explore/education.

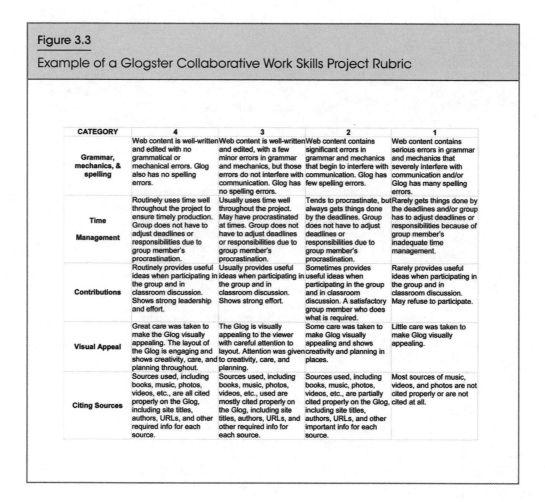

**Figure 3.3**

**Example of a Glogster Collaborative Work Skills Project Rubric**

| CATEGORY | 4 | 3 | 2 | 1 |
|---|---|---|---|---|
| Grammar, mechanics, & spelling | Web content is well-written and edited with no grammatical or mechanical errors. Glog also has no spelling errors. | Web content is well-written and edited, with a few minor errors in grammar and mechanics, but those errors do not interfere with communication. Glog has no spelling errors. | Web content contains significant errors in grammar and mechanics that begin to interfere with communication. Glog has few spelling errors. | Web content contains serious errors in grammar and mechanics that severely interfere with communication and/or Glog has many spelling errors. |
| Time Management | Routinely uses time well throughout the project to ensure timely production. Group does not have to adjust deadlines or responsibilities due to group member's procrastination. | Usually uses time well throughout the project. May have procrastinated at times. Group does not have to adjust deadlines or responsibilities due to group member's procrastination. | Tends to procrastinate, but always gets things done by the deadlines. Group does not have to adjust deadlines or responsibilities due to group member's procrastination. | Rarely gets things done by the deadlines and/or group has to adjust deadlines or responsibilities because of group member's inadequate time management. |
| Contributions | Routinely provides useful ideas when participating in the group and in classroom discussion. Shows strong leadership and effort. | Usually provides useful ideas when participating in the group and in classroom discussion. Shows strong effort. | Sometimes provides useful ideas when participating in the group and in classroom discussion. A satisfactory group member who does what is required. | Rarely provides useful ideas when participating in the group and in classroom discussion. May refuse to participate. |
| Visual Appeal | Great care was taken to make the Glog visually appealing. The layout of the Glog is engaging and shows creativity, care, and planning throughout. | The Glog is visually appealing to the viewer with careful attention to layout. Attention was given to creativity, care, and planning. | Some care was taken to make Glog visually appealing and shows creativity and planning in places. | Little care was taken to make Glog visually appealing. |
| Citing Sources | Sources used, including books, music, photos, videos, etc., are all cited properly on the Glog, including site titles, authors, URLs, and other required info for each source. | Sources used, including books, music, photos, videos, etc., used are mostly cited properly on the Glog, including site titles, authors, URLs, and other required info for each source. | Sources used, including books, music, photos, videos, etc., are partially cited properly on the Glog, including site titles, authors, URLs, and other important info for each source. | Most sources of music, videos, and photos are not cited properly or are not cited at all. |

Over the past decade, it has become easier and easier to make websites. Today, there are many free and inexpensive software programs for website creation. Here are a few:

❱ Google Sites
https://sites.google.com

Google Sites is a free service that allows students and teachers to create websites for any purpose. Many students use them as online portfolios. These sites can be open to the public or set so that only students and teachers who are registered for Google Apps through their school can see the pages. The websites can have single or multiple authors and are easy to create using a wide range of web page templates.

### ▶ SchoolFusion
http://schoolfusion.com

On this website, teachers can easily create robust web pages and blogs called Fusion Pages. A teacher-friendly interface makes the process of editing, adding, and updating content simple. When users join a Fusion Page, they are automatically given a unique calendar and access to Web 2.0 collaboration tools. This safe online community keeps students engaged, learning, and collaborating.

### ▶ Ning
www.ning.com

Ning appeals to educators who want to create closed social networks for their classrooms or organized around specific interests. Features of the site include user controls, forums, document and video posting, blogs, photo albums, and an events calendar.

### ▶ Intuit Website Builder
www.intuit.com/website-building-software

This inexpensive software allows you to design and build a website in minutes, even if you've never attempted to create one before. It's easy to use the design tools by dragging and dropping text, images, and other elements. Intuit offers hundreds of fully functional, navigation-ready website templates featuring multiple pages and sample text that you might easily use in your own site.

### ▶ PBworks
http://pbworks.com

This cloud-computing service can help educators create a resources page for class notes, presentation slides, schedules, policies, and examples of student work. For group projects or student portfolios, students can build collaborative pages, start discussions, post content, upload homework, and share their work. For parent outreach, teachers can post assignments, key dates, and volunteer lists.

## ⏻ Communication and Collaboration Software

Now more than ever, technology allows students to collaborate on projects without the constraints of time or geography. Because we have already discussed blogs and wikis at length, we will not go into them in detail here, but as our previous examples have illustrated, both blogs and wikis provide the means for students to communicate and share ideas as they work cooperatively.

What we will focus on here is on how a teacher might pair instant messaging and VoIP with the aforementioned communication software and expand formal cooperative learning experiences. Combining VoIP with sites that facilitate user-content sharing—such as instant messaging for quick chats, blogs for discussions, Google Sites for collaborating on and sharing information and schedules, and Delicious or Diigo for sharing web resources—facilitates powerful collaboration at any time of day and from any geographical location. Here's an illustration. For a Latin III class, students Jake, Shantel, and Dion are combining their notes on a Google site to create a teaser for an iMovie about Julius Caesar. The site allows the students to collectively summarize their notes and draft a script. Now they are ready to make some decisions about when and where to film and who will play each role.

They decide to log onto Skype (www.skype.com), a service that allows multiple users to talk for free, regardless of location, through their computer. After creating Skype accounts and installing a webcam for the microphone, they agree to meet virtually at 7:00 the next evening. Shantel is able to participate from her laptop, even though she is in another state visiting relatives. As the conversation takes place, they add notes to a document using TypeWith.me about who has which responsibilities. They are able to save the document for future reference. They can also send links to each other using Skype's chat feature as they talk, allowing everyone to see the same resources at the same time. Then, they create a project calendar using Google Calendar so that everyone can see due dates and meeting times. After creating their calendar, they add it to their project's Google site.

As the above example illustrates, cooperative learning is not so much learning to cooperate as it is cooperating to learn (Wong & Wong, 1998). Rapid advances in network infrastructure and bandwidth in our schools have made this approach more feasible than ever. Now students can collaborate through the web with other students in their school, subject experts, and multiuser game players. They can even collaborate across the globe!

Web-enabled collaborative learning has evolved dramatically from its initial use as a simple way for students to look up information together on websites. The web has become much more than an electronic reference book; today, it's a thriving medium for collaboration in business, education, and our personal lives.

One of the most well-known and successful web collaborations is the JASON project (www.jasonproject.org), an organization focused on engaging students in hands-on scientific discovery. JASON's standards-based Expeditions curricula are geared to students in grades 4–9. With the help of multimedia tools and Internet broadcasting technology, participating students become part of a virtual research community, accompanying real researchers in real time as they explore everything from oceans to rainforests to polar regions to volcanoes. Students can also take advantage of all of the online activities available through Team JASON Online.

Another example of a project that demonstrates cooperative learning through technology is the Flat Classroom Project (www.flatclassroomproject .org), which is strongly influenced by Thomas Friedman's *The World Is Flat* (2005). Cofounded by Vicki Davis of Westwood Schools in Camilla, Georgia, and Julie Lindsay of the Beijing International School in China, this project involves middle and high school students collaborating with peers across the globe to identify key emerging technological and global trends. The students collaborate via videoconferences, blogs, wikis, and multimedia and experience firsthand how open-source software, workflow software, and Voice over Internet Protocol are "flattening the world."

Collaboration suites such as Google and tools such as the iPad are increasingly making technology-assisted teamwork between students and teachers the norm. Here are just a few of the thousands of applications that help students brainstorm, problem solve, create, and collect information together:

❱ TypeWith.me
http://willyou.typewith.me

This simple, free online resource allows multiple users to take notes, summarize, and chat together in real time. Each user's contribution is designated with a unique highlight color.

▶ TitanPad
http://titanpad.com

This free resource offers the same features as TypeWith.me.

▶ FaceTime
www.apple.com/mac/facetime

This app, available from the iTunes store, allows seamless audio and video communication between two parties using Macintosh devices or laptops.

▶ Syncpad
http://mysyncpad.com

This app, also available from the iTunes store, allows multiple students to simultaneously draw on a virtual whiteboard using their Macintosh devices. Figure 3.4 shows an example of the Syncpad in use.

**Figure 3.4**

Example of Collaborative Problem Solving Using Syncpad

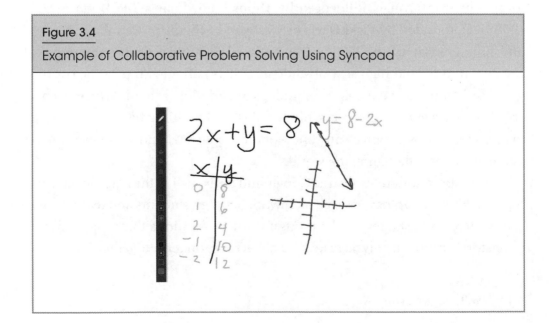

▶ DoodleToo
www.doodletoo.com

This program, also available as an app from the iTunes store, allows multiple users to collaborate by drawing, writing, and chatting.

▶ Google Calendar
www.google.com/calendar

Shared calendars allow students to organize group activities from home as well as from school. Teachers can monitor student groups remotely this way as well. One of the most popular calendar-hosting sites is Google Calendar, which allows participants to view and edit group calendars.

## WebQuests

WebQuests are inquiry-oriented activities that allow students in a class or from multiple locations to work together to learn about a particular subject or to tackle a particular project or problem. WebQuests are designed to use learners' time well, to focus on using information rather than looking for it, and to support learners' thinking at the levels of analysis, synthesis, and evaluation (Dodge & March, 1995). A well-designed WebQuest task is practical and engaging and elicits student thinking. It provides a goal to channel student energies and also clarifies the teacher's learning objectives. Here are some websites that will help you find or design effective WebQuests:

▶ Quest Garden
http://questgarden.com

This website hosts a variety of examples and tools to help teachers get started using and creating WebQuests.

▶ WebQuest Taskonomy
http://webquest.sdsu.edu/taskonomy.html

Here, you'll find a taxonomy of the 12 most common types of WebQuest tasks.

▶ Zunal WebQuest Maker
www.zunal.com

This site contains tools and resources for finding and creating WebQuests.

## Web-enabled Multiplayer Simulation Games

The advent of multiplayer computer games has opened a new avenue of interaction: allowing individuals to interact with other individuals simultaneously through a computer game interface. The difference between these web-enabled games and typical multiplayer computer games is that the web-enabled ones allow human-to-human interaction through a simulated computer interface over the Internet rather than *simulating* that interaction through artificial intelligence within the game program. In other words, the interface, surroundings, characters, situations, and challenges are simulated, but the interactions are human to human and real. As the idea of cooperative learning revolves around the concept of students interacting with each other for a common purpose in learning, it's logical to conclude that well-designed multiplayer computer games would lend themselves to facilitating cooperative learning, provided that they are used properly and offer opportunities for problem solving and continual learning in an enjoyable, engaging environment (Lobel, 2006; Gee, 2009). Indeed, according to Kriz and Eberle (2004), "Gaming simulation is an interactive learning environment that makes it possible to cope with complex authentic situations that are close to reality. At the same time, gaming simulation represents a form of cooperative learning through teamwork" (p. 6).

Here are some great games designed to educate collaboratively:

▶ Civilization V
www.civilization5.com

Sid Meier's Civilization is one of the most successful strategy game series ever created. This game lets multiple players match wits against history's greatest leaders as they employ exploration, construction, diplomacy, and conquest to build and rule an empire to stand the test of time.

▶ Girls Inc. Team Up
www.girlsinc.org/gc/page.php?id=6.2

This is an elementary problem-solving game in which a team of girls, each of whom has a unique ability, needs to solve spatial puzzles.

▶ The Sims
http://thesims.ea.com

The Sims is a life-simulation game that allows players' avatars to interact with one another as they go about daily life. Students can learn social and cooperative skills by playing the game and paying specific attention to the body language of their avatars and to their reactions to different situations.

Communication with students in other cities, states, and countries broadens the perspective of students and challenges them to learn about other cultures, languages, and issues throughout the world. The expansion of global telecommunication networks has made this possible even in some of the world's most remote regions. Students can use e-mail to collaborate with e-mail pen pals from far away. There are many examples of websites that facilitate correspondence and project-based learning between students and other communities. Here are some of the best:

▶ ePALS
www.epals.com

This is one of the Internet's largest communities of collaborative classrooms engaged in cross-cultural exchanges, project sharing, and language learning.

▶ The Teachers Corner
www.theteacherscorner.net/penpals

This website allows teachers to search for classroom keypals by grade level as well as location. Clicking on a grade level brings up a world map showing pushpins on the locations of available keypals.

## Shared Bookmarking

Before the web supported the quick and easy sharing of web links, many teachers used to log onto each computer in a computer lab and bookmark the sites they wanted students to go to for a project. Although this kept the students on task with the appropriate websites, it was very time consuming for the teacher. Now all a teacher has to do is bookmark her best resources on a social bookmarking site and make one link to it that stays on the computers all year. Students can use the teacher site at home or at school without having to remember a lot of URLs. For cooperative learning projects, students can set up their own social bookmarking sites to categorize (tag) websites and share them with others in their group. Here are some of the more popular social bookmarking websites:

▶ Diigo
www.diigo.com

Diigo allows you to save your bookmarks online and organize them by tags. You can also create groups so that other Diigo users can save to a common place for a project or topic of interest. The site allows users to network with one another to compare saved sites.

▶ Google Bookmarks
www.google.com/bookmarks

This site allows you to store, categorize, and access your bookmarks using your Google login.

▶ Delicious
www.delicious.com

With Delicious, you can keep your favorite websites, music, books, and more in a place where you can always find them; share your favorites with students and colleagues; and discover new and interesting things by browsing popular and related items.

▶ Evernote
www.evernote.com

Here you can store screenshots, pictures, documents, and websites and organize them by tag or topic.

## Course Management

In addition to blogs and wikis discussed in earlier sections, teachers can create online learning communities for their students through web-enabled course management system (CMS) programs. These services allow teachers to securely share resources, facilitate online discussions, and post information. Students share ideas, communicate as a group, and learn collectively. Many universities use these services regularly. We list some common online services here:

▶ Moodle
http://moodle.org/

This is a free CMS—an open-source software package designed to help educators create effective online learning communities.

▶ Blackboard
www.blackboard.com

The Blackboard Academic Suite enables institutions to access any learning resource at any time from any place.

▶ Google Apps for Education
www.google.com/educators/p_apps.html

Google Apps for Education lets school tech administrators provide e-mail, sharable online calendars, instant messaging tools, and even a dedicated website to faculty, students, and staff for free.

There are many resources available on the Internet to help you and your students embrace collaborative learning. Here are two that we have found to be particularly useful:

▶ Jigsaw Classroom
www.jigsaw.org

This is the official website of the jigsaw classroom, a cooperative learning technique that helps students work together to learn content and skills.

▶ The University of Wisconsin—Stout
www.uwstout.edu/soe/profdev/rubrics.shtml

Several rubrics related to cooperative learning are available here.

# Helping Students
# Develop Understanding

# 4

# Cues, Questions, and Advance Organizers

We group *cues, questions,* and *advance organizers* together in this chapter because they all focus on enhancing students' ability to retrieve, use, and organize information about a topic. *Cues* are "hints" to students about the content of a lesson, providing information on what the students already know as well as some new information on the topic (Marzano, Pickering, & Pollock, 2001). *Questions* allow students to access previously learned information on the topic, and teachers to assess what the students do not already know. *Advance organizers* are introduced before a lesson to draw attention to important points, identify relationships within the material, and relate material to students' prior knowledge (Lefrancois, 1997; Woolfolk, 2004). The most effective advance organizers provide an organized conceptual framework that is meaningful to the learner and that allows the learner to relate concepts in the instructional material to elements of that framework (Martorella, 1991; White & Tisher, 1986).

Using cues, questions, and advance organizers at the beginning of a lesson or unit focuses learning on the important content to come. Cues, questions, and advance organizers can motivate students by tapping into their curiosity and interest in the topic. In addition, using higher-order questions helps students deepen their knowledge by requiring the use of critical thinking skills (e.g., making inferences, analyzing perspectives).

We have eight recommendations for classroom practice:

## RECOMMENDATIONS

- Focus on what is important.
- Use explicit cues.
- Ask inferential questions.
- Ask analytic questions.
- Use expository advance organizers.
- Use narrative advance organizers.
- Use graphic advance organizers.
- Use skimming as an advance organizer.

Technology's potential applications are readily evident in this strategy, as teachers and students can use a variety of technology tools to create well-organized, visually appealing organizers. In this chapter, you will see what we mean, as we examine ways to use *word processing applications*, *data collection and analysis tools*, *organizing and brainstorming software*, *instructional media*, and *instructional interactives*.

We can recommend several resources that focus on different levels of questions and provide excellent examples:

▶ Bloom's Taxonomy Blooms Digitally
http://techlearning.com/article/8670

This 2008 article by Andrew Churches suggests appropriate verbs for use at each level of Bloom's taxonomy for both digital and traditional learning activities.

▶ For the Best Answers, Ask Tough Questions
http://faculty.philau.edu/kayk/KKay/articles/BestAnsers.pdf

This is an outstanding article on the topic of essential questions, written by Joyce Valenza and originally published in the April 20, 2000, issue of the *Philadelphia Inquirer*. An essential question is one that requires the student to make a decision or create a plan. It requires more than simple research and regurgitation of answers. The article includes links to other resources addressing the topic of essential questions.

▶ Blooms Digitally
www.usi.edu/distance/bdt.htm

This interactive graphic provides links to a variety of appropriate online tools for use at each level of Bloom's taxonomy.

▶ Why Is It Important for Students to Learn About Bloom's Taxonomy?
http://larryferlazzo.edublogs.org/2011/05/07/why-is-it-important-for-students-to-learn-about-blooms-taxonomy

This excellent blog post by Larry Ferlazzo, published on May 7, 2011, discusses the importance of explicitly teaching what Bloom's taxonomy is to students. The article includes some great examples and links to many resources on Bloom's taxonomy.

▶ The Differentiator
www.byrdseed.com/differentiator

This unique website allows teachers to select items from lists of thinking skills, content areas, resources, products, and grouping strategies, then automatically creates a "Students will" statement.

## ⏻ Word Processing Applications

Word processing programs are extremely versatile and well suited as tools to create advance organizers, whether expository, narrative, or graphic. *Expository* advance organizers include brochures, definitions, rubrics, and programs. *Narrative* advance organizers are usually stories, articles, or artistic works. *Graphic* advance organizers are usually tables, charts, or artistic works.

Teachers can use expository, narrative, and graphic advance organizers alone or combine them to form compelling introductory materials that will help students focus on the essential concepts and themes that will prepare them to learn. For instance, if you are taking your students on a field trip, have them conduct research on the Internet beforehand and create a simple brochure using word processing software. The brochure might contain useful information students can refer to during the trip, including maps, facts, and pictures. You might also have them copy and paste it into an agenda that you have created with a word processor and saved to your school's server or other commonly accessible location. Prior to embarking on the trip, students could skim the brochure as an additional advance organizer.

Another application of word processing programs is the use of table-making features to create an advance organizer for note taking. At the beginning of a lesson, the teacher gives students a two-column notes template with key terms, concepts, or themes for the day's instruction listed in the first column. As the lesson progresses, the students can gradually fill in this skeleton with explanatory text, web links, and pictures. This helps students organize their thoughts around the essential information and gets them thinking about what they know about the topic even before the teacher has fully begun the lesson. This expository advance organizer could be posted for all to see on a computer projector or saved to a central server for the students to download. Furthermore, because the notes are digital, students can easily revise them and e-mail them home for study.

To create a note-taking template in Word, click on **Insert > Table** and enter the number of columns and rows you want the initial table to have. Don't worry if you misjudge the size of the table; you can easily insert or delete rows and columns later.

## ⏻ Data Collection and Analysis Tools

Although spreadsheet software may not be the first technology tool you think of when you want to create an advance organizer, it may actually be the best choice when a lesson is very unique or you want to use spreadsheet functions in a rubric. Rubrics are excellent advance organizers because they prepare students to apply their abilities, knowledge, and critical thinking skills. Combining the expository information in a rubric with artistic narrative organizers is an effective strategy for preparing students to learn.

Here's an example. Mrs. Kedzierski, a high school language arts teacher, is planning a poetry writing lesson. For a narrative advance organizer, she gives students a selection of poems that set the mood for a major historical period: the Renaissance. The vocabulary, tone, and story line of poems by Shakespeare, Donne, and Jonson help activate students' prior knowledge and awaken their curiosity. After students read several of Shakespeare's sonnets, they write their own, as if they too were living in Elizabethan England. Of course, writing from this perspective is not easy and requires some up-front guidance. Mrs.

Kedzierski decides to create a rubric to pass out to the students before they begin their writing.

Although Mrs. Kedzierski is familiar with online rubric-making sites, she prefers to create her own in Microsoft Excel or in a word processing program using the table-making features. When using Excel, she first types her lesson criteria (e.g., *follows sonnet format, uses vocabulary appropriate to the time, sets story in Elizabethan period*) into the cells. Then she applies her desired formatting, colors, and fonts. She decides to program the spreadsheet to automatically tabulate the rubric score as she grades the poems. She does this by highlighting the cell under the rubric sub-scores column and choosing the **fx** on the formula bar. Then she selects the **SUM** function and makes sure the summation selects the proper range of sub-scores, such as **D1:D4**. Now she has a rubric she can use quickly and easily over and over again.

## ⏻ Organizing and Brainstorming Software

One of our recommendations is that teachers use explicit cues. By that, we mean your cues should be straightforward and provide students with a preview of what they are about to learn. Although it's common to think that cues should be subtle or ambiguous—like hints—in the classroom, a direct approach is most effective. Simply tell students what content they are about to learn.

For illustration, consider Ms. Douglas, a 6th grade science teacher who starts a unit on the physical properties of bridges by announcing to her students that they will be looking at different types of bridges, the parts of bridges, and the reasons why different bridges serve different purposes. She uses an Inspiration organizer (see Figure 4.1) to show the students their learning goal.

Notice that Ms. Douglas has also included an *essential question* in this Inspiration organizer. Asking students to use background knowledge to answer essential questions aligns with research showing that higher-order questions produce deeper learning than lower-order questions do (Marzano, Pickering, & Pollock, 2001). Because Ms. Douglas's students are doing this activity in conjunction with their study of forces of motion, she gives explicit cues that will help them connect the content. She explicitly states, "As you think about your answer to the essential question of what factors architects need to consider before building a bridge, also think about Newton's Third Law of Motion: that for every action, there is an equal and opposite reaction."

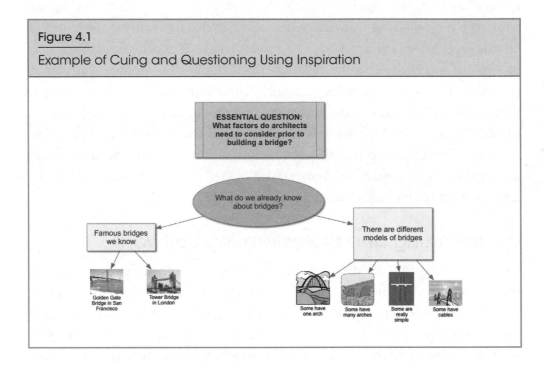

**Figure 4.1**

Example of Cuing and Questioning Using Inspiration

As a teacher, when you provide cues and questions like the ones Ms. Douglas provides, students have a clearer sense of what they are going to learn. To aid the learning process, look for opportunities to activate students' background knowledge, thereby providing a direction for exploration. The technology, in turn, provides you with editable visual aids and multimedia resources that appeal to a number of learning styles. Auditory learners have the added benefit of being able to listen many times to information in order to understand it better. Visual learners use the pictures and video as visual clues to understanding the content. The motion portrayed in the video can reach kinesthetic learners by helping them to picture the motion of forces associated with bridges.

Let's take a look at how Ms. Douglas might use the same software to create an advance organizer to further her 6th graders' study of bridges. Kidspiration and Inspiration software are ideal tools for creating advance organizers, and specifically graphical organizers. Whether these organizers are used digitally with students or printed out for them to complete by hand, organizing and brainstorming software allows learners to add and organize information as it is being introduced.

Ms. Douglas's goal is to get her students to apply the concepts they learned during a study of Newton's Laws of Motion to real-world purposes. Particularly, she wants to have them learn about different types of bridges and how engineers decide which type of bridge to build in various situations. She uses Inspiration to create an advance organizer. It includes blank areas to label the types of bridges and the forces acting upon them. She leaves blank sections and instructs her students to fill these in with a drawing of each type of bridge, complete with arrows showing the stresses. She also includes a word bank to introduce new vocabulary terms.

Next, Ms. Douglas incorporates multimedia into this process of cueing and questioning. She provides her students with a collection of links to online resources featuring instructional media and instructional interactives, where they can find the information they'll need to complete the advance organizer. The resources listed here can themselves be categorized as expository or skimming advance organizers:

• How Bridges Work (http://science.howstuffworks.com/bridge.htm). This website offers detailed explanations of how things work. The articles are broken into chapters, and vocabulary terms are in bold.

• PBS Building Big: Bridges (www.pbs.org/wgbh/buildingbig/bridge/index.html). This series of tutorials offers applets and short games to introduce the physics behind bridges, domes, skyscrapers, dams, and tunnels.

• NOVA Online: Super Bridge (www.pbs.org/wgbh/nova/bridge/). This simulation has students learn about different types of bridges and then apply their skills by deciding which bridge works best in various situations.

• BrainPOP (www.brainpop.com/technology/scienceandindustry/bridges/). This short movie introduces basic vocabulary and concepts behind bridges.

As the students are introduced to new vocabulary terms and concepts, they fill in the blank sections. Figure 4.2 shows one student's completed organizer.

Later, as the students delve deeper into the concepts, the teacher can add to this organizer. The word bank can grow as the students learn more vocabulary. If she chooses, Ms. Douglas can even use this organizer as a final assessment piece by giving students a blank graphic organizer at the end of a unit and having them fill in the text and drawings.

**Figure 4.2**

Completed Advance Organizer Created in Inspiration

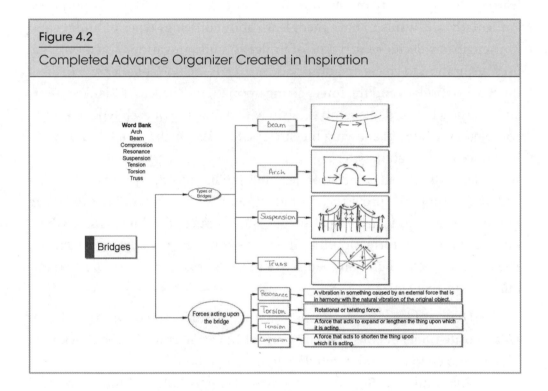

Let's look at another example of using organizing and brainstorming software for activating prior knowledge. Ms. Corum, an elementary school teacher, is beginning a unit on mathematical problem solving and wants her students to have a clear understanding of how complex mathematical problems are solved. She also wants to formatively assess their understanding before she introduces a model of the problem-solving process.

Ms. Corum gets her students to focus on the topic of problem solving by having them team up in groups of three and take turns explaining how they would go about solving a given word problem. She instructs them to focus on the steps in the process rather than the outcome. After about 10 minutes, she leads them into the next part of the lesson by opening her Webspiration Classroom (www.webspirationclassroom.com) account on a projected computer screen. The students watch as she types in this question as the main idea: "What are the steps you should take to solve a math word problem?" Then Ms. Corum selects the RapidFire tool on the toolbar, which can generate an idea map out of words and phrases, and hands the computer over to a student assistant who facilitates the students' brainstorming using a mixture of cues and questions. Because RapidFire generates an idea map automatically as words are typed in, it helps keep the attention of the students on the brainstorming rather than the technology. As students enthusiastically offer their suggestions, the student assistant records them for the class to see on a projection screen. The completed idea map is shown in Figure 4.3.

**Figure 4.3**

Example of Idea Gathering in Inspiration Using RapidFire

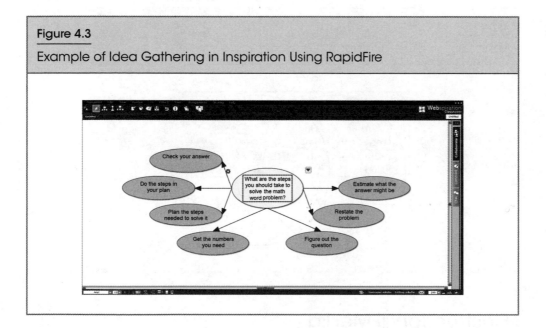

## Graphic Organizers on the iPad

The iTunes store has dozens of apps that provide graphic organizers for students and teachers. In Chapter 1, we showed you how MindMeister could be used to create a KWHL chart. This same app can be used to create graphic organizers as students learn new material.

Teachers and students can draw directly on their iPad graphic organizers using one of many drawing tools. Here's an example. Ms. Standing Bear teaches high school biology in a school where each student has an iPad. As the students start to learn about the differences between eukaryotic and prokaryotic cells, they are instructed to open the Venn diagram blackline master that they have previously saved in their Photos app. Ms. Standing Bear downloaded the Venn diagram for her students by logging onto her ASCD account and saving the image from *A Handbook for Classroom Instruction That Works.* Next, she has the students open a drawing app and choose the Venn diagram as their background. Now they can write and draw the differences between the two types of cells as they learn. Figure 4.4 shows an example of one student's organizer.

**Figure 4.4**

Venn Diagram Created Using a Drawing App on the iPad

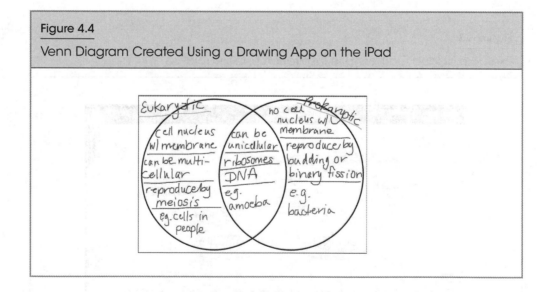

## ⏻ Instructional Media

One effective way to use cues and questions is through online discussions. Although assessing online discussions can be tricky, searching the keyword "blog" at http://rubistar.4teachers.org returns many pages of helpful rubrics on the subject.

Here's an example of how to use cues and questions in online discussions. Mr. Hiser, a high school government teacher, is teaching a class on how a bill becomes a law. He has lots of great multimedia to use in his lesson, but he wants to make sure students stay engaged and on target with their learning. He wants to avoid showing long movies where students become bored, miss the point, or drift off to sleep. Fortunately, his school has set up My Big Campus (www.mybigcampus.com) accounts for each student. He instructs the students to log onto their accounts and enter his class section on their computers. Here he has posted a link to a 20-minute segment of the documentary *How a Bill Becomes a Federal Law*, from the Leonore Annenberg Institute for Civics. He has also posted online cues along with time codes that correspond to the parts of the video which he'd like the students to answer questions about that he has posted in the blog section of the students' accounts. The students independently watch the videos on their computers with headsets on, pausing the video at the designated time codes as needed to answer the questions on the blog. Mr. Hiser monitors the blog and posts further cues and questions to spur discussion and clarify any misconceptions.

Here's another example of using instructional media to introduce new concepts. Ms. Mitchell, a preK teacher, is getting ready to introduce her class to the letter *M*. She decides to begin with a multimedia advance organizer. She goes to www.sesamestreet.org and searches the site for the letter *M*. She finds a number of good videos and decides to use one called "Law & Order: The Missing *M*." Not only does this video do a great job introducing the letter *M*, but she finds it funny. She also finds another video, "The Alphabet with Kermit," that she thinks would help her students focus on the topic.

The next day in class, Ms. Mitchell has her students come to the reading area in the front of the room and brings her computer up on the projector. She tells her class that they are going to learn a new letter and shows them the Kermit video, in which a four-year-old boy sings the Alphabet Song but accidentally forgets the letter *M*. Kermit tells the boy he did a great job with the song but forgot the letter *M*. At that point, Ms. Mitchell switches to the "Law & Order: The Missing M" video. This advance organizer focuses the students on what they are going to learn for the rest of the lesson—the letter *M*. They then move into a number of cutting and coloring activities, all centered on *M*.

In yet another example, Ms. Simpson, a 10th grade language arts teacher, wishes to provide her students with a frame of reference as they begin reading John Steinbeck's *The Grapes of Wrath*. She projects a PowerPoint slide show of images that capture the living conditions of displaced farm workers during the Great Depression. She reasons that the visuals will help her mostly affluent students, who have no real idea of hunger or hopelessness, gain a better sense of the hardships of that time period. While she knows that the pictures of the Dust Bowl period will make an impression on her students, she speculates that a movie will have an even greater impact. She conducts a Google Video search and selects several clips she feels will give her students a clearer idea of what it might have been like to have lived through the Dust Bowl period. You can find video clips online from the following resources:

▶ Discovery Education Streaming
http://streaming.discoveryeducation.com

Use this educational video collection to create an advance organizer at the onset of a learning activity. Assessment questions are also included with many of the videos.

▶ The Internet Archive
www.archive.org

Home to the "Way Back Machine" and Internet archives, this resource also has multiple video clips from the 20th century.

▶ Google Video
http://video.google.com

This subsection of Google searches specifically for video clips using the keywords that you enter.

▶ Watch Know
www.watchknow.org

This directory features hundreds of thousands of good videos suggested by educators. They are reviewed, approved, and assigned to appropriate categories via wiki.

▶ Creative Commons
www.creativecommons.com

Creative commons is a nonprofit organization that offers flexible copyright licenses for creative works. This engine searches for flexible copyright material—graphics, sounds, and publications—that are meant for public use.

# ⏻ Instructional Interactives

Instructional interactives can also provide advance organizers for students. For example, Mrs. Lewers, a 6th grade teacher, is teaching her class about constellations, nebulas, and planets of the night sky. She really wanted to take them to an observatory so they could see the planets and nebulas, but field trips had been restricted in her district. Fortunately, her class has recently received a set of iPads. She arranges to have the Star Chart app loaded onto all of her students' iPads. This app allows her students to hold their iPads toward the sky and see an accurate picture of the planets, stars, nebulas, and constellations. Because the app is connected to the iPad's GPS, the students are able to see the night sky clearly even though it is the middle of the afternoon (see Figure 4.5). Ashlyn, one of Mrs. Lewers's students, is quickly able to find Polaris, the North Star, and sees the lines connecting the stars that make up the Little Dipper. She is able to see the horizon line as well. Using Star Chart as an advance organizer, Ashlyn has a much better idea of what to look for as she attempts to identify the constellations at home over the following two weeks. She is able to take her iPad home and compare the Start Chart display to the real night sky. This allows her to do her homework even on cloudy nights.

## Social Bookmarking

Teachers might consider gathering resources for advance organizers using a social bookmarking service. For instance, they could start a Diigo group for a specific topic, as was mentioned in Chapter 3. Teachers can create groups that focus on specific content, grade levels, or projects. Each resource can be given a "tag"—that is, a one-word descriptor of its content. Teachers may even tag certain resources as good advance organizers: For example, a BrainPOP Jr. movie on the "ch" sound could be saved to a Kindergarten literacy Diigo group with the tags "ch," "multimedia," and "AdvanceOrganizer." One group of high school educators decided to create a Diigo group to pool together resources that would help them integrate nanotechnology into their existing science curricula. After each teacher created a Diigo account, one of the teachers created a NanoTeach group, named after the McREL research study in which they were participating. He then invited the other interested teachers to join his group. Their collection of resources can be found at http://groups.diigo.com/group/nano_teach.

### Figure 4.5
Screen Shot of Star Chart Showing Polaris and the Little Dipper

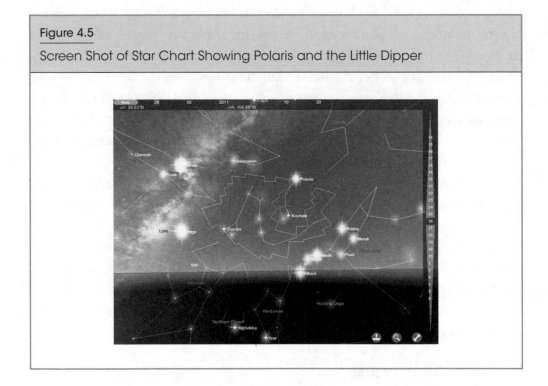

# 5

# Nonlinguistic Representations

Nonlinguistic representations enhance students' ability to use mental images to represent and elaborate on knowledge. To back up slightly, knowledge is stored in two forms: *linguistic* form (as language) and *nonlinguistic* form (as mental images and physical sensations). The more individuals use both types of representation, the better they are able to reflect on and recall knowledge. Teachers usually present new knowledge in linguistic form; that is, they either talk to students about new content or ask them to read about new content. When teachers branch out to help students use nonlinguistic representations as well, the effects on achievement are strong because they tap into students' natural tendency for visual image processing (Medina, 2008), helping them to construct meaning of content and skills being learned and to recall it better later. For example, diagrams and models are used in mathematics and science to help represent phenomena that students cannot observe, such as the arrangement of atoms in a molecule and how that arrangement changes during an interaction. In other subjects, students can use nonlinguistic representations such as graphic organizers to organize information into a conceptual framework. The ultimate goal for using these strategies is to "produce nonlinguistic representations in the minds of students" so they are better able to process, organize, and retrieve information from memory (Marzano, Pickering, & Pollock, 2001, p. 73).

We have five recommendations for classroom practice using nonlinguistic representations:

## RECOMMENDATIONS

- Use graphic organizers.
- Make physical models or manipulatives.
- Generate mental pictures.
- Create pictures, illustrations, and pictographs.
- Engage in kinesthetic activities.

Technology plays an obvious role in facilitating the creation of graphic organizers and helping to generate mental pictures and pictographs. According to Marzano's original meta-analysis (1998), using graphic representations had one of the highest impacts on student achievement, with an average effect size of 1.24. Another developing role of technology includes kinesthetic activities. New hardware and software that allow the user to respond to and give information through physical sensations, such as the Nintendo Wii and the Xbox Kinect, have exploded into the commercial market in the past decade. The opportunity for classroom learning, while yet to be realized, has great potential. Other examples of using kinesthetic activities with technology include Lego/Logo robotics, science probeware, and iPad apps that interact with the user's geographic location and movements.

In this chapter, we look at the following categories of technology that can help teachers provide and help students create mental pictures and pictographs: *word processing applications, data collection and analysis tools, organizing and brainstorming software, database and reference resources, multimedia, instructional interactives,* and *kinesthetic technology.*

## ⏻ Word Processing Applications

Word processing software allows students to easily add clip art and photos to their writing. This strategy is especially helpful when working with emergent readers or English language learners, who particularly benefit from visual cues (Hill & Flynn, 2006). Adding pictures to notes also has been shown to aid in understanding and retention of new content (Marzano, 1998).

Here's an illustration. Ms. Byers, a kindergarten teacher who is helping her students learn the sound of the letter *D*, brings up a word processing document on a computer projector, changes the type to 26-point Century Gothic (a font that young readers find very legible), and asks her students to think of words that start with the *D* sound. As students respond, she types a list of words, adding bold and underline formatting to the letter *d*. Ms. Byers then goes back and shows them how to insert clip art. She explains everything she does: "To add a drawing to each word, I'm going to place my cursor—that's the blinking line that you see—in front of each word. Then I'm going to go to "Insert." Can anyone tell me what *Insert* would start with? Good, the letter *I*. Who sees the letter *I* up here in my menu? That's right; it's the fourth word in that row."

Ms. Byers continues cuing her students as she goes through the steps of adding clip art. While the kindergarten students will not necessarily be able to insert clip art on their own for a while, they are seeing their teacher model the process. She lets various students choose the clip art that she pastes beside each word, and this way she uses pictographs to help her students remember words that begin with the *D* sound. When they are finished, the list looks like Figure 5.1.

**Figure 5.1**

Graphics-Enhanced Notes: The Letter Sound "D"

*Clip art images © 2012 Jupiterimages Corporation.*

Ms. Byers can now print the document and put copies in students' take-home folders, on the bulletin board, on each student's desk, on her classroom website, or any other place where the students will see the words and pictures and get a nonlinguistic reminder of the sound of the letter *D*.

A similar activity could be done using iPad apps such as AudioNote and DrawFree or the iPod voice recorder. AudioNote allows students to draw pictures while recording audio of what they are learning. Upon playback, the sections of the drawing that correspond to the audio played will automatically be highlighted in blue. Figure 5.2 shows an example of a student's use of AudioNote to explain the relationship among eighths, fourths, and halves.

**Figure 5.2**

Screenshot of a Student's Work in AudioNote

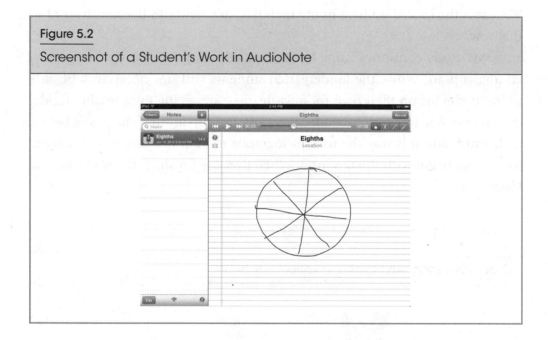

This same technique can and should be used with older students to help them remember processes or new vocabulary words. Figure 5.3 shows a student's drawing of her understanding of the water cycle using the PaperDesk iPad app. As she learns key vocabulary, she also records these words to help her remember them later.

## ⏻ Data Collection and Analysis Tools

Spreadsheet software, along with digital probes and digital microscopes, provides effective ways for students to collect and analyze data using nonlinguistic representations.

**Figure 5.3**

Student Work Created in PaperDesk

## Spreadsheet Software

One of spreadsheet software's primary purposes is to enable users to easily create graphs and charts from data entered. Although spreadsheet software is most often used in business settings, it can be a valuable tool for creating nonlinguistic representations of data.

One effective way to use spreadsheet software in this manner comes from David Warlick (http://davidwarlick.com), an educational technology consultant and speaker. In an activity he demonstrates for teachers, he begins by accessing data from the U.S. Geological Survey (http://neic.usgs.gov/neis/gis/qed.asc) that show software activity in the past 30 days (see Figure 5.4). Most people look at this and can make little sense of these strings of numbers. Warlick imports the data into a spreadsheet, does a little reformatting, and generates an *XY* scatter plot. Here are the steps to take to convert the information in Figure 5.4 into nonlinguistic form using Microsoft Excel:

1. Select **Data > From Web** and put http://neic.usgs.gov/neis/gis/qed.asc in the address field.

2. Choose the little arrow at the top left of the window to select the entire page to import. Click **Import**, then **OK**.

3. Your data should now appear in the spreadsheet. Remove any extraneous material that may have been imported and ensure that the columns of data are graphed on the correct axis. Highlight all the data under column A and select **Data > Data Tools > Text to Columns**.

4. A window should appear, asking how the data is described. Select **Delimited**, then click **Next**.

5. Change the delimiters selection to **Comma** and unselect any other choices, such as **Tab**. Click **Next**, then **Finish**. Your data should now be displayed in neatly arranged columns with the following headings: Date, TimeUTC, Latitude, Longitude, Magnitude, and Depth.

6. Select the columns that show the Date, TimeUTC, Magnitude, and Depth and delete them. This removes the extraneous material for this particular activity, leaving only the latitude and longitude data.

7. The goal is to plot these coordinates on an *XY* plane, but latitude and longitude are in the opposite places to do this. In other words, if you leave the column order as it is, you'll create a sideways map of the world. So select the Longitude column, **Cut** the column, highlight the column to the left of the Latitude data, and then choose **Paste** to arrange the columns so that the Longitude column is first, followed by the Latitude column.

8. Next, highlight all the data in both columns and choose **Insert > Scatter > Scatter with Only Markers**.

9. To make the patterns in your plot clearer, choose **Chart Tools > Format > Size** and select the arrow shape, then select **Lock Aspect Ratio > Close**. Now drag the corners of your chart to enlarge it. You can select the title and delete or change it. Use **Chart Tools > Layout > Legend** to turn off the legend. Under the same menu, turn on the vertical and horizontal **Axis Tiles** and label them "Longitude" and "Latitude."

10. Choose any of the data markers by clicking once on one of them in the plot. Then choose **Chart Tools > Format > Current Selection > Format Selection**. Select **Marker Options** and make the size smaller by changing it to "2." The patterns in your plot should now be easier to analyze.

Your completed chart should look something like Figure 5.5.

---

**Figure 5.4**

**Unformatted Seismic Data Downloaded from the U.S. Geological Survey**

```
Date,TimeUTC,Latitude,Longitude,Magnitude,Depth
2011/08/23,09:37:57.5,37.099,-104.711,3.2,  5
2011/08/23,07:17:58.4,37.076,-104.637,3.7,  5
2011/08/23,07:01:35.1,37.109,-104.55,3.2,  5
2011/08/23,06:56:59.4,37.110,-104.722,3.5,  5
2011/08/23,06:04:56.1,42.100,142.480,4.8, 46
2011/08/23,05:46:19.1,37.118,-104.622,5.3,  4
2011/08/23,04:56:52.9,12.010, 44.042,4.9, 10
2011/08/23,03:55:57.4,14.321,-90.055,4.4, 22
2011/08/23,03:20:01.9,-56.172,-27.076,4.9,110
2011/08/23,02:48:52.0,37.056,-104.726,3.0,  5
2011/08/23,01:23:00.4,33.155, 76.839,5.1, 42
2011/08/23,00:41:14.7,-22.071,-179.193,4.6,520
2011/08/22,23:30:20.1,37.039,-104.531,4.6,  5
2011/08/22,22:38:37.7,35.565,-97.361,2.5,  6
2011/08/22,22:24:53.8,52.769,-169.84,4.6, 57
2011/08/22,22:18:50.9,-18.291,-177.727,5.0,630
2011/08/22,20:12:20.5,-6.41,103.985,6.0, 31
2011/08/22,17:39:38.6,-18.334,168.111,5.0, 37
2011/08/22,16:25:21.6,38.552, 69.586,4.8, 25
2011/08/22,16:02:08.1,-18.25,-177.966,4.6,629
2011/08/22,15:26:11.1,37.421,141.434,4.4, 45
2011/08/22,14:55:32.1,-7.42,128.126,4.9,162
```

A teacher who follows these steps will have changed what was initially a meaningless string of numbers into a nonlinguistic representation of those data. Students will be able to see the plot points of the data and can begin to answer the following questions:

- Which line represents the equator?
- Which line represents the prime meridian?
- Where are the Aleutian Islands of Alaska?
- Where are the fault lines of California?
- Can the "Ring of Fire" be seen?
- Why are the data denser in some areas than others?
- How are the major plots showing at the 150-degree longitude mark related to natural disasters that have been on the news lately?
- Could we overlay these data on a map of the world?

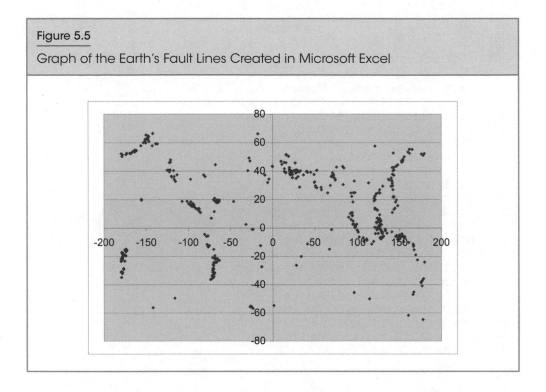

**Figure 5.5**

Graph of the Earth's Fault Lines Created in Microsoft Excel

Other spreadsheet technology would also work well for this activity. For instance, Inspiration's InspireData allows students to enter data, then organize and sort them using nonlinguistic symbols and pictures in the Plot View. There are several options: Venn diagrams, stack graphs, and pie charts. Students can label the material in various ways, apply color schemes to indicate different data categories, and sort by label, color, and plot type.

One of the best uses of technology in the classroom is to allow students to look at information differently and think critically. In a traditional setting, Ms. Frazier, a 9th grade social studies teacher, would ask her students to research data on the United States and China and look at the economic differences between the two countries. Her student, Jill, would go to the library and look up the information and have data that were current a few years ago. Jill might go online and search each country, sort through the thousands of hits, and try to make sense of the vast data sets presented. A better tool to use, however, could be WolframAlpha (www.wolframalpha.com). Jill types in the query "United States and China" and immediately is presented with a clear set of current economic data on the two countries (Figure 5.6). Rather than spend the bulk of her time looking *for* valid and current data, Jill is now looking *at* the data and trying to make meaning. She sees, for example, that the United States and China rank numbers one and two respectively in most categories, but that in terms of GDP per capita the United States is 20th and China is 136th. In GDP real growth, however, the United States is 127th and China is 20th. Looking at these data Jill can begin to create a hypothesis about where the two countries might be at a point in the future.

**Figure 5.6**

WolframAlpha Chart Comparing the GDPs of the United States and China

Economic properties:

| | United States | China |
|---|---|---|
| GDP | $14.6 trillion per year (world rank: 1st) (Q2 2010 estimate) | $5.308 trillion per year (world rank: 2nd) (Q2 2010 estimate) |
| GDP at parity | $14.6 trillion per year (world rank: 1st) (Q2 2010 estimate) | $9.418 trillion per year (world rank: 2nd) (Q2 2010 estimate) |
| real GDP | $14.37 trillion per year (price-adjusted to year-2008 US dollars) (world rank: 1st) | $4.327 trillion per year (price-adjusted to year-2008 US dollars) (world rank: 3rd) |
| GDP per capita | $46 000 per person per year (world rank: 20th) (Q2 2010 estimate) | $3920 per person per year (world rank: 136th) (Q2 2010 estimate) |
| GDP real growth | +2.5% per year (world rank: 127th) (Q1 2010 estimate) | +9% per year (world rank: 20th) (2008) |
| Gini index | 0.408 (world rank: 69th highest) (2000) | 0.415 (world rank: 63rd highest) (2005) |
| consumer price inflation | −0.36% per year (world rank: 157th) (2009) | −0.7% per year (world rank: 164th) (2009) |
| unemployment rate | 9.26% (world rank: 65th highest) (2009) | 4.3% (world rank: 144th highest) (2009) |

*Source: http://www.wolframalpha.com/input/?i=United+States+and+China. (accessed September 14, 2011)*

While Jill used WolframAlpha, her friend Lena used a site her dad told her about—Gapminder (www.gapminder.org). Like WolframAlpha, Gapminder presented Lena with economic data on the two countries, but Gapminder showed the long-term historic data beginning in 1856 and forecasting through 2014 (Figure 5.7). She could clearly see how the gap between the two countries changed over time and use today's data and historic trends to make an informed hypothesis.

**Figure 5.7**

Gapminder Chart Showing Relative Economic Growth
Over Time of the United States and China

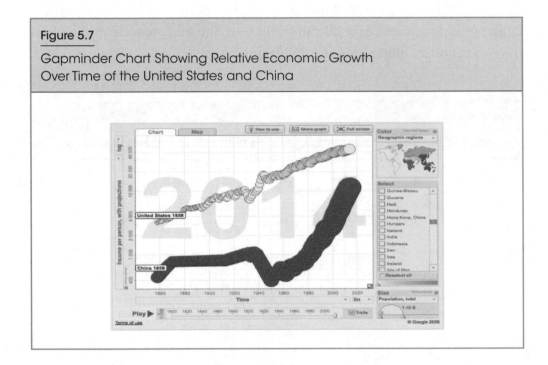

While some students in the class spent their time collecting data and had a finished report that presented the current GDP of both countries accurately, Jill and Lena used their time to analyze data and create reports with predictions of what those data would look like in the future based on trend data. Instead of simply collecting data they were working at higher cognitive levels to analyze and evaluate those data.

## Digital Probes and Digital Microscopes

Technology has come a long way in providing the tools that allow students to go beyond repetitive calculations, hand graphing, and sketching. Today's digital probes and digital microscopes feature photography and video functions that enable students to acquire information and images—some of which are types of nonlinguistic representation—for analysis, synthesis, and evaluation.

Obviously, probes and microscopes are useful tools in science class, but all subjects can use parts of these tools to enhance the curriculum. For instance, language arts and social studies classes might make use of digital scopes' photography and video functions in dramatic productions, anthropological investigations, and reenactments. Music classes might use sound probes to analyze music. Mathematics classes might use probe data to illustrate practical examples of graphing equations. Even so, let's use two science topics to illustrate the use of these two related technologies: First, how students can use digital probes to compare the temperatures and luminosity of incandescent and compact fluorescent lightbulbs, and second, how students can use digital microscopes to examine both crystal patterns and *triops*, tiny prehistoric crustaceans that are among the oldest living species on Earth.

Of course, to investigate the temperature and luminosity of lightbulbs, students could also use the naked eye or standard thermometers and stopwatches, both of which were "high-tech" at one time. The next step would be to use graph paper and colored pencils to create graphs that incorporate observational data. Then they might present this information by using a ruler to draw a large, approximate graph on a piece of poster board. These approaches are certainly sound; indeed, many of us learned by these very methods. Still, it is easy to see that modern technology has a lot to add in terms of efficiency, accuracy, analysis, and presentation. Likewise, students could observe crystals or triops with a magnifying glass, but a digital microscope greatly enhances this activity. Today's technology allows us to take still pictures, insert digital labels, record video clips, and use the resulting images in a presentation. This is fast and easy and produces professional-looking results.

## Digital Probes

For just about any science measurement that you can think of, you can collect data with a digital probe. Usually when you purchase probeware, it comes with software for data logging, analyzing, and graphing. Once students have learned the fundamentals of graphing, they can skip the boring, mistake-prone process of data entry and the time-consuming routine of creating hand-drawn graphs and get right to higher-level problem solving and thinking. Vendors such as Vernier, Pasco, HOBO, and Fourier specialize in different areas, such as wireless (Bluetooth) data transfer, long-term data logging, and all-in-one elementary multiprobes, but all of them allow the user to collect data and put them into a graphic form for further analysis.

Here's an example of incorporating digital probes into a lesson. Mr. Enapay's 8th grade students are in the middle of a science inquiry investigation. After a lesson on types of energy, Mr. Enapay has his students predict the relationship between gravitational potential energy and kinetic energy. He explains to students how to use Pasco's SPARKvue software using the formulas for gravitational potential energy ($PE=mph$) and kinetic energy ($KE= \frac{1}{2} mv^2$) to compare the relationship between these two types of energy in a moving object such as a bouncing ball or pendulum. Last year, his students tried to use a clock to graph data by hand, but it took a long time and was not very accurate or easy to analyze. He is hoping things go smoother this year with the probes.

Mr. Enapay's students use motion probes to collect potential and kinetic energy data simultaneously, as seen in Figure 5.8. SPARKvue instantly creates graphs out of the data. When students compare the data to their predictions, they gain a deeper conceptual understanding of energy. Students save their graphs for later use in a report or presentation.

Mr. Enapay observes that by using probes, his students spend much less time calculating and representing data, which is on the lower level of Bloom's taxonomy, and more time working at the higher levels: analyzing and evaluating graphic patterns.

In Vernier's elementary-friendly software application, Logger Lite, the interface has large, easy-to-read buttons, which help young students to see the data. Ms. Cobb, a kindergarten teacher, uses a digital probe and Logger Lite to help her students understand the concept of insulation. She begins by asking them why they think that their mittens and gloves keep their hands warm in the winter. Some students hypothesize that the mittens themselves are warm. To test this theory—and to demonstrate the concept of insulation—Ms. Cobb takes a reading of the classroom's temperature by setting the probe on her desk. While the numerical degrees might not be meaningful, the students are able to see the line that represents the temperature, and they will be able to observe the line falling or rising as the temperature changes. Ms. Cobb then places the probe inside an empty mitten. The students observe that nothing changes. However, when a volunteer comes up and places his hand in the mitten with the probe still in place, the students see that the temperature begins to rise. They now have a better understanding that it is the hand inside a mitten that actually creates heat, and the mitten contains that heat. By using the software, Ms. Cobb presents her kindergarteners with a vivid, nonlinguistic picture of the data that they can understand without having to decipher numbers and degrees.

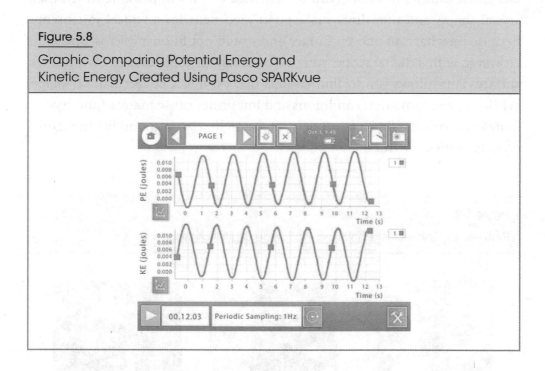

**Figure 5.8**

Graphic Comparing Potential Energy and
Kinetic Energy Created Using Pasco SPARKvue

## Digital Microscopes

Most microscope manufacturers make a microscope that can export images to a computer. However, the most versatile digital microscopes are those that can be used in a traditional, mounted configuration and as a handheld field scope. Unlike traditional microscopes, digital scopes have the built-in capacity to take pictures, movies, and time-lapse images. Some types also can project onscreen images, such as pages in a book or magazine articles, when they're plugged into a computer's USB port for data transfer and power. Scope vendors and manufacturers such as ProScope, Konus, Ken-A-Vision, and Scalar sell various models of handheld and mountable digital USB scopes. ProScope has also released a wireless microscope that will project to an iPad using the AirMicroPad app.

Teachers can have students use digital microscopes both during their investigations and afterward to create diagrams and graphics for students' analyses and presentations. Figure 5.9 shows pictures of microscopic topaz crystals taken with a ProScope. With the unaided eye, it's impossible to tell their crystal shape, and they don't make good specimens for a typical microscope because they have an uneven surface and would not fit on a microscope slide. However, with a digital scope, you can take magnified pictures of their uneven surface. This allows you to find crystals that exhibit a perfect natural shape. While uneven formation conditions and impurities cause many of the crystals to deform, you can find a few that form just right. Can you find the hexagonal crystals in these pictures?

**Figure 5.9**

Pictures of Crystals Taken with a ProScope Digital Microscope

Digital scopes also provide a way to produce video clips of live microscopic specimens. Figure 5.10 shows another image captured with a ProScope: the first frame in a video clip documenting a triop swimming in a Petri dish.

Triops, tiny creatures that date back to the Triassic Period, live in intermittent pond environments. They hatch, breed, and die within 90 days, and their eggs can last for decades waiting for a strong rain to fill the pond.

**Figure 5.10**

Video Image of a Triop Taken with a ProScope Digital Microscope

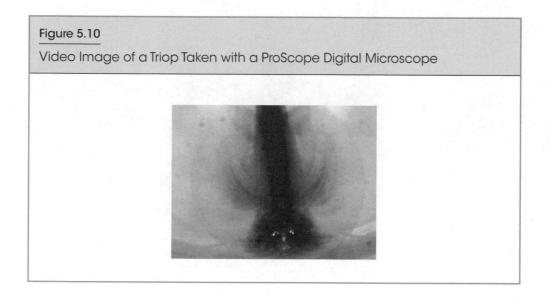

Finally, many digital scopes allow students to create time-lapse movies. Figure 5.11 shows a frame from a time-lapse movie documenting plant growth, created by Mr. Fuglestad's science students at Stillwater Junior High School in Stillwater, Minnesota. Projects that involve monitoring changes over time and recording data reinforce the science skills of observation. And with digital scopes, students can capture phenomena that might otherwise go unnoticed.

## ⏻ Organizing and Brainstorming Software

Graphic representations serve as mnemonic devices that facilitate the classification, organization, storage, and recollection of information into and out of long-term memory. This is especially true for students with learning styles that favor visual forms of learning. Organizing and brainstorming software gives teachers and students ways to create a variety of descriptive patterns to build conceptual understanding of everything from new vocabulary words to complex systems.

**Figure 5.11**

Frame of a Time-Lapse Movie on Plant Growth

*Special thanks to Stillwater Junior High and science teacher Pete Fuglestad.*

Inspiration, SmartTools (used with SmartBoards), and even the Microsoft Office SmartArt tools can all be used to organize ideas and represent curricular concepts. You might start by using words and phrases in a pattern organizer and then add to them with visual, audible, and moving depictions. In this section, we demonstrate the value of the six common types of pattern organizers: conceptual/descriptive (combined for our example), generalization/principle, time-sequence, episode, and process/cause-effect.

## Conceptual/Descriptive Pattern Organizers

Teachers can combine conceptual and descriptive pattern organizers to use in many ways and to many ends, including teaching facts and characteristics about a person, place, thing, event, or vocabulary word. This pattern type is more open-ended than the others and easy to create with students during classroom discussions. You can find some examples in Inspiration's Templates folder. See, for example, the Vocabulary Word template located under Language Arts and the Supporting Idea template located under Thinking Skills.

Figure 5.12 shows a descriptive pattern organizer for learning the vocabulary word *mnemonic*. It's a modification of the Vocabulary Word template found in Kidspiration's Reading and Writing Activities folder, created by a 5th grade teacher and his students to model how he wanted them to create their own descriptive pattern around vocabulary words. The students started the activity with words and then inserted images to deepen the learning and reinforce knowledge retention.

**Figure 5.12**

**Conceptual/Descriptive Pattern Organizer Created with Kidspiration's Vocabulary Word Template**

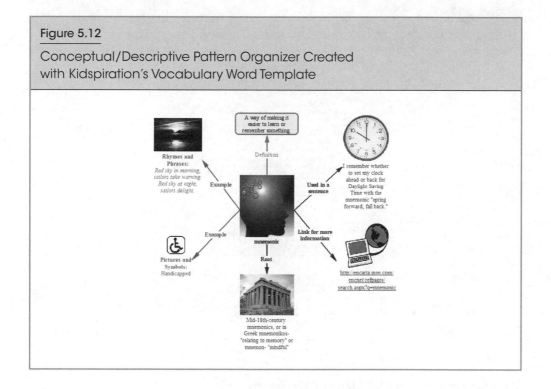

## Generalization/Principle Pattern Organizers

As their name suggests, generalization/principle pattern organizers work especially well in mathematics and science subjects. To illustrate, Ms. Scott's algebra students have been using quadratic equations for some time, and she expects them to understand the equations' applications. For a homework assignment, she provides an algebra principle and asks her students to make a pattern organizer with at least three different application examples. Because the students have previously worked with these mathematical principles and have already demonstrated their applications, no additional direct instruction is necessary. One of her students' organizers appears in Figure 5.13. This particular organizer was created using bubbl.us mind mapping software (http://bubbl .us), which is especially easy for elementary students due to its simple interface.

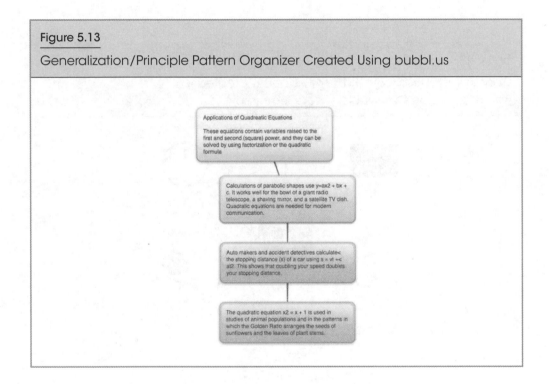

**Figure 5.13**

Generalization/Principle Pattern Organizer Created Using bubbl.us

## Time-Sequence Pattern Organizers

A time-sequence pattern organizer is terrific for teaching students historical progression. Say that Mrs. Campbell, a secondary social studies teacher, wants her students to understand the pace and events of the "Space Race" that started with Sputnik 1 in 1957 and ended with the Apollo-Soyuz mission in 1975. She guides students in using Inspiration to create a Space Race Time Sequence like the one in Figure 5.14. She tells them to show both Soviet and U.S. missions and incorporate symbols for the different types of space missions.

Alternatively, Mrs. Campbell could ask students to create a similar time-sequence pattern organizer by using the Word Drawing tools. One technical hint she gives is to use the grid at **Draw > Grid > Snap objects to grid** and **Draw > Grid > Display gridlines on screen**. Mrs. Campbell also advises her students to use the clip art located within Word at **Insert > Clip Art** or online at http://office.microsoft.com/clipart/ so that they can be sure the images they select and use are not copyright-restricted. It is important for teachers to both model and monitor adherence to copyright laws and to demonstrate best practices for "digital citizenship." Today's technology makes it easier than ever for students to copy and use digital content, including copyrighted material. However, teachers can use the very same technology to identify plagiarism by searching text strings from students' work online. We encourage teachers to teach their students fair use and copyright laws. For more information, see Technology & Learning's Copyright and Fair Use Guidelines for Teachers, available at www.techlearning.com.

---

**Figure 5.14**

Time-Sequence Pattern Organizer Created in Inspiration

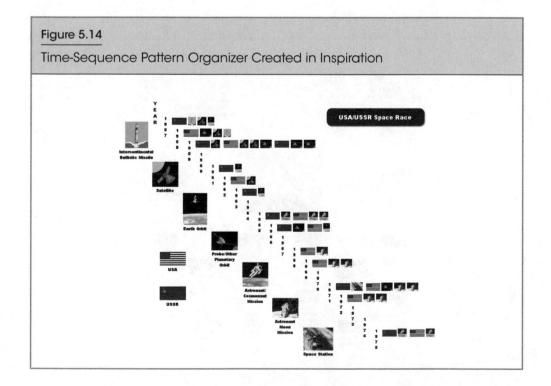

## Episode Pattern Organizers

Episode pattern organizers are useful for depicting complex events where many different people, places, times, and processes all contribute to the overall concept. This type of graphic organizer also contains a time-sequence pattern within it. Our example is an extension of Mrs. Campbell's Space Race assignment. She chooses one of the best time-sequence organizers and uses it as part of a new episode pattern organizer as a way of discussing the many factors involved with the Space Race. Mrs. Campbell creates the organizer seen in Figure 5.15 in Inspiration, then uses **File > Transfer to Word Processor** to place it in Microsoft Word. During class, she projects this organizer on screen and hyperlinks the time-sequence to the episode pattern organizer in Microsoft Word by using **Insert > Hyperlink > Place in This Document > Space Race Time Sequence**.

---

**Figure 5.15**

Episode Pattern Organizer Created in Inspiration

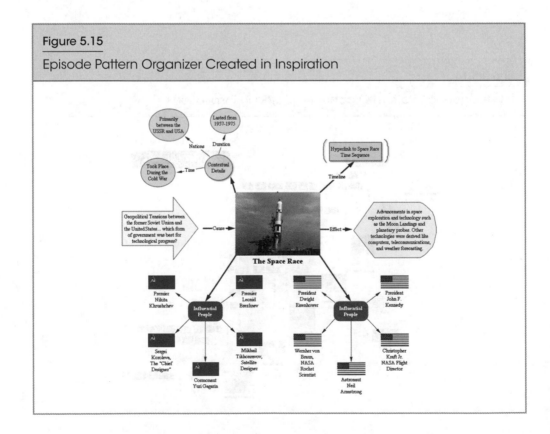

## Process/Cause-Effect Pattern Organizers

The final example, in Figure 5.16, is a process/cause-effect pattern organizer. Here, a high school advisor opens a discussion of goals with freshmen participating in a group counseling session. The advisor uses the organizer to communicate the importance of sound planning practices and encourages the freshmen to make their own customized organizers. The visual helps students connect the decisions they make in high school to events later in life by allowing them to see possible cause-and-effect relationships at a glance. The organizer not only sparks discussion but guides it as well.

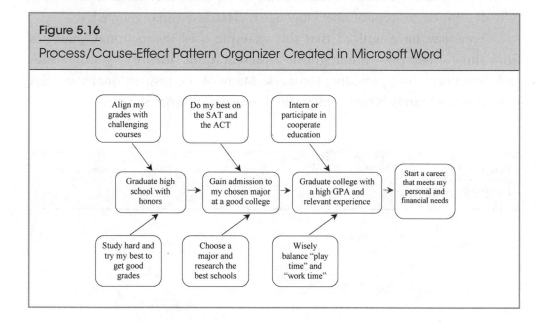

**Figure 5.16**

Process/Cause-Effect Pattern Organizer Created in Microsoft Word

## ⏻ Database and Reference Resources

Students will often find themselves at a loss for the right word or using the same words repeatedly. Applications such as Visuwords (www.visuwords .com), Snappy Words (www.snappywords.com), Thinkmap's Visual Thesaurus (www.visualthesaurus.com), and Merriam-Webster's Visual Dictionary Online (http://visual.merriam-webster.com) offer nonlinguistic ways to help students understand vocabulary, use proper parts of speech, compare synonyms, and generally improve the quality of their writing. These applications do this by graphically representing words and definitions so that students can readily see the comparisons and classifications within the language.

Here's an example of one such application in use. Mr. Chen, a 6th grade teacher, asks his students to use Visuwords to increase the number, variety, and sophistication of adjectives in their writing. Students enter words into the search box on the Visuwords website and double click on nodes to expand them. They use the color-coded key to find the parts of speech that they are trying to use and the many synonyms for the words. (An example of the results for the search "excellent" can be seen in Figure 5.17.) Not only are Mr. Chen's students improving their vocabulary and writing skills, they are gaining a more fully developed concept of how language is classified and organized.

You may have noticed that this example uses instructional strategies from three categories—nonlinguistic representations, identifying similarities and differences, and providing feedback. Many of the instructional strategies work this way; rarely is one strategy used in isolation from the rest.

---

**Figure 5.17**

Example of Visuwords

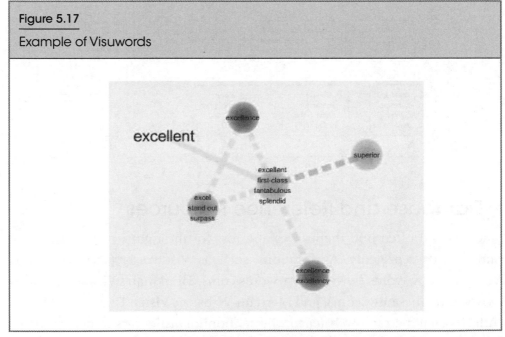

*Reproduced courtesy of Visuwords online graphical dictionary (website: visuwords.com)*

Some Google applications stand out as excellent tools for creating nonlinguistic representations. Students can use Google Sky to explore the far reaches of outer space, for example, or Google Maps to create their own routes and customized explorations. Google Earth is useful: A three-dimensional model of the Earth, it can be used to help students learn more about any topic that has a geographical component. The app allows users to view aerial and satellite imagery, the bottoms of the deepest oceans, evidence of climate patterns over time, and more.

Here's an example. Westborough, Massachusetts, social studies teachers Ingrid Gustafson and Carol Alcusky created an award-winning lesson for Google's Ancient Rome in 3D Curriculum Competition. (The lesson can be found at www.google.com/educators/romecontest.html.) The lesson called for groups of four to five students to use a variety of Google apps to design, write, illustrate, and edit an online newspaper featuring information on ancient Rome. Among the apps the students used was Google Earth—in particular, a layer within the app called 3D Ancient Rome that models ancient Rome in great detail (see Figure 5.18). This layer allowed students to identify icons representing roads, hills, bridges, and historic sites, as seen in Figure 5.19. Examples of completed projects can be found at http://sites.google.com/site/theroman record. To find additional classroom examples and lesson plans for use with Google Earth, go to http://sitescontent.google.com/google-earth-for-educators.

Another great Google app for use in the classroom is SketchUp, a drafting program that is free to educators. (Information about how to get Google SketchUp can be found at http://sketchup.google.com/intl/en/industries/edu/primary.html.) At https://sites.google.com/site/architecturewq, you can see an example of an architecture WebQuest that makes good use of SketchUp. The WebQuest was created by Leanna Johnson for St. Paul Lutheran School in Farmington, Missouri, using a template created by Patricia McGee and Deborah Claxton from the work of Bernie Dodge. The WebQuest requires students to use SketchUp and other resources to learn about spatial geometry. They work independently to find out why understanding perimeter and area is vital to the work of an architect. Throughout the process, they visit websites that prepare them for several design projects. A detailed rubric ensures that the mathematics standards used in the lesson are assessed. Figure 5.20 shows an example of a model house created with SketchUp by a 6th grade student named Spencer.

**Figure 5.18**

Screenshot of Google Earth's Ancient Rome Layer

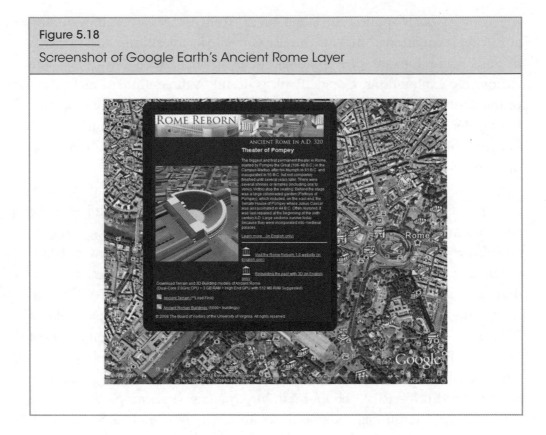

Some other great apps for creating nonlinguistic representations in the classroom can be found at the following websites: www.flashearth.com, http:// maps.nationalgeographic.com/maps, www.freecad.com, and www.autocadws. com/mobile.

## ⏻ Multimedia

One of the most effective forms of nonlinguistic representation is multimedia. Since teachers first started showing reel-to-reel films in their classrooms, countless educators have observed that movies and videos help engage students in content. Today, we can take engagement much further by shifting multimedia learning from something that's teacher-directed to something that's teacher-facilitated. Research indicates that multimedia has the most effect on student learning when the student is the creator (Siegle & Foster, 2000). Although

PowerPoint presentations and movies are great teaching aids and do lead to higher levels of student engagement, the most engaging learning comes from having the students create the presentation or movie themselves as a part of the learning process. Many believe that movie-editing tools that have become ubiquitous in schools are leading to a new "digital literacy," in which students need to know the language of camera angle, colors, soundtrack, and fonts in much the same way that they need to know the grammar of written and spoken language. George Lucas (2005) likens this evolving literacy to the onset of reading and writing in the general population as a result of the printing press.

### Figure 5.19

### Images from Google's Ancient Rome 3D Layer

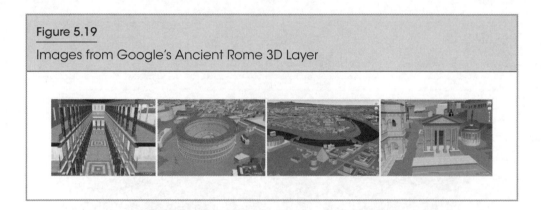

As we've mentioned previously, it is essential that students understand the significance of copyright and fair use, and this can be especially imperative when they engage in multimedia projects. Students should know, for example, that according to Section 4.2.3 of the Consortium of College and University Media Centers' *Fair Use Guidelines for Educational Multimedia* (1996), they may not use more than 10 percent or 30 seconds of a copyrighted song or film. Students should be aware of these guidelines, but should also be introduced to open-access sources that have more relaxed laws regarding student use. For instance, they can go to www.jamendo.com and download entire songs free of charge for an education-related movie. Websites such as http://creativecommons.org help students and teachers to locate audio, video, images, text, and educational resources for their projects.

Multimedia is a combination of single mediums, such as video, audio, and interactivity. Generally, we can think of multimedia in the classroom as projects that include at least two of the following: audio, video, graphics, animations, and text. Thus, multimedia projects might include presentations, animations, and movies created using such tools as Inspiration, PowerPoint, Keynote, and iMovie. These types of projects help students create a mental image of the concepts and themes they are trying to learn. Think back to a memorable project you did in school. Did it involve some sort of imagery or visual aids? As we have stated before, knowledge connected with nonlinguistic representations is remembered more deeply than that connected with linguistic forms alone.

Figure 5.20

Spencer's House Created Using Google SketchUp

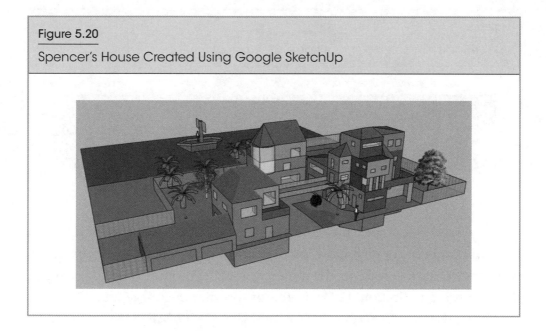

## Presentations

The advancement of presentation technology is one of the most powerful educational technology innovations. With some creativity, a computer, a projector, and presentation software, students can create presentations that rival those of professionals. PowerPoint, Keynote, and Google Presentations are three popular tools used for classroom presentations. Browse these websites to get some ideas about student and teacher presentations:

▶ Jefferson County Schools—PowerPoint Collection
http://jc-schools.net/ppt.html

This is a large collection of K–12 student and teacher PowerPoint presentations in all subjects.

▶ PowerPoint in the Classroom
www.actden.com/pp

This is a fun, colorful website with two cartoon characters to guide you (or your students) through the basics of PowerPoint.

▶ Keynote User Tips
www.keynoteuser.com/category/tips/

This site has themes, tips, links, troubleshooting, and other cool stuff for Apple's Keynote presentation software.

▶ Keynote Theme Park
www.keynotethemepark.com/index.html

This is an ideal website for finding free theme downloads, recommended links, news, and tips.

As students begin a multimedia project, too often their first step is to launch some software and begin to haphazardly, if enthusiastically, create something. Presentations, and movies even more so, require significant planning and organization. Otherwise, students can get carried away in the fun aspects of production and not pay enough attention to the content, resulting in a "PowerPointless" presentation. Remember, content is what it's all about. Good presentations should follow the same steps as moviemaking, which we will discuss later in this section.

Students should begin a multimedia project just as they would any other research project and should only move into the presentation software *after* they have completed their background research, planning, and draft writing. (An exception to this guideline is when the objective of the lesson is to learn a particular software skill.) In general, students should try and answer the tried and true questions of *who, what, where, when, why,* and *how.* As they delve deeply into the whys and hows of a project, they practice problem solving and analysis and use other higher-level thinking skills. Of course, the teacher's responsibility is to refine these questions based on the new content, students' learning goals, and the type of project being undertaken.

For teachers preparing students to engage in a multimedia project, developing the scoring rubric is a critical step. When you are adapting or creating a multimedia project rubric, ask yourself several questions: How long do you really want the students' presentations to be? How much computer space is available? Who is the audience? Which software is compatible? Here are some specific items to consider in a project rubric:

1. Content accuracy
2. Length of presentation (number of slides)
3. Slide layout (e.g., amount of text and number of graphics, titles, sounds, animations)
4. Background graphics appropriate for audience and theme
5. Software requirements (e.g., Quicktime, Java, Flash, Windows Media Player)
6. File size (compressing pictures will help a lot with this)
7. Storage and delivery requirements
8. Color schemes

When planning, it is preferable to build in enough time for every student to present his or her project to the entire class. With so much to teach, time is always a concern, and we realize that you may not be able to allow all of your students to present in each unit. A good compromise is to randomly select a small number of presenters—perhaps three to five students per assignment. Of course, students who do not present must still turn in a digital or printed copy of their project. Alternatively, you could ask all students to present a shortened version of their presentation. This way, all students practice creating projects and learn more about the communication skills required to present.

Figure 5.21 shows an example of a student-created slide for a presentation on Martin Luther King Jr.'s influence on the United States. Most of the slides in this presentation do not contain as many types of multimedia as this one, nor should they. However, this slide is a good example of how sound, video, text, and imagery can be combined in an effective presentation. Notice how the slide has a title, template, and logo. It also has hyperlinked sound and video. The sound and video files are saved in the same folder as the PowerPoint file, with hyperlinks attached to the words "Watch the Speech" and "Listen to the Speech." Also, notice how the text has been placed over areas of the images that are not critical but have been shadowed to maintain the images' original look and allow for enough contrast to read the text. This shadowing is done by putting the text in a text box, changing the text color to contrast with the background, highlighting the text box, and choosing **Format > Text Box > Colors and lines** > (choose a color) > **Transparency = 50% > OK**.

**Figure 5.21**

Slide in a PowerPoint Multimedia Presentation

*License for photos of Martin Luther King Jr. granted by Intellectual Properties Management, Atlanta, GA, as exclusive licensor of the King Estate. Photo of the March on Washington reproduced with permission of AP/Wide World Photos.*

Prezi (http://prezi.com) and Nota (http://notaland.com) are two tools that not only help students create engaging multimedia projects but also allow them to share their projects online. Prezi allows users to make dynamic, nonlinear presentations and is ideal for showing whole-to-part relationships (e.g., specific locations and events during a long journey, how the various parts of a cell work together). Nota makes it easy for students to collaborate on multimedia projects online and can also be used for collaborative note taking that includes rich multimedia components.

## Animations

As children, many of us made animations. We used a tablet of paper and drew stick figures, making slight changes in the stick figures' positions on each page. Then we quickly flipped through the pages and watched our rudimentary animation. Whether it is our stick figure flipbooks or an animated movie like Pixar's *The Incredibles*, all animations share basic beginnings. Here are two quality online resources that will help you and your students learn more about animation:

▶ Animation Factory
www.animationfactory.com/help/tutorial_gif.html

This site has tutorials from Animation Factory by Jupiterimages and a collection of royalty-free animated clip art on the Internet. It features more than 400,000 animations, video backgrounds, templates, backdrops, and web graphics.

▶ Go! Animate
http://goanimate.com/

This site makes it easy for students to create animated clips.

Here is one of the simplest ways to teach students to animate. Explain to your students that they will animate their ideas by creating a series of progressing diagrams and ask them to begin by drawing a *template frame* as the starting point for the scene they want to animate. (You may have noticed that the background scenery in old cartoons doesn't change much. This is because those cartoons were made using a template frame.) This frame can be drawn in any software program that will generate a picture, such as Word, PowerPoint, or Photoshop. Next, explain to students that they can add, subtract, or modify images within the template frame using copy, paste, and rotate commands as well as other drawing tools. Have students save the frame they created by number and scene (unless there is only one scene). Then ask students to save their modified frame as the next frame in the series and continue animating until all of the frames are complete. Finally, they should save the edited version in a movie format, using moviemaking software such as iMovie or Windows Movie Maker.

In Figure 5.22, you can see some student-created frames for an animation demonstrating a chemical reaction in which concentrated sulfuric acid dehydrates sucrose to produce carbon and water. Notice the slides' sequential

## Figure 5.22

## Frames for an Animation

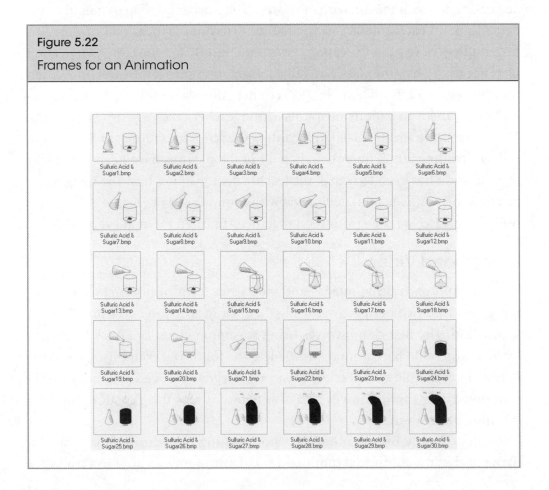

titling and how the student drew the beaker and reaction chamber once and then rotated and moved these elements in subsequent slides. Each slide is one frame of the animation; when connected together in a series, they create the illusion of movement.

Other approaches to animation include using still images, time-lapse photography, and manipulated objects, such as paper cut-outs, puppets, or clay figures (claymation). Not surprisingly, the creative and kinesthetic aspects of animation of manipulated objects can be particularly engaging for young students. Consider the example of a 1st grade teacher who will conclude a unit on the Amazon rainforest by assessing students' understanding of the rainforest's animals and their habitat. She announces that the class will be creating a claymation movie, and that each student will be using clay to create two animals that live in the Amazon rainforest. The teacher goes on to help the students look up each animal's eating habits, determine which level of the rainforest it lives in (e.g., in the canopy, at ground level), and find three interesting facts about it. Then the class turns this information into a movie script. When filming begins, each student places his or her animals on the correct backdrop and poses them in various positions as the teacher takes a series of pictures. The students are also involved in recording the script narration, reinforcing the skills of reading aloud fluently. When all of the pictures have been taken and the narration has been recorded, the teacher demonstrates how the images can be combined into an animated movie with sounds overlaid. Figure 5.23 shows Audra's anteater, a frame from the 1st graders' finished claymation movie.

## Movies and Video

We approach using movies and video as a form of nonlinguistic representation from two perspectives: using them *for* instruction and using them *as* instruction. The first case involves using streaming video or DVDs to engage learners and build background knowledge. The following example of how Mrs. Robinson, a middle school science teacher, integrates movies into her instruction on writing in the content area also demonstrates this function, but in a slightly different way.

First, Mrs. Robinson modifies a story-writing rubric using RubiStar. She then attaches the completed rubric to a list of astronomy vocabulary terms that

**Figure 5.23**

Frame from a Claymation Movie

students have been learning. She gives students the assignment to write a story using at least ten of the following astronomy terms in correct context:

| | | |
|---|---|---|
| Escape velocity | Meteoroid | Satellite |
| Geosynchronous orbit | Pressure | Thrust |
| Gravity | Radiation | Weight |
| Ionosphere | Reaction engine | |
| Magnetosphere | Rotation | |

After Mrs. Robinson gives students the rubric and list of vocabulary words, she asks them to read the terms carefully, think about what each one means, and think about how they could incorporate the terms into the assignment according to the standards set by the rubric. The next thing she does surprises students and heightens their interest in the assignment. Mrs. Robinson adds a third element to the assignment: a nonlinguistic representation in the form of a music video. She tells the students to get comfortable, turns down the lights, and projects the music video of the song "Major Tom (Coming Home)" by

Peter Schilling (inspired by David Bowie's 1969 song "Space Oddity") from a free downloaded version she found on the Internet at www.vh1.com/artists/az/schilling_peter/artist.jhtml. Sometimes she shows a student-made music video of Bowie's original song, found at http://video.google.com (search: *Daydreaming to David Bowie*). By the time the brief video is over, Mrs. Robinson's students have generated mental pictures that give the vocabulary context. Now they have plenty of creative ideas and are well prepared to use the vocabulary terms in their stories.

The second way movies are used in the classroom involves students actually creating the movies themselves to demonstrate their knowledge and skills. Generally, students enjoy the challenge, creativity, and collaboration that go into creating movies, and research shows that students have a higher level of understanding and retention when they learn using media and technology (Reeves, 1998; Siegle & Foster, 2000). You also can use the movies they create over and over again as examples for other students. Let's take a look at the steps students should follow to create their own movies.

**Step 1: Writing the script.** The script consists of the exact words that the student actors will read or speak. To be sure of the timing, the actors should read the script aloud and time it. Remind them to allow time for pauses or transitions between ideas.

**Step 2: Storyboarding.** The purpose of the storyboard is to give students an idea of the images, settings, and props they will need for the movie. Tell them that as they read their scripts, they might decide that "a picture is worth a thousand words." Instead of describing something dramatic, why not show it?

At this point, students should transfer the script to the lines on the storyboard, breaking it into sections dictated by the images that should accompany the lines. In the box for each section, students might describe or draw a picture that reminds them of the image they want at that point in the movie. If they are using still images, they should notate where those images are stored on the computer, or note that they need to take the picture. If they use websites, they should write the sites' URLs. Figure 5.24 shows two examples from a student-movie storyboard. Note that the students have titled the scene, numbered each shot, and included the relevant lines from the script, along with tips for filming and editing.

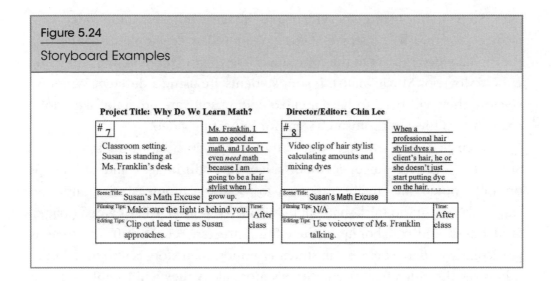

**Figure 5.24**

Storyboard Examples

**Step 3: Shooting the video.** In the classroom, this step involves resource allocation. Most classrooms have a limited number of still and video cameras available. Before issuing a camera to students, review their scripts and storyboards for completion and verify that they have conducted at least one full practice speaking their lines with props. Also, if students plan to shoot still pictures, they should have all needed materials. If they plan to have a voiceover effect in their movies, they should record the spoken words on camera beforehand. It is easier to import a video clip and separate the audio during the editing process.

Here are some tips on recording video to pass along to students:

• Begin recording three to five seconds before the actor starts talking. You might need this space during the editing process.

• Use a tripod to keep the camera steady.

• Use a digital microphone rather than the one on the camera. This will improve the sound quality. A clip-on microphone works well.

• It is not necessary to shoot the video sequentially. If you are using different scenes, you can shoot all the video in one scene before moving to the next, even if the scenes you shoot aren't in the same order as in the movie.

• *Remember:* Every time the video camera stops recording, the video software makes a new video clip.

**Step 4: Importing the video and images.** Importing the video into iMovie (Macintosh) or Movie Maker (Windows) is as simple as connecting the digital video camera to the computer's Firewire or USB port and launching either iMovie or Movie Maker. If your students are using a different Windows version, they will need to have a video editing software program like Adobe Premiere. Follow your software's steps for importing video.

**Step 5: Video editing.** Now is the time to go back to the storyboard. Students should have a collection of video clips, still images, and audio clips on a computer. They might also want to use the computer's microphone to "lay down" an audio track that will play under a series of still or video images. Students should collaborate in the editing process. Feedback from others is particularly valuable because, in students' minds, their story is well told, but as others see the video with fresh eyes, it's more likely they will be able to point out parts that are confusing or scenes that seem to be missing. Once the clips are in the correct order, students might need to edit individual clips, removing unwanted sections. They should edit all clips before adding any transitions between them.

Once the movie is rough-edited, students can add a title at the beginning and credits at the end. Remind them in the assignment guidelines to cite sources in the credits. This is a great opportunity to teach or review proper citation formats. One good reference site is hosted by Duke University Libraries at www.lib.duke.edu/libguide/cite/works_cited.htm. It has examples of various kinds of citations in APA, MLA, *Chicago*, Turabian, and CSE formats. As previously mentioned, it is important to model and monitor copyright compliance.

**Step 6: Adding music.** Now students will add appropriate music. While students will want to use their own CDs or music they have obtained online, it is important to model ethical behavior. Because the movies they are creating are for educational purposes, they may incorporate copyrighted music, provided that they purchased this music legally and limit the selected clips to no more than 30 seconds or 10 percent of the song's full length, whichever is less. You might want to direct students to use the sound clips in the moviemaking software or go to www.jamendo.com and find the style and length of music that meets the needs of their movie. Most music on Jamendo is copyright-free, but students need to remember to cite the source in the credits.

**Step 7: Saving and sharing the movie.** Now students should make sure they have saved their movie in its final form. This usually involves condensing all the separate pieces into one movie file. At this point, they are ready to share the movie with the class, the school, the community, and maybe even the world via the Internet.

A few other resources for multimedia creation can be found at the following websites:

▶ DigiTales
www.digitales.us

Bernajean Porter's website provides tools and examples to help teachers and students begin the process of digital storytelling. A section on evaluating student projects includes rubrics and scoring guides.

▶ San Fernando Education Technology Team's iCan Film Festival
http://homepage.mac.com/sfett/html_movie/Ican/4.html

Guided by their teacher, Marco Torres—an Apple Distinguished Educator and 2005 California Teacher of the Year—students have created and archived great examples of student videos.

▶ Animation 101
http://library.thinkquest.org/25398/Clay/ClayHowTo.html

This website offers great tutorials to help your students get started using hand-drawn and stop-motion animation.

▶ Make Beliefs Comix
www.makebeliefscomix.com

This free website allows students to create great-looking comic books around classroom lessons easily and quickly.

▶ Zooburst
www.zooburst.com

This site allows students to design great interactive virtual pop-up books.

More and more educators are now using recorded lessons to differentiate instruction, review material, and "flip" the classroom so that lectures become homework, leaving time for more engaging activities during the school day. Here are a few resources that exemplify this idea:

▶ The Flipped Class Network
http://vodcasting.ning.com/

This open network provides a social sharing and learning space for educators who are interested in the idea of the "flipped classroom." The website is the brainchild of Aaron Sams and Jon Bergmann, two high school chemistry teachers in Colorado.

▶ Khan Academy
www.khanacademy.org

This collection of 2,400 lessons has become a leading example of how video can be used for "anytime, anyplace" learning. Content includes mathematics, humanities, and science lessons.

## ⏻ Instructional Interactives

Let's look again at the use of multimedia *for* instruction rather than *as* instruction. McREL's meta-analysis *A Theory-Based Meta-Analysis of Research on Instruction* (Marzano, 1998) discusses specific teaching strategies and the effect sizes on student achievement. Marzano found "the use of computer simulation as the vehicle with which students manipulate artifacts produced the highest effect size of 1.45 (n=1), indicating a percentile gain of 43 points" (p. 91).

There are great computer simulations available on the web, some for free and others by subscription. One outstanding example of a free simulation resource is the National Library of Virtual Manipulatives (http://nlvm.usu.edu/en/nav/vlibrary.html). This site provides scores of interactive Java applications. Students select from a matrix organized by content area (numbers and operations, algebra, geometry, measurement, and data analysis and probability) and by grade level (preK–2, 3–5, 6–8, and 9–12). Figure 5.25 shows an example of an algebra simulation for high school students. Each simulation at this site also includes a link to national standards it addresses, a teacher/parent guide, and instructions for the student.

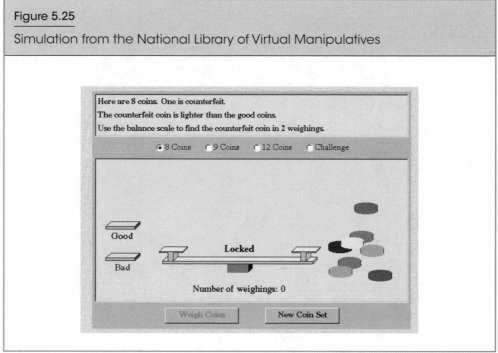

**Figure 5.25**

Simulation from the National Library of Virtual Manipulatives

Here are 8 coins. One is counterfeit.
The counterfeit coin is lighter than the good coins.
Use the balance scale to find the counterfeit coin in 2 weighings.

⦿ 8 Coins ⦾ 9 Coins ⦾ 12 Coins ⦾ Challenge

Good

Bad

Locked

Number of weighings: 0

Weigh Coins    New Coin Set

*Reproduced courtesy of the MATTI Association, Utah State University.*

Elementary students will love the multimedia simulations at www .iknowthat.com. This site has interactive multimedia applications for preK–6 language arts, mathematics, science, social studies, the arts, and problem solving, and is also available as an app for the iPad and iPod Touch. If a subscription-based site is an option, www.explorelearning.com is a great source for simulations. It offers a catalog of modular, interactive simulations, called gizmos, in mathematics and science for teachers and students in grades 6–12. One example is the "mouse genetics" gizmo in Figure 5.26. In this simulation, students breed "pure" mice with known genotypes that exhibit specific fur and eye colors and thus learn how traits are passed on via dominant and recessive genes. They can store mice in virtual cages for future breeding and get statistics of fur and eye color every time a pair of mice breeds. They can use Punnet to predict results. While it's true that students can read about genotypes in a textbook, using a simulation like this one allows them to see the effects of genetics over a hundred generations in less than two minutes.

### Figure 5.26

### ExploreLearning's Mouse Genetics Gizmo

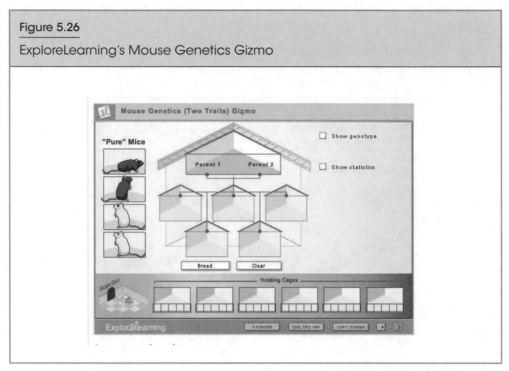

*Reproduced courtesy of ExploreLearning.*

Here are some other quality web resources that can support the use of nonlinguistic representations:

▶ Knowitall.org
www.knowitall.org

Knowitall.org is South Carolina ETV's educational web portal, a collection of fun, interactive websites for K–12 students. The site is searchable by both subject and grade level and has support resources for teachers and parents.

▶ Interactive Mathematics Activities
www.cut-the-knot.org/Curriculum/index.shtml

Java-based mathematics games are categorized by discipline. This site is appropriate for high school and even college students. In addition to algebra and geometry, there are games for logic, calculus, probability, and more.

▶ Conflict History
www.conflicthistory.com

The Conflict History website allows students to browse the timelines of conflicts across the globe. Clicking on an event shows where and when it took place and provides a link for finding more information.

▶ Shodor
http://shodor.org/interactivate/activities/

This website offers scores of interactives covering numbers and operations, geometry, algebra, probability, statistics, modeling, trigonometry, and calculus. A version is also available as an app for the iPad.

▶ Our Timelines
www.ourtimelines.com

This free web resource allows students to create a timeline of a person within the context of events that happened during his or her lifetime. Categories of events include historical events, technological advances, and disasters.

## ⏻ Kinesthetic Technology

An increasing number of digital resources support kinesthetic learning. Most of us remember flutephones, those plastic recorder-like instruments from our elementary days. They weren't designed to sound much like a real instrument, but they did allow students to experience making music and reading real notes on a page. Now there are a variety of iPad apps that not only allow students to experience music making and note reading, but also do a great job of sounding like real woodwind, brass, string, and percussion instruments. Some elementary music teachers are even connecting such apps to amplifiers and using them to put on concerts. Some physical education teachers are using Konani's "Dance, Dance, Revolution" video game to actively engage students in workouts that are both strenuous and fun. The Nintendo Wii and Kinect for Xbox 360 both track users' movements, allowing for many educational games that actively involve students in kinesthetic learning. Likewise, VTech (www.vtechkids.com) offers a number of tools for engaging preschoolers in kinesthetic activities to help them learn numbers, letters, and colors.

Technology has the potential to affect nonlinguistic representations more than any other strategy. As tools become more sophisticated, realistic, and accessible, students will have the ability to virtually explore their surroundings, visualize information, and express themselves through an ever expanding variety of means. Used to their fullest capability, these tools can provide students with endless ways to better understand their world.

# 6

# Summarizing and Note Taking

The instructional strategy *summarizing and note taking* focuses on enhancing students' ability to synthesize information and distill it into a concise new form. Here, teachers work on helping students separate important information from extraneous information and state the information in their own words.

Based on McREL's research, we have three recommendations for using summarizing in the classroom:

## RECOMMENDATIONS

- Teach students the rule-based summarizing strategy.
- Use summary frames.
- Engage students in reciprocal teaching.

Note taking is similar to summarizing in that it enhances students' ability to organize information in a way that captures the main ideas and supporting details, helping students to process information. Although note taking is one of the most useful study skills a student can cultivate, teachers rarely teach it explicitly as a skill in itself.

Based on McREL's research, we have three recommendations for using note taking in the classroom:

## RECOMMENDATIONS

- Give students teacher-prepared notes.
- Teach students a variety of note-taking formats.

• Provide opportunities for students to revise their notes and use them for review.

Technology, in the form of typewriters and word processors, has been playing a role in note taking for many years. Now, however, the sophistication of the software can turn it into a true learning experience. Technology can scaffold, or provide support, while students are learning the summarizing process. In this section, we show you how the following technologies help to scaffold and organize the summarizing and note-taking processes: *word processing applications, organizing and brainstorming software, multimedia,* and *communication and collaboration software.*

## ⏻ Word Processing Applications

A word processor is a computer application used to produce printable material. Word processors run the gamut from the robust Microsoft Word to the free Google Docs program. All provide teachers a way to strengthen summarizing and note taking.

### Summarizing

One classroom recommendation for teaching students to summarize in the classroom is to use rule-based summarizing. Using this strategy provides students with a process to apply as they summarize and gives them a structure to guide them when attempting what can otherwise be a confusing task. Figure 6.1 shows the steps for rule-based summarizing that, with slight modifications, apply to both younger and older students.

---

**Figure 6.1**

**Rule-Based Summarizing**

Steps
1. Take out the material that is not important to understanding.
2. Take out words that repeat information.
3. Replace a list of things with a word that describes the things in the list (e.g., use the word *trees* for *elm*, *oak*, and *maple*).
4. Find a topic sentence. If you can't find a topic sentence, write one.

You can use the Track Changes feature in Microsoft Word to both demonstrate rule-based summarizing and have students practice the process. First, open Word and go to **Review > Track Changes** to activate the Track Changes feature. Then click the arrow under **Balloons** and choose **Show Revisions in Balloons** (see Figure 6.2).

**Figure 6.2**

**Configuring Track Changes in Microsoft Word**

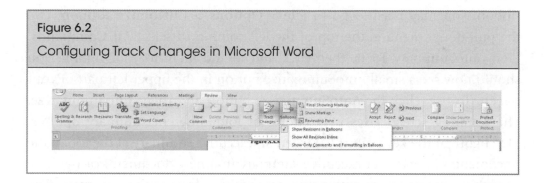

Here's how Ms. Sanborn, a 7th grade science teacher, uses the Track Changes feature to show her students how to summarize a selection from their textbook. She begins by selecting a passage from her textbook and pasting it into a blank Word document. After saving the document, she activates Track Changes as we've explained and begins applying the summarizing rules. As Ms. Sanborn finds redundant sentences, she highlights them and presses the delete key. As you see in Figure 6.3, those sections appear crossed out and in red. You can also see where she simplifies the terms "continents and tectonic plates" to "land surfaces."

**Figure 6.3**

**Microsoft Word Document Showing Tracked Changes**

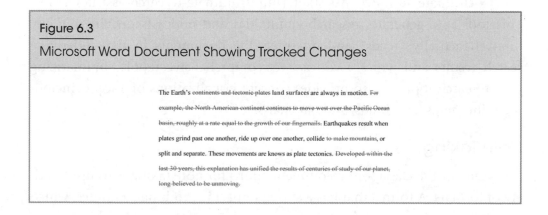

By modeling the process for her students using the word processor, Ms. Sanborn is able to show them how to summarize the text in a way that makes it easier for them to understand the content.

Another useful feature in Word that many teachers don't know about is the AutoSummarize tool. It does exactly what the name suggests: takes a selection of text and provides a summary. To add AutoSummarize to your ribbon, you may need to go to **File > Options > Customize Ribbon**. Use the pull-down menu at the top of the left column to select **All Commands**. Find AutoSummary Tools, then click **Add** to add them to your ribbon. You should now see a small AutoSummarize button in the upper left part of your screen. To use, click the **AutoSummarize** button and then **AutoSummarize**. The resulting screen gives us a choice of four different summary options: (1) Highlight the key points; (2) insert an executive summary at the top of the document; (3) insert an executive summary in a new document; or (4) hide everything except the executive summary without leaving the document. The first option—highlighting the key points—is a particularly good teaching tool. The AutoSummarize feature is available in Word 2007, but has been removed from Word 2010. If the feature is not available to you, try one of the following web-based resources:

• Text Compactor (http://textcompactor.com) or the Online Summarize Tool (www.tools4noobs.com/summarize). These free resources allow you to paste in a large body of text or URL, which they then automatically summarize. These tools can also be used to provide feedback to students just learning how to summarize.

• Ultimate Research Assistant (http://ultimate-research-assistant.com). This tool auto-generates research summaries and podcasts on virtually any topic. It actually "reads" and interprets the documents in the underlying search results and writes a concise yet comprehensive report summarizing your research topic. It also provides concept visualizations of a topic, including mind maps, tag clouds, and bar charts.

## Note Taking

One of the classroom recommendations for note taking is to use a variety of formats. A format that has a strong impact is combination notes, which employ outlining, webbing, and pictographs in addition to words. Graphic representation has been shown to produce a percentile gain of 39 points in student achievement (Marzano, 1998). In the combination notes format, students begin with an inverted *T* on their paper. They record facts and notes on the left side of the page, use drawing or other nonlinguistic representations on the right, and then write a one- or two-sentence summary under the bar of the *T*. In the example in Figure 6.4, you see combination notes used during a 1st grade class's discussion of the parts of a computer. The four parts of the computer the teacher discussed are listed on the left side, a drawing of the four parts is on the right, and there's a short sentence at the bottom to summarize the discussion.

**Figure 6.4**

Combination Notes Created in Microsoft Word

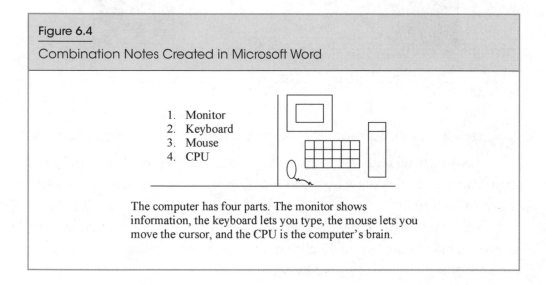

1. Monitor
2. Keyboard
3. Mouse
4. CPU

The computer has four parts. The monitor shows information, the keyboard lets you type, the mouse lets you move the cursor, and the CPU is the computer's brain.

Combination note templates can be easily created using word processing, drawing, or presentation software. The Notebook Layout View feature in the Macintosh version of Microsoft Word also supports note taking. (This feature is not currently available for the Windows operating system.) To activate this feature, click the button in the lower left corner of the screen in Word. This view helps students to organize notes as they type them. They can also easily add drawings and voice recordings. Figure 6.5 shows an example of a student's notebooks using Notebook Layout View.

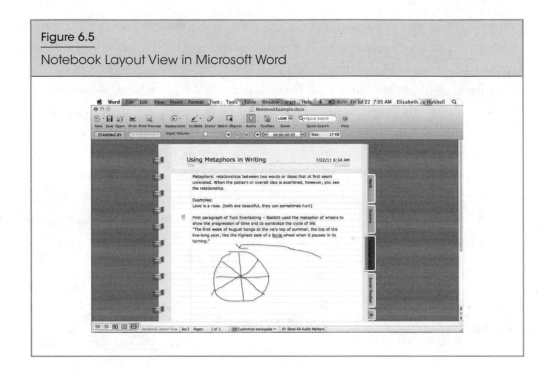

**Figure 6.5**

Notebook Layout View in Microsoft Word

Here are some iPad apps that can help students take and organize notes:

• **Notes.** This note-taking app is built into the iPhone, iPod Touch, and iPad. Using a simple yellow legal pad interface, students can take notes by typing or using a stylus.

• **Evernote.** This app syncs with the user's online Evernote account. The user can collect notes by highlighting text, taking screenshots, or uploading pictures. Notes can be organized by tags.

• **AudioNote.** This app allows students to draw or type notes while recording a voiceover. Upon playback, the app will highlight specific sections that were being drawn during a particular point in the audio recording.

• **Infinote.** This app organizes notes using a virtual "corkboard" upon which students can place virtual "sticky notes."

• **PaperDesk.** This app allows the user to choose from a variety of paper styles (e.g., white notebook paper, graph paper, yellow legal pads) on which to take notes. The app also includes an audio recording feature that allows students to verbally capture key points.

# ⏻ Organizing and Brainstorming Software

The features in organizing and brainstorming software support distinct ways of enhancing summarizing and note taking.

## Summarizing

Using summary frames is one of the explicit recommendations for classroom practice. Summary frames are a series of questions the teacher asks students, designed to highlight the critical elements of specific kinds of information and tests. *Classroom Instruction That Works, 2nd Edition* (Dean, Hubbell, Pitler, & Stone, 2012), presents six types of summary frames: *narrative, topic-restriction-illustration (T-R-I), definition, argumentation, problem/solution,* and *conversation.* A summary frame is really an advance organizer or set of teacher-prepared notes intended to help students focus on what is important as they are reading or watching a video. Consider the example of Ms. Pringle, who is teaching her 3rd graders about the different families of instruments. She finds a great web resource created by the San Francisco Symphony at www.sfskids .org. But before she directs her students to the site, she uses Kidspiration to create a *definition frame* that will help her students focus as they explore the instrument families of the orchestra (see Figure 6.6). A definition frame asks the following questions:

- What is the term to define?
- What is the general category to which the term belongs?
- What are the characteristics that set this item apart from other elements in the set?
- What are some types of the item being defined?

Ms. Pringle divides her students into four expert groups, one for each major orchestral family. Students in each group use the SFS website to become "experts" on their assigned family and summarize the information from the website using the definition frame. Then Ms. Pringle places the students into new groups of four, each with an expert in a different orchestral family. The students share the information they have learned with the other three members of their group. This jigsaw activity allows students to help each other with the definition frame as they summarize.

**Figure 6.6**
**Definition Frame Created in Kidspiration**

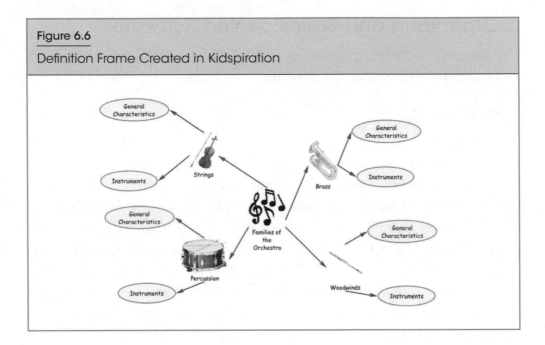

During class, Ms. Pringle finds that some students are having difficulty coming up with the general characteristics of their instrument families. She decides to use a second type of summary frame, the *topic-restriction-illustration* (T-R-I) frame, to help them. The T-R-I frame presents students with these three guiding questions:

- What is the general topic or statement?
- What information narrows or restricts the topic or statement?
- What examples illustrate the topic or restriction?

Ms. Pringle has students who were having difficulty identifying the general characteristics of their instrument families listen to a narrated version of Benjamin Britten's *A Young Person's Guide to the Orchestra* on TeacherTube.com. Using the T-R-I frame's guiding questions, the students are able to better define the families of the orchestra.

Here's another example: Mr. Winslow is teaching his 6th graders a unit titled "Pollution: It's a Dirty Word." After a short lecture about different types of power plants, he shows some videos he has downloaded that depict the pollution from coal-fired plants. He also shows short videos of the nuclear disaster at Chernobyl and the aftermath of the 2011 tsunami in Japan. The class sees the pollution from coal plants, but students also see the possible problems with nuclear power plants. To help his students summarize their thinking, Mr. Winslow chooses to use a *problem/solution* frame. The problem/solution frame directs students to look at an issue through the lens of these five guiding questions:

1. What is the problem?
2. What is a possible solution?
3. What is another possible solution?
4. What is another possible solution?
5. Which solution has the best chance of succeeding?

Mr. Winslow uses a template from the template library at webspiration classroom.com: **Starter Docs > Thinking & Planning > Problem-Solution Essay**. Shown in Figure 6.7, this template guides students as they work in groups to define the problem and propose possible solutions. It gives them a clear structure for looking at the problem and helps them see that possible solutions might lead to unintended consequences.

### Figure 6.7

#### Graphic Organizer Created in Webspiration

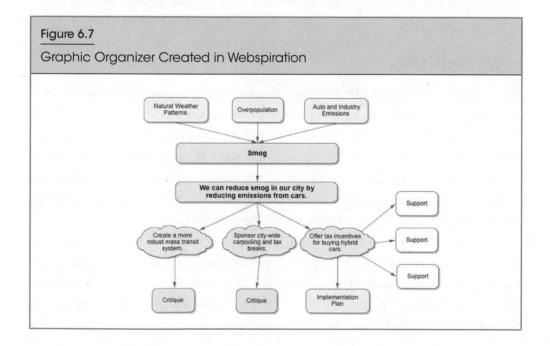

## Note Taking

Most teachers insist that their students take notes. After all, how will students study without them? Unfortunately, too few students really understand what it means to take good notes. The classroom recommendations for note taking include using a variety of note-taking formats and giving students teacher-prepared notes. Inspiration has a large number of templates that are terrific aids to teachers and students in the note-taking process.

Here's an example. Ms. Simpson, a 10th grade language arts teacher, uses PowerPoint and videos as advance organizers to begin a unit on John Steinbeck's *The Grapes of Wrath*. She then assigns a few chapters of the book for weekend reading. When the students return to school on Monday, she has them sit in base groups and discuss the character traits of the main character, Tom Joad. She wants their discussion to focus on the traits that she thinks Steinbeck intentionally developed, so she uses Inspiration to put together some notes to guide the base group conversations. Some students are more comfortable dealing with text than with graphics, so after Ms. Simpson creates the Inspiration document, she clicks **File > Transfer to Word Processor** and is able to give students both a graphic and an outline version of her teacher-prepared notes. She then guides the students to find specific examples from the book for each trait.

## ⏻ Multimedia

Not only can students create summaries and notes of multimedia content, they can also use multimedia to enhance and present their summaries and notes. For instance, three high school students use a wiki to collaborate on a project where they create a "teaser" for a movie about the life of Julius Caesar. They all take their notes separately during class, but using the wiki, they combine and summarize their notes to create their script. We'll discuss this example further in the upcoming section on communication software.

When students experience multimedia, they sometimes get caught up in the entertainment factor and neglect the critical analysis of the content necessary to create useful notes they can use for further study. When teachers introduce multimedia into their classrooms, they must ensure that students stay focused on distinguishing trivial content from essential content, coalescing minor points into major themes, and personalizing their notes based on their learning styles.

The same is true when students create multimedia summaries: They are often tempted to focus on presentation rather than substance. Obviously, spending lots of time selecting fonts and backgrounds is not time well spent; identifying and analyzing the essential components of the content is. On the plus side, using multimedia to summarize and take notes is fun, which engages students in the content. For example, students might interview their grandparents about a historical event or era they lived through. This is a tried-and-true lesson that teachers have used for many years, but with technology enhancements, it has become the type of project that parents archive with their family keepsakes.

Here's a more specific illustration. Mr. Medina assigns his middle school social studies students to interview senior citizens at a nearby activity center about the civil rights movement. Students videotape the interviews and watch them with their groups when they are back in class. During the viewings, they discuss, take notes, and summarize the interviews into common themes. Then they create a "news broadcast" about the civil rights movement, using clips of actual interview footage. Because each group has only three minutes for its news broadcast, it's essential that students apply their summarizing skills to create a product that is concise yet thorough.

In another example, Mrs. Cho wishes to combine moviemaking and the *conversation* summary frame for a character education lesson for her 6th grade students. She has her students work in groups of three to film a nonviolent bullying scene, then exchange the tapes and go through the steps of a conversation frame:

1. How did the characters greet each other?
2. What questions or topic was insinuated, revealed, or referred to?
3. How did their discussion progress?
4. What was the conclusion?

Using this frame, the class is better able to analyze exactly what constitutes "bullying"; later, the students use their definition to create agreed-upon rules for how to treat each other and other schoolmates.

Another great way to use multimedia to summarize and take notes is with slide show–based combination notes. Various applications, such as Power-Point, Prezi, Keynote, and Google Presentation, can be used for this activity. The two-column format links essential concepts on the left with multimedia enhancements on the right of a slide. Along the bottom of the slide, an overall statement summarizes the combination notes. Figures 6.8 and 6.9 show a teacher's assignment and template created in PowerPoint.

Figure 6.10 shows an example of a student's use of combination notes to summarize the book *The Outsiders* by S. E. Hinton. Although the images, sound, and video that the student selected may not seem like ones you would choose, the student chose examples that are personally meaningful. This is especially important because the notes serve as a personalized tool for him to study and remember the themes in the book.

Note that the students are using an *argumentation* frame for themes. The four elements they have to address are evidence, claim, support, and a qualifier for their theme, using the following questions:

1. *Evidence*: What information does the author present that leads to a claim?

2. *Claim*: What does the author assert is true? What basic statement or claim is the focus of the information?

3. *Support*: What examples or explanations support the claim?

4. *Qualifier*: What restrictions on the claim or evidence counter to the claim are presented?

In this example, the claim is that the lowest and highest social classes are just as capable of noble or malicious acts.

Another way to visualize a summary is by creating a word cloud. At word cloud generators like tagxedo.com or wordle.net, users can create a visually descriptive summary of just about any major topic. One way of doing this is to go to wikipedia.org and search for a topic you are trying to teach or learn about. Once you have found it, select **Print/export > Printable version** from the left sidebar. Copy and paste the text into one of the aforementioned word cloud generators, and you instantly have a visually rich summary. You can even change shapes and colors. An example of a word cloud summary of the Watergate scandal using Wordle is seen in Figure 6.11.

**Figure 6.8**

Guidelines for a PowerPoint Combination Notes Assignment

### Combination Notes Criteria
### *The Outsiders*

- Use the combination notes template.
- Identify at least three major themes.
- Enhance each theme with relevant graphics, sounds, links, or video clips (different types for each theme).
- At the bottom of each notes slide, include a brief statement summarizing the preceding themes.
- Use legible fonts between 16 and 40 points.
- Ensure color contrast is visually appealing and easy to read.
- Randomly selected students will present their notes orally to the class.
- Less is more. Too much text can make your presentation too cluttered. Save detailed explanations for oral remarks.

*Clip art images © 2012 Jupiterimages Corporation.*

**Figure 6.9**

Combination Notes Template Created in PowerPoint

### Title

Identify the Major Themes | Multimedia Theme Enhancements

Summary Statement

*Clip art images © 2012 Jupiterimages Corporation.*

### Figure 6.10
### Combination Notes Created in PowerPoint

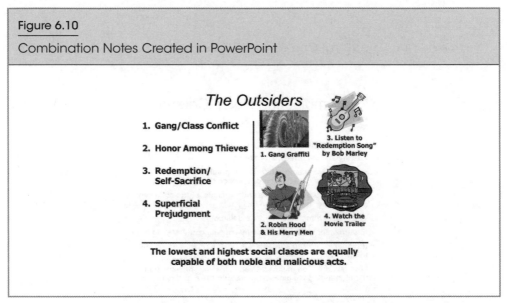

*Photograph by Les Chatfield (leslie_chatfield@yahoo.co.uk).*
*Clip art images © 2012 Jupiterimages Corporation.*

Many teachers and students see summarizing and note taking as individual activities, and often they are. However, there are ways to summarize and take notes collaboratively, and there are several websites that facilitate this:

▶ Google Docs
https://docs.google.com

This free suite of office applications lets students import existing documents, including spreadsheets and presentations, or create new ones from scratch. Documents are stored on the cloud and are accessible on any browser. Other users can be invited to help edit the documents.

▶ Your Draft
www.yourdraft.com

This free online editor allows fast and flexible drafting. Users can give others the right to edit, or only to read their page and add replies.

▶ Writeboard
www.writeboard.com

**Figure 6.11**

Summary of the Watergate Scandal Created in Wordle

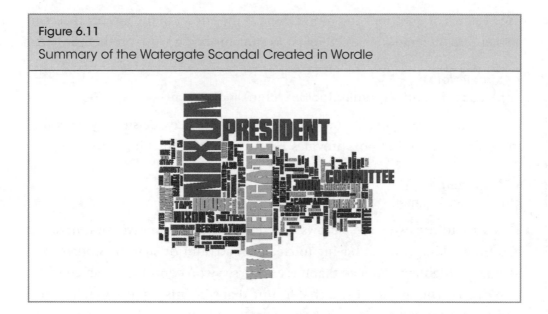

This website allows users to create sharable documents, save every edit, revert to previous versions, and compare changes.

▶ NoteStar
http://notestar.4teachers.org

NoteStar allows students to take information from the web, organize it, and automatically create citations in either MLA or APA style. Teachers can also establish projects and assign individual students sections of the project to complete. This site is designed for students in grades 4–12.

▶ ThinkFree
www.thinkfree.com

Similar to Google Docs, ThinkFree is a free office suite available online. Users can collaborate to prepare documents, spreadsheets, and presentations.

▶ ThinkTank
http://thinktank.4teachers.org

Designed for grades 3–8, ThinkTank allows students to use online tools to zero in on a project topic. The site is organized in a kind of narrative frame in that it uses a series of questions to prompt users as they develop the project. This site also allows integration with NoteStar as students begin work on their project.

▶ Cornell Notes
http://coe.jmu.edu/LearningToolbox/cornellnotes.html

Many schools use Cornell Notes as a school- or districtwide strategy. This site, from the Learning Toolbox, provides a good tutorial on making Cornell Notes.

▶ Typewith.me
http://typewith.me

This easy-to-use web tool allows for real-time collaborative summarizing and note taking without having to create an account or sign in. Students are assigned a highlight color so that it is easy to see who contributed which selection of text. The site also has a chat feature that students can use to talk about their work. Students invite collaborators by simply sharing the unique URL of their document. (Similar websites to this one are http://primarypad.com and http://titanpad.com.)

▶ Lit Summary Podcast
www.learnoutloud.com/Catalog/Literature/American-Classics/
Lit-Summary-Podcast/24192#3

Each episode of this podcast contains an audio summary of a classic book in Western literature.

▶ Township High School Summary Frames
www.d214.org/staff_services/si_summary_frame.aspx

This website from Township High School in Arlington Heights, Illinois, offers many downloadable examples of summary frames alongside directions for using them.

▶ The Jigsaw Method
http://olc.spsd.sk.ca/de/PD/coop/page4.html

This website from Saskatoon Public Schools in Saskatchewan, Canada, offers some great resources on the Jigsaw Method for helping students to summarize a large body of knowledge collaboratively.

# ⏻ Communication and Collaboration Software

Although e-mail and group folders on a server can certainly support summarizing and note taking, there are new tools that provide much more intuitive and seamless ways for students to collaborate as they take notes and summarize. Collaborative web-based tools such as wikis and blogs allow groups to share resources, edit web pages, and easily find and categorize information by means of "tags," or short descriptors of resources. In this section, we show the role that wikis and blogs can have in collaborative summarizing and note taking.

## Wikis

Mr. Simmons, a 10th grade English teacher, is wrapping up his class's study of Shakespeare's *Julius Caesar*. For a final project, which will serve to assess his students' understanding of the play, he asks students to make a short movie trailer—a preview-style advertisement—for a movie about the life of Julius Caesar. Before giving the assignment, he creates a rubric by modifying RubiStar's multimedia criteria and grading on the qualities of voice, soundtrack, economy, historical accuracy, and enticement. The assignment follows:

> Create a teaser (trailer) for an imaginary movie about the life of Julius Caesar. You can use live motion, clay animation, cut-out animation, or drawn animation. Your movie needs to include voiceover narration, a soundtrack, and scenes from Caesar's life as depicted in Shakespeare's play. You may work independently or in self-selected groups of up to three people. See our class website to access the rubric for more detailed information about this assignment.

A group of students—Jake, Shantel, and Dion—decide to do a live-action trailer. The first thing they need to do is combine the individual notes that they took throughout the class's study of the play into a collective set of notes. Next, they'll need to summarize these collective notes into the beginning of a script for their project. They decide to use the PBWorks wiki (http://pbworks.com) to help them collaborate.

PBWorks has a number of easy-to-understand tutorials to help the students quickly learn how to create and personalize a wiki. Following the guidelines available, Jake creates the wiki (http://caesar.pbworks.com) and copies and pastes his notes from various lectures onto a page that he creates and names CaesarBio. He also finds a picture of a bust of Caesar on the Wikipedia website and copies it to his page. Shantel and Dion read his posted notes and copy and paste some of their own, resulting in a collaborative page of facts about Julius Caesar.

In the wiki that Jake began, Shantel creates three new pages: Resources, Assignment, and Storyboard. She also adds a sidebar for easy navigation. On the Resources page, she links to Wikipedia and her own del.icio.us account, which contains her saved web links that she has tagged as "Caesar." This allows the group to easily share resources as they write their script. Next, Dion posts the original assignment from Mr. Simmons so that they all can stay focused on the topic. He also copies and pastes Mr. Simmons's rubric on a separate page.

Now to the project itself. Shantel suggests that they first type a script and then work on the storyboard. Jake agrees, so all three students begin to edit and shape their trailer's script. The students are able to work on the script separately from home, together during their lunch hour or study hall, and either individually or collaboratively in the school media center before and after school. The wiki serves as a common area for them to take notes, summarize information, and plan and carry out their project. If Mr. Simmons or any member of the group wishes to see changes made throughout the process, they are available for viewing in the "history" of each wiki page, along with an indication of who saved each change. Most wikis, including PBWorks, have this feature.

Before assigning this project, Mr. Simmons had taught his students the six different summary frames that are discussed in detail in *Classroom Instruction That Works, 2nd Edition*. To help them summarize their teaser, he suggests that they use a narrative summary frame. This, he explains, will work well for the play by guiding them through questions that commonly relate to fiction and helping them identify the characters, setting, initiating event, internal response, goal, consequence, and resolution of the play. For their trailer, Jake, Shantel, and Dion decide to omit the consequence and resolution so that it won't "give away" the end of the movie.

## Blogs

Blogs provide a very effective way to implement the strategy of *reciprocal teaching*. This highly structured form of peer teaching has four components: (1) summarizing, (2) questioning, (3) clarifying, and (4) predicting. After the students have read a section independently, one student *summarizes* the information for the class. Other members of the class or the teacher may help during this process. The student then asks the class *questions* in order to highlight important sections of the text. Then the same student asks classmates to *clarify* confusing information. Finally, the student asks for *predictions* about what will follow the passage they just read.

The reciprocal teaching format can be used not just with reading and face-to-face conversation but also with web-based educational movies and blogs. For example, Ms. Holt, a 4th grade teacher, wishes to employ reciprocal teaching as her students are learning about different forms of energy. Blogs provide the means for students to use the strategy of reciprocal teaching but allow time for more in-depth conversation that can extend beyond the allotted time in the classroom. Ms. Holt logs on to BrainPOP, and the entire class watches the short, Flash-based movie *Forms of Energy*. As they are watching, she types the vocabulary terms from the movie on a blog: *potential, kinetic, chemical, electrical, light, mechanical, thermal,* and *nuclear*. She then selects Jonah to leads the class's discussion on the blog.

Jonah signs on to the blog and begins by *summarizing* what he understood from the movie: that energy can come from a variety of places, and that potential energy is stored energy, while kinetic energy involves motion. He then types in some *questions* about each of the types of energy for his classmates to answer. By the next day, they respond with their understanding and come up with several examples of each type of energy. They are able to read these together as a class using a projector. Ms. Holt is thrilled with the level of conversation that her students are having.

On the second day, Jonah *asks for clarification* on nuclear energy. This seems confusing for all, so they watch that segment of the *Forms of Energy* movie again. Ms. Holt also clarifies nuclear energy by posting on the blog and receives numerous "a-ha!" responses. Finally, Jonah *makes the prediction* that they will next learn about which forms of energy are safer and cheaper. He notices that one of the videos related to *Forms of Energy* on BrainPOP is *Fossil Fuels,* so he also *makes the prediction* that they will be learning about how fossil fuels are used to create energy.

The blog serves as an archive of their class's discussion for later review and as a part of their assessment. Ms. Holt shares the blog's URL with parents, who enjoy getting a peek at the conversations taking place in the classroom.

# 7

# Assigning Homework and Providing Practice

*Homework* and *practice* give students a chance to review and apply what they have learned.

In the last few years, the research findings on the effectiveness and importance of homework have been mixed (Kohn, 2006; Marzano & Pickering, 2007), yet most teachers continue to assign homework and believe that there is a good reason to do so. Many factors can affect the amount of influence that homework has on achievement, including the degree of parental involvement, homework quality, students' learning preferences, the structure and monitoring of assignments, and home environments (Hong, Milgram, & Rowell, 2004; Minotti, 2005). Cooper, Robinson, and Patall's (2006) meta-analysis of research on homework practice provides support for the positive effects of homework. Using narrative and quantitative techniques, the analysis integrated the results of research on homework from 1987 through 2003 and revealed a positive relationship between homework and achievement, with an effect size of 0.60. Still, other researchers have found no positive relationship between homework and achievement (Vatterott, 2009).

At its best, homework can provide opportunities for students to familiarize themselves with new concepts as well as to practice, review, and apply what they've learned. It provides opportunities for them to deepen their understanding of the content and to gain proficiency with their skills, and extends learning beyond the classroom walls. The practices recommended in this section can help teachers and students get the most out of homework and avoid some of the pitfalls.

We have three recommendations for classroom practice:

## RECOMMENDATIONS

- Develop and communicate a district or school homework policy.
- Design homework assignments that support academic learning and communicate their purpose.
- Provide feedback on assigned homework.

Having students practice a skill or concept enhances their ability to reach the expected level of proficiency. However, it seems that not all types of practice will yield improved performance. For example, "traditional" practice—that is, reviewing notes or rereading texts—has little effect on achievement, but is still better than no practice at all (McDaniel, Roediger, & McDermott, 2007). To be effective, practice should be overt, which means it involves students in actively recalling material through quizzing, rehearsal, or self-assessment (e.g., by using flash cards or labeling). When these forms of "practice testing" occur frequently (two or three times between acquisition or presentation of material and final assessment of knowledge), the effect on student achievement is increased (Karpicke & Roediger, 2008). Testing students at regular intervals throughout the learning period also has a positive impact on learning (Carpenter, Pashler, & Cepeda, 2009; Rohrer, Taylor, & Sholar, 2010).

Practice is also more likely to be effective when students are required to practice more than one skill at a time (Hall, Domingues, & Cavazos, 1994; Rohrer & Taylor, 2007). A possible explanation is that students must practice identifying the process that they need to follow as well as the process itself. In addition, when students can access and use corrective feedback about their performance to determine what and how to practice, retention and achievement of the skill or knowledge are improved (Pashler, Rohrer, Cepeda, & Carpenter, 2007). Practice also appears to be more effective when distributed over time rather than massed into a single session: In general, students need to practice upwards of 24 times before they reach 80 percent competency (Anderson, 1995; Newell & Rosenbloom, 1981).

Based on these findings, we have three recommendations for providing practice:

### RECOMMENDATIONS

- Clearly identify and communicate the purpose of practice activities.
- Design practice sessions that are short, focused, and distributed over time.
- Provide feedback on practice sessions.

Technology facilitates homework and practice by providing a wealth of resources for learning outside of the classroom, making it easy for students to work on collaborative homework assignments and providing "drill and practice" resources that help students refine their skills.

Many technologies that are used for practice have the ability to track a student's progress over time and provide more challenging tasks accordingly. According to research on strategies that help students who are struggling, computer-assisted instruction (CAI) contributes to the learning of at-risk students because it is nonjudgmental and motivational, provides frequent and immediate feedback, can individualize learning to meet students' needs, allows for more student autonomy, and provides a multisensory learning environment (Barley et al., 2002).

In this chapter, we look at the categories of technology that enrich a classroom's homework and practice program: *word processing applications, data collection and analysis tools, multimedia, instructional interactives,* and *communication and collaboration software.*

## ⏻ Word Processing Applications

Most people think of word processing software as a one-trick pony: You use it to type papers and that's it. However, the varied tools in word processing applications make it much more than simply an electronic typewriter.

In other sections of this book, we discuss many of the tools available in Microsoft Word, which is one of the most common word processing software products. But we haven't yet touched on the research capability within the program. Almost every teacher knows to send student researchers to search engines like Google or Yahoo!, but far fewer know that students can also search within Word. Right-clicking any word brings up a dialog box that features the **Look Up** command. Clicking on this command opens a window on the right-hand side of the page that allows students to search such resources as dictionaries, thesauruses, and even the Bing search engine for more information on the chosen word.

One real advantage to using this tool rather than opening a browser program and using a search engine is that the search results tend to be more focused than those generated by a general-purpose search engine. For younger students and other fledgling researchers, this can be a significant benefit. Students who search from within a Word document are less likely to be sent on "wild goose chases" or to be diverted from the assignment by the web's many distractions.

Here's an illustration of how students might use Word for research. Ms. Thompson is teaching her 5th graders about the Holocaust. For the unit's final project, she offers her students a choice of topics, some of which are student-generated, and a choice of formats: a slide-show presentation, a movie, or a standard report.

Emma decides to do a report, as she has already created a presentation and a movie for previous units. As she works on her report on her home computer, she comes across the word *persecution* in a text that she's reading in Word. Although Emma knows she has heard this word before, she isn't certain of its meaning, so she right clicks on the word and chooses **Look Up**. The definitions provided help a little, but she still isn't sure that she completely gets the word's meaning. So Emma clicks on the thesaurus link in the research tool and reads some of the synonyms for persecution: *bullying, harassment,* and *discrimination.* The combination of the definition and the synonyms gives Emma a good idea of what the word means.

After she finishes the first draft of her report, Emma checks the grade level of her writing, as Ms. Thompson had taught her to do, using the Word spelling and grammar tool (see Chapter 1). She sees that her Flesch-Kincaid grade-level rating is only 4.9. Emma knows that she can increase the sophistication of her writing by using some of the new vocabulary words the class has been learning, changing some of the adjectives to more descriptive ones that she recognized in Word's thesaurus, and combining some of the short sentences she has a tendency to use.

## ⏻ Data Collection and Analysis Tools

Whether it's on a home computer, classroom laptop, or school lab computer, using spreadsheets for homework and practice is typically about students using data to master concepts and skills. Students can practice by calculating, manipulating, and displaying data to gain deeper understanding.

Here's an example. Ryan Turnage teaches physical education and is a football coach at Caroline High School. His colleague, Mrs. Baker, teaches algebra. Mrs. Baker asks Coach Turnage to help motivate some of the players to practice their data analysis skills. Because he is in charge of the football team's strength and conditioning program, he decides to have his players track their workouts: how much weight they are lifting and the number of repetitions they are doing at each session. A computer lab is located just across from the locker room, so after each workout, he has his players open a spreadsheet to enter their data. Coach Turnage also has them correlate the data with their heart rate, which he has them take in the computer lab as they wait for the computers to boot up. Finally, the players save their spreadsheets to a central server folder for later use. At the end of the season, the players and coaches can check the progress of each player's workouts, and the players graph these data in Mrs. Baker's algebra class.

After the students become comfortable using spreadsheet software, Mrs. Baker has them use spreadsheets to deepen their understanding of parabolic functions. As part of her unit on graphing quadratic equations, she gives her students standard homework assignments focused on solving parabolic functions and hand-graphing. Next she brings technology back into the mix, instructing students to enter the answers to their homework problems into spreadsheets so that they can quickly see how changes in constants and signs change the parabolic graphs.

## ⏻ Multimedia

One way some innovative teachers and schools are using technology to enhance and even redefine homework and practice is the "flipped classroom." Pioneered in 2007 by Jonathan Bergmann and Aaron Sams, two chemistry teachers from Woodland Park High School in Woodland Park, Colorado, the flipped classroom is transforming how some teachers disseminate information and organize class activities. The basic idea is that students can listen to the "lecture" part of the class as podcasts or vodcasts at home or on the bus and engage in applying what they learn under the teacher's guidance during class time. In this way, the role of the teacher changes from "presenter of content" to "learning coach," and the teacher can spend most of her time talking to and working with students—answering questions, working with small groups, and guiding the learning of each student individually. (You can read more about the flipped classroom online at www.thedailyriff.com/articles/how-the-flipped-classroom-is-radically-transforming-learning-536.php.)

Another good example of instructional media is the Khan Academy (www.khanacademy.org). With over 2,400 videos covering K–12 math, biology, chemistry, and physics, and even finance and history, it is easily the most exhaustive free collection of instruction on the Internet. The content is presented in easily digestible 10- to 20-minute chunks especially intended for viewing on the computer. In addition, the conversational style of the videos is the tonal antithesis of what people traditionally associate with math and science instruction. There is even a teacher dashboard that allows the teacher to track how students are doing as they progress through the lessons.

BrainPOP (www.brainpop.com) and BrainPOP Jr. (www.brainpopjr.com) contain hundreds of short, Flash-based movies covering English, social studies, mathematics, science, health, art, and technology. Each movie is followed by a 10-question quiz that can be printed off or emailed to the teacher. Most content is available in both English and Spanish. There is also a BrainPOP app for the iPad that provides a free movie every day. Although the sites are subscription-based, they are worth considering.

Clearly, using and creating multimedia requires a high degree of technology accessibility for students. Some schools check out computers and equipment to students, while others enjoy the benefits of one-to-one laptop programs in which students have a laptop assigned to them for the whole year. If they do not have a family computer to use, they can use their school laptop. When access is not a problem, multimedia homework is an opportunity to deepen understanding and gain proficiency. Practicing with multimedia allows students to shape the experience to their individual learning style and increase their level of understanding to mastery.

In addition to learning *from* multimedia such as educational games and interactive simulations, students can learn *with* multimedia by creating their own projects at home or at school to develop their understanding and practice skills.

When students create multimedia projects like those discussed in Chapter 5, they undertake many of the project's tasks outside of class. After planning their scripts and storyboards, students can search their homes and neighborhoods for imagery to incorporate via video. This creates more opportunities for creativity than the typical classroom and school offer.

Another example of creating multimedia for homework and practice is teacher or student construction of games using a presentation tool such as Keynote or PowerPoint. Students create a game using hyperlinks and action buttons. Like any multimedia project, the game needs to be well planned before the actual design begins. Sarah Lodick created such a game in PowerPoint while completing her student teaching for the University of Georgia. She wanted her mathematics students to learn basic graphing skills using the Cartesian coordinate system, so she created a game called BattleGraph (see Figure 7.1), based on the Battleship board game, in which students customize the game or play it directly. The game uses $x$- and $y$-coordinates to place ships on a graphical ocean. A player also uses $x$- and $y$-coordinates to try to locate and hit the opposing player's ships. Even students without home access to computers can play the game, as it can be printed out in hard copy form. BattleGraph is available online at http://sarah.lodick.com/edit/powerpoint_game/battle graph/battlegraph.ppt.

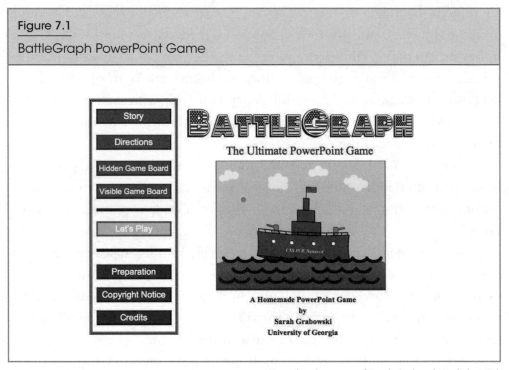

**Figure 7.1**

BattleGraph PowerPoint Game

*Reproduced courtesy of Sarah Grabowski Lodick, MEd.*

## ⏻ Instructional Interactives

Well-made software programs allow teachers to choose which learning objectives students need to practice, offer sophisticated and seamless multimedia to keep the learner engaged, and provide immediate feedback and scaffolding in order to help students understand and practice a concept. Here are some resources that recognize the best educational software:

▶ *ComputED Gazette's* Education Software Review Awards and Best Educational Software Awards
www.computedgazette.com/page3.html

These awards, also known as the EDDIEs and the BESSIEs, recognize innovating software for education. Categories include Early Learning, Early Elementary, Upper Elementary, Middle School, High School/Post-Secondary, Internet Tools, Educational Websites, and Teacher Productivity Tools.

▶ **The Software and Information Industry Association's CoDIE Awards**
www.siia.net/codies

Entries for these annual awards are nominated by users. The awards recognize software in various industries, including education. Among the awards is the Education Newcomer Award.

▶ **Discovery Education's Best Educational Software**
http://school.discovery.com/parents/reviewcorner/software/

Discovery Education's educational software review is compiled after testing software with children and parents. Testers look for well-designed products that encourage students as they learn. Each review provides a detailed synopsis of appropriate age, content, and caveats.

Interactive resources for educational purposes can be grouped into two categories: long-term, project-based interactives that incorporate simulations or games, and simple teaching and learning aids that focus on a limited concept or skill. The distinction between the two types is primarily in the scope of the learning objectives and the depth of the critical thinking involved. Interactives in the first category allow students to take many learning routes that are differentiated for their readiness level and interests and include feedback mechanisms that are both real-time and longitudinal. The best of these interactives have four features: They diagnose the student's learning needs, prescribe a learning progression, interact with the student, and adapt the learning progression based on the student's progress. Some examples of these are Cognitive Tutor (www.carnegielearning.com/specs/cognitive-tutor-overview), Dimension U (www.dimensionu.com), GiSE (www.gise.rice.edu/gamelinks.html), PBS Kids' Cyberchase (www.pbs.org/parents/cyberchase), Ed Heads (http://edheads.org), the Fast ForWord Reading Series (www.scilearn.com/products/fast-forword-reading-series), and ExploreLearning's Gizmos (www.explorelearning.com). While very useful, the interactives that focus on a limited concept or skill are not as multifaceted as others that take students all the way through Bloom's taxonomy into deep and varied levels of critical thinking. They are, however, excellent tools for introducing and practicing basic skills and concepts.

Consider this example. Mrs. Dempsey's 3rd grade class is learning about acids, bases, and the pH scale. Although the students do several related experiments and activities at school, Mrs. Dempsey wants to ensure that they will remember the material when the unit is complete. Several weeks after the close of the unit, she asks them to go through the activities from the Kitchen Chemistry PBS Zoom website (http://pbskids.org/zoom/games/kitchenchemistry/virtual-start). The website allows them to conduct virtual experiments by "mixing" substances to test for carbonation.

At the end of the tutorial is a section to print out a reward certificate. To confirm that her students completed the activities, Mrs. Dempsey asks them to either print the reward certificate and hand it in or save it as a screen shot and e-mail it to her. Later, she will use a BrainPOP quiz to test for retention.

In another example, a 1st grade class is working on short vowel sounds, but some students are ready for more challenging work. One of their teacher's favorite resources for building reading skills is the Starfall website (www.starfall.com), which is a great resource for providing focused practice time on a particular skill. During this particular class session, all Mrs. Dempsey's students go to the Learn to Read section of the website. Some do the short-vowel activities while others concentrate on long vowels and consonant blends. Each vowel sound links to a corresponding e-book where students can click on unfamiliar words and hear them "spoken." Students can also play a game designed to help build their knowledge of specific vowel sounds. The variety of activities and flexible presentation style mean each student is able to work on skills that best meet his or her needs, and the teacher is able to differentiate instruction during practice sessions.

Here are some other recommended websites to use for homework and practice:

❱ BBC Skillswise
http://bbc.co.uk/skillswise

This resource from the BBC includes a Numbers section and a Words section. Within these sections are concept areas containing worksheets, games, and quizzes appropriate for grades 3–8. Among the concepts covered are punctuation, fractions, suffixes, and multiplication.

❱ National Library of Virtual Manipulatives
http://nlvm.usu.edu/en/nav/vlibrary.html

This resource from Utah State University contains many virtual manipulatives to help students in grades preK–12 better understand mathematics concepts. Some of the manipulatives include base blocks, geoboards, algebra tiles, algebra balance scales, and various puzzles.

❱ Flashcard Exchange
www.flashcardexchange.com

This resource allows teachers and students to generate custom virtual flashcards and access flashcards others have created. Teachers can create study guides for students or allow students to create their own. Students also can play "memory" with the card stack.

❱ Hurricane Strike!
http://meted.ucar.edu/hurrican/strike/index.htm

This simulation from the University Corporation for Atmospheric Research in Boulder, Colorado, takes students through tutorials about hurricanes and helps them apply what they've learned to make decisions as a hurricane approaches.

❱ Rocket Math
Apple App Store and Android Marketplace

Rocket Math is a free math app appropriate for children of all ages. Children are able to practice basic mathematical functions or work on telling time, handling money, and identifying three-dimensional shapes. As players successfully complete math problems, all of which are formatted into game-like interfaces, they earn virtual money. That money can then be used to build a personalized rocket ship.

## ⏻ Communication and Collaboration Software

Chapter 1's discussion of providing feedback covered how to use the Microsoft Word Track Changes and Insert Comments features to give feedback to students about their writing. Although these tools are an ideal way to let a few authors edit a piece of writing for peer review, there can be complicating factors. To edit a document collaboratively, all students must either have access to a shared folder (which may not be possible away from school) or must e-mail the document to other group members. Editing a document via e-mail can be confusing and cumbersome with a large group—often resulting in one version overwriting another or multiple versions of one document. In these circumstances, another option is to select communications software designed to facilitate collaboration.

Here's an example. Several students in a high school family/consumer sciences class agree to perfect their recipe of steak au poivre as a final project. First, they will practice making the dish individually at home, and then they will compare recipes and results. What they need is a way to share their recipe adjustments. They decide to use Writeboard (http://writeboard.com), one of several services that allow multiple users to edit a document via the web in a manner similar to a wiki. (Other web resources that offer similar services are listed in Chapter 6.) Writeboard allows users to compare different versions of their page and see changes made, much as with Track Changes in Word. As you can see in Figure 7.2, the changes between the 4th and 11th versions of the recipe are shown via highlighted text and gray strikethroughs.

Students now have access to resources that help them communicate in real time to teachers, peers, or outside facilitators. Something as simple as using a blog to foster discussions can provide rich out-of-school experiences for students, often allowing them to share input that they may not be willing to share in a face-to-face setting. Teachers have made use of tools such as Google Chat, Skype, texting, and Twitter to extend the learning far beyond the time and space of the classroom. (For more examples of how social media provides rich out-of-school learning experiences, you may wish to read the article "Social Media Find Place in Classroom," published in *USA Today* on July 25, 2011, and available online at www.usatoday.com/news/education/2011-07-24-schools-social-media_n.htm).

## Figure 7.2

## Screenshot of Writeboard Showing Changes Between Versions

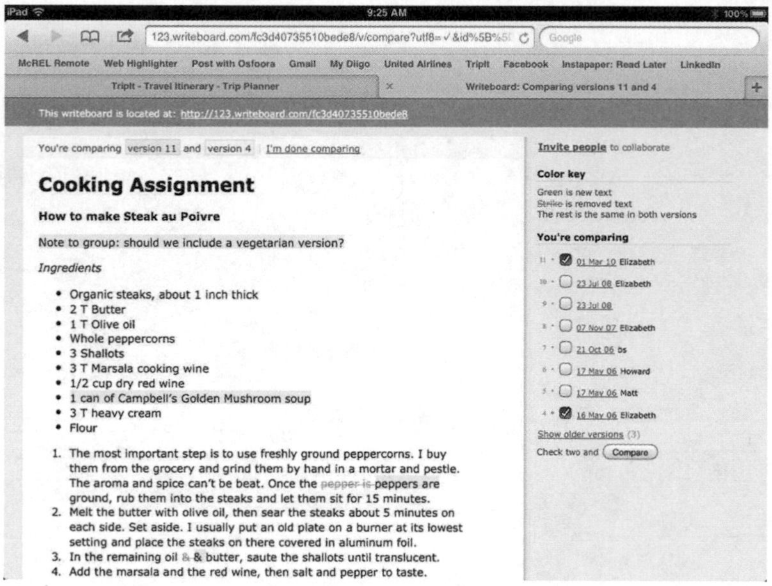

# Helping Students Extend and Apply Knowledge

# 8

# Identifying Similarities and Differences

Asking students to *identify the similarities and differences* in the content they are learning helps them to structure their understanding of the content. During the process, they make new connections, experience fresh insights, and correct misconceptions. These complex reasoning procedures lead students to deeper understanding.

The following processes are integral to this strategy (Marzano, Pickering, & Pollock, 2001):

• *Comparing*—this is the process of identifying similarities between or among things or ideas. The term *contrasting* refers to the process of identifying differences; most educators, however, use the term *comparing* to refer to both.

• *Classifying*—this is the process of grouping things that are alike into categories on the basis of their characteristics.

• *Creating metaphors*—this is the process of identifying a general or basic pattern in a specific topic and then finding another topic that appears to be quite different but that has the same general pattern.

• *Creating analogies*—this is the process of identifying relationships between pairs of concepts—in other words, identifying relationships between relationships.

These processes help move students from existing knowledge to new knowledge, concrete ideas to abstract ideas, and separate concepts to connected concepts. Students use what they know as an anchor for new learning. As a result, many people consider these processes to constitute the core of all learning (Bransford, Brown, & Cocking, 2000; Chen, 1999; Fuchs et al., 2006; Gentner, Loewenstein, & Thompson, 2003; Holyoak, 2005).

Based on McREL's research, we have three recommendations for classroom practice:

### RECOMMENDATIONS

- Teach students a variety of ways to identify similarities and differences.
- Guide students as they engage in the process of identifying similarities and differences.
- Provide supporting cues to help students identify similarities and differences.

Technology facilitates the process of identifying similarities and differences by helping to create graphic organizers for comparing, classifying, creating metaphors, and creating analogies. In this chapter, we show how to use the following resources to help your students identify similarities and differences: *word processing applications, communication and collaboration software, data collection and analysis tools,* and *organizing and brainstorming software.*

## ⏻ Word Processing Applications

Graphic organizers are a time-tested way of representing similarities and differences, and we discuss them at length in the section on organizing and brainstorming software in this chapter. But what if you don't have the necessary software? No problem. You can show your students how to use drawing tools in their word processing programs to draw diagrams, charts, or other templates to compare and classify items or illustrate a metaphor or an analogy. For example, Microsoft Word's SmartArt menu contains a variety of Venn diagrams to help students compare and contrast concepts. You can find a selection of Venn diagrams by clicking on **Insert > SmartArt > Relationships**.

Another option is to create classification tables and templates. Remember that classifying is the process of grouping things into definable categories on the basis of their attributes. Word processors make this easy. In the example shown in Figure 8.1, Ms. Fisher gives her students a list of geography terms using Google Docs. Students define the key categories they feel are best to group the items, then sort the terms into the categories they create. Due to the collaborative nature of Google tools, students are able to do this activity in small groups, with each of them at his or her own laptop. Students classify terms by elevation and then classify again based on geography terms that relate most strongly to water or land. Throughout the process, students view the terms in new ways.

## Figure 8.1

### Classification Activity Created in Google Docs

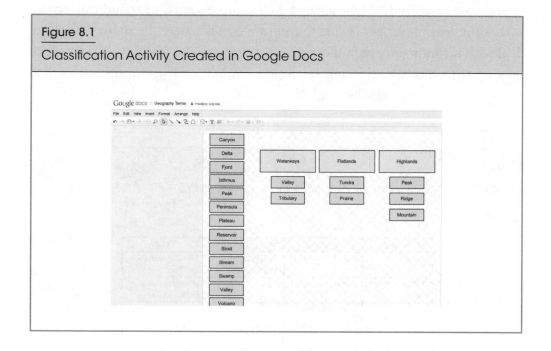

Figure 8.2 shows a second example. Here, Mr. Andrews takes his literature students' work with classification to a more abstract level in order to build their understanding of different literary genres. He presents students with a list of titles and the categories of Blue, Purple, Red, and Yellow, which, he explains, will represent four categories that the students will define for themselves. Then he begins the classification activity by asking students to suggest common themes among these books. Students also brainstorm other classification possibilities, such as grouping the books by genre, time period, or another characteristic (e.g., short and long, easy and hard, male authors and female authors).

Students then work individually to create their own categories and classify the books in the list by placing them in the appropriate category.

Throughout the activity, the students must return to their categories, reconsider them, and think about the books and categories in new ways. They also must think about their classification rationales and how they will defend their choices. The activity concludes with Mr. Andrews asking his students to exchange completed charts and see if others can identify the classification criteria they're using. Try this yourself with the example in Figure 8.2. Can you figure it out? The student who created this example used Blue to indicate books with a theme of revenge; Purple to indicate books where the main characters deal with a conflict between the individual and society; Red to indicate books dealing with race equality and relations; and Yellow to indicate books that contain "coming of age" themes.

### Figure 8.2

### Book Classification Table Created in Microsoft Word

| Blue | Purple | Red | Yellow |
|---|---|---|---|
| Hamlet | Huckleberry Finn | To Kill a Mockingbird | The Catcher in the Rye |
| A Tale of Two Cities | The Outsiders | | Where the Red Fern Grows |
| | Gone with the Wind | | |
| | | | |

**Define your categories and categorize the following books from the Junior-Senior reading list:**

- Hamlet
- Where the Red Fern Grows
- Huckleberry Finn
- To Kill a Mockingbird
- The Catcher in the Rye
- A Tale of Two Cities
- The Outsiders
- The Grapes of Wrath
- Gone with the Wind
- Death of a Salesman
- Wuthering Heights

So far, we've looked at some examples that engage students in sorting and classifying. Now let's look at how students might work on the related skill of recognizing and creating analogies, which require students to identify a similarity between two elements.

Mr. Purcell uses word processing software, a laptop, and a projector with his elementary class to create and display an "Analogy of the Day" thinking puzzle (see Figure 8.3). He starts this year with teacher-created examples, primarily simple ones such as this:

Hot is to Cold as Night is to _____.
Hard is to _____ as High is to Low.

As students get better at solving the analogy comparisons over a period of months, Mr. Purcell allows individual students to take over the Analogy of the Day activity and create a new puzzle for each day, providing one-on-one help if needed. Mr. Purcell also uses this opportunity to familiarize those students who don't have home access to technology with some easy operational tasks. Artistic students (and teachers, too) can use the Drawing tools of a word processor to create illustrative graphics. The Internet is also a great resource for graphics to add to analogy puzzles. Those in Figure 8.3 were acquired from www.clipart.com.

**Figure 8.3**

Analogy of the Day Puzzle Created in Microsoft Word

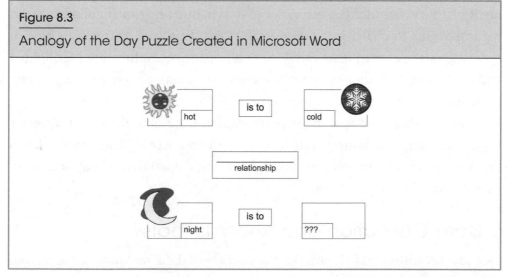

*Clip art images © 2012 Jupiterimages Corporation.*

## ⏻ Communication and Collaboration Software

Here's an example of communication and collaboration software put to good use in the classroom. Mrs. Lincoln, a middle school teacher, wants to make sure her students understand how Martin Luther King Jr.'s "I Have a Dream" speech resonates with their lives. Her school has Google Apps for Education—a suite of free and easy-to-use applications for use within a protected school domain. Each student has a Google account and an online portfolio organized on his or her individual Google site. Mrs. Lincoln first downloads the text of the "I Have a Dream" speech from www.americanrhetoric.com/speeches/mlk ihaveadream.htm and pastes it into a Google text document. Then she saves the document as a template and keeps a copy in her Google account. Because her students all have Google accounts, she has their usernames saved, which makes sharing the document easy. Each student is invited to read the copy of the text document and given collaboration rights.

Mrs. Lincoln first shows the students a video of the speech as an advance organizer. Then, after providing a lesson on metaphors and how they are used to convey meaning, she asks the students to begin analyzing the text of the speech at different starting points. Their job is to find one metaphor, highlight it with the Google Docs highlighting tool, and describe its meaning in parentheses (see Figure 8.4). As the students work, Mrs. Lincoln projects the document on the computer projector. Soon, a dynamic array of highlighting and writing begins to evolve into a rich tapestry on the screen as the deep hidden meaning of the speech is revealed. After all of the metaphors are highlighted and explained, Mrs. Lincoln leads the students in making sense of each metaphor and fine-tuning the explanations in the document.

By collaborating with their peers, students are able to see the speech's larger meaning and lasting connections to today's world. The ability of students to collaborate in real time through a Google document makes this activity effective, efficient, and fun.

## ⏻ Data Collection and Analysis Tools

Spreadsheet software facilitates the comparison of data, making it an ideal tool to use with students to help them identify similarities and differences.

**Figure 8.4**

Example of Metaphor Analysis Using Google Docs

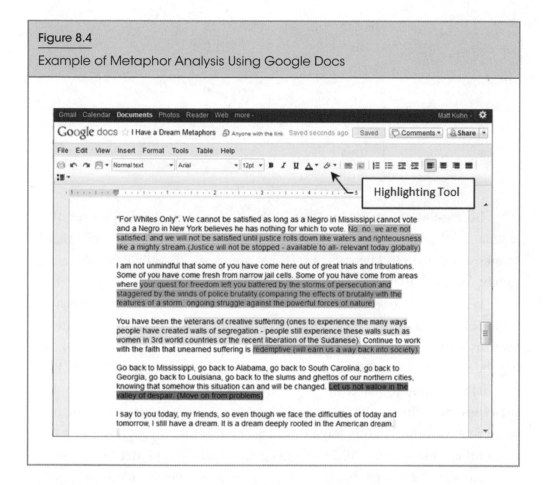

Spreadsheet templates can help teachers implement this strategy. For example, Ms. Li's 2nd graders are studying the planets of the Milky Way, including their sizes, masses, and gravitational pulls. To clarify the concept of gravitational pull, Ms. Li wants her students to grasp how their weight—a function of gravity—would vary on the planets in our solar system. She begins her planning by researching how to calculate one's weight on the various planets. (Two resources that address this are www.factmonster.com/ipka/A0875450.html and www.teachervision.fen.com/astronomy/lesson-plan/353.html.) She finds that making these calculations is a matter of multiplying one's weight on Earth by the gravity of the other planet in relation to the Earth's gravity. If Earth's gravity is 1, the relative gravity of the other planets are as follows:

| | |
|---|---|
| Mercury | .38 |
| Venus | .9 |
| Moon | 0.17 |
| Mars | .38 |
| Jupiter | 2.38 |
| Saturn | .92 |
| Uranus | .89 |
| Neptune | 1.13 |

Because Ms. Li wants her 2nd graders to focus on the differences of the gravitational pulls rather than the mathematics of multiplying decimals, she creates a template in Microsoft Excel that automatically calculates the child's weight on the planets when the child enters his or her weight.

Let's take a closer look at how this template works. Ms. Li enters a formula for each cell from B2 through B11. She first clicks on cell B2, which is Mercury's row. Then in the formula bar, she types the formula **=B1\*.4**, telling the software to multiply whatever value that is typed into B1 (the child's weight) by .4, and to place this product in cell B2. When she clicks in cell B3, she types the formula **=B1\*.9**, telling the software to multiply the value in B1 by .9. She continues in this way until each cell from B2 through B11 has a formula for calculating the child's weight on that particular planet.

Now all the student has to do is enter his or her weight in cell B1, and the spreadsheet will automatically calculate the weight on the different planets. If Ms. Li has already created a graph chart to visually show the results, the chart also will update automatically. Figures 8.5 and 8.6 show the spreadsheet with a child's weight of 50 pounds and the resulting chart. With the bar graph, students have a nonlinguistic representation of their weights on different planets. Ms. Li goes on to use these data to talk with her students about the similarities and differences in the planets' sizes, masses, and gravitational pulls. By comparing the differences, students begin to analyze the differences in planetary sizes and other characteristics that could affect their weight.

In another school, Mrs. Lokken, a 10th grade science teacher, uses Excel to show similarities and differences with older students. In her class, students have been collecting data on sunrise and sunset times for cities across the

**Figure 8.5**

**Completed Comparison Spreadsheet: My Weight on Different Planets**

| Enter your weight in pounds here: | 50 |
|---|---|
| Mercury | 19 |
| Venus | 45 |
| Earth | 50 |
| Moon | 8.5 |
| Mars | 19 |
| Jupiter | 119 |
| Saturn | 46 |
| Uranus | 44.5 |
| Neptune | 56.5 |

**Figure 8.6**

**Comparison Chart Created in Microsoft Excel: My Weight on Different Planets**

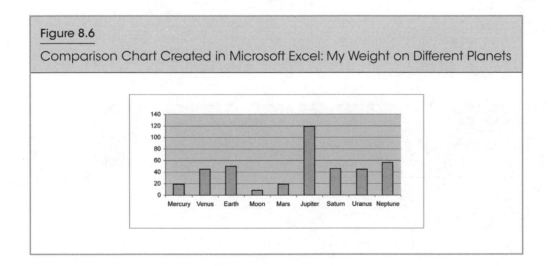

world from www.timeanddate.com. The learning goal is for students to see how a location's latitude affects the length of its days during various time spans throughout the year. After they collect selected cities' sunrise and sunset times for one month, the students work collaboratively in groups of three to enter the data into a spreadsheet and to find the length of each city's day throughout the month of August (see Figure 8.7). When students subsequently chart their data on a scatter plot, they are easily able to compare the lengths of days (see Figure 8.8).

### Figure 8.7

Comparison Spreadsheet Created in Microsoft Excel:
Sunrise and Sunset Times in Various Cities

| ◇ | A | B | C | D | E | F | G | H |
|---|---|---|---|---|---|---|---|---|
| 1 | | Melbourne, Australia | Miami, FL, USA | Buenos Aires, Argentina | Juneau, AK, USA | Quito, Ecuador | Moscow, Russia | |
| 2 | Latitude | 37° 52' S | 25° 47' N | 34° 20' S | 58° 18' N | 0° 14' S | 55° 45' N | |
| 3 | Aug 2 sunrise | 7:19 | 6:48 | 7:46 | 4:51 | 6:17 | 5:37 | |
| 4 | Aug 2 sunset | 17:33 | 20:06 | 18:14 | 21:15 | 18:23 | 21:34 | |
| 5 | Aug 4 sunrise | 7:17 | 6:49 | 7:45 | 4:55 | 6:17 | 5:40 | |
| 6 | Aug 4 sunset | 17:35 | 20:05 | 18:16 | 21:10 | 18:23 | 21:30 | |
| 7 | Aug 11 sunrise | 7:09 | 6:52 | 7:38 | 5:11 | 6:16 | 5:54 | |
| 8 | Aug 11 sunset | 17:41 | 20:00 | 18:21 | 20:53 | 18:22 | 21:14 | |
| 9 | Aug 18 sunrise | 7:00 | 6:55 | 7:30 | 5:26 | 6:15 | 6:07 | |
| 10 | Aug 18 sunset | 17:48 | 19:54 | 18:26 | 20:35 | 18:21 | 20:58 | |
| 11 | Aug 30 sunrise | 6:44 | 7:00 | 7:15 | 5:52 | 6:11 | 6:30 | |
| 12 | Aug 30 sunset | 17:57 | 19:42 | 18:34 | 20:02 | 18:18 | 20:28 | |
| 13 | | | | | | | | |
| 14 | | | | | | | | |
| 15 | | | | | | | | |

### Figure 8.8

Completed Comparison Chart:
Scatter Plot Showing the Variation in Day Length for the Month of August

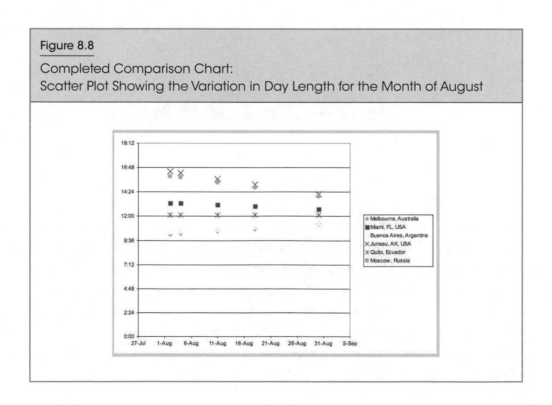

With the charts set up, Mrs. Lokken and her students can use them as tools for content analysis. Here are some questions she asks:

• What predictions can you make about how the graph will look in December?

• Why is Quito's length of day unaffected by the change in seasons?

• Why do you think Miami shows only a small change?

• What are some reasons why the icons representing Buenos Aires and Melbourne are nearly superimposed?

• Is there a date when all cities will generally be on the same line? If so, on which line? On which date? When will this reoccur?

In this example, note the extent to which technology facilitates the processes of analyzing the similarities and differences, explaining the trends found, and predicting future patterns. Consider how difficult and impractical this activity would have been without technology.

Now let's consider how an elementary teacher might combine the instructional strategy of analyzing similarities and differences with the strategy of nonlinguistic representation during a science lesson on density by using data collection tools to measure the mass and volume of various objects.

Mrs. Wesolowski wants to teach her 5th grade class the concept of density as a characteristic of materials. Her goals are to make sure all her students understand that density is how much mass is packed into a certain volume and to dispel common misconceptions about the relationship between volume and mass. For instance, most students think that larger objects are always more massive and vice versa. They also think that materials have all the same characteristics or all different characteristics. Mrs. Wesolowski's goal is to have her students understand the possible combinations of similarities and differences in material characteristics.

She decides to guide her students through a set of three density experiments by independently varying volume, mass, and density. To measure mass, they'll be using a digital scale instead of a traditional balance. The objects students need to measure all have small masses, and the fine accuracy the digital scale provides allows them to capture minute but significant differences in mass for their calculations. The students are also able to connect the digital scale to a computer by USB cable to take multiple measurements.

Mrs. Wesolowski gives her students a spreadsheet template to multiply length by width by height to calculate volume and then divide mass by volume to get the density in grams per cubic centimeter (g/cm³). After leading her class through a science inquiry planning process, including making some predictions, she guides her students through the following three experiments:

1. Students collect and calculate volume, mass, and density data on a rectangular sponge. Then they soak the same sponge in melted wax and let the wax harden. Students again collect the data and calculate density. By keeping the volume the same but changing the mass (with the wax), they are able to see that density is dependent on the concentration of mass.

2. Students use scissors to trim a rectangular sponge until its mass equals that of a 1 cm³ density cube on the digital scale. (These cubes are available from science education supply retailers.) Once the masses are equalized, students again collect data and calculate the density of both objects. By keeping the mass the same but varying the volume, students can see that density also is dependent on volume.

3. Now that the students have used data collection to calculate density and compare objects, they see that density is related to both mass and volume independently. In a third experiment, they combine the first two experiments. Using red and blue Lego building blocks that are identical in shape and size, they construct one all-red cube and one all-blue cube, building the blue cube larger than the red one. Again the students collect volume and mass data and then calculate volume with the spreadsheet. Some students are surprised to find that the densities of the two cubes are the same. Then they realize that density is a characteristic of the material (plastic). Even if both the mass and volume are different, the ratio of mass to volume is the same. The different colors of the cubes underscore the idea that objects can look different in many ways but still have the same density.

As you can see, in this lesson, technology is the key to accurate comparisons. It also facilitates quick computations so that students can focus on the density concepts. Now let's look at an example of how observational data collection facilitates identifying similarities and differences through classification.

Mr. Brewer gives his 4th grade students a matrix for classifying "bugs." He doesn't tell them about the various categories they might use, such as insect (e.g., beetles), arachnid (e.g., spiders), and myriapod (e.g., centipedes); he will introduce these categories later, after the students have had a chance to think critically about the characteristics that will help them identify similarities and differences to classify bug specimens.

With the organizer distributed, Mr. Brewer now provides the students with an assorted collection of bug specimens encased in plastic, which he found at his science education supply retailer. Using a ProScope, his students view magnified images of the specimens and use the matrix to classify them. At first, students categorize by all sorts of traits, such as color, size, and eye shape. Eventually, with some guidance from Mr. Brewer, students see that number of legs, antennae, and body segments are important defining characteristics. Some students also subcategorize the specimens by the presence of wings, fangs, and both wings and fangs. As Figure 8.9 shows, the students rearrange their matrix into three categories, using the observational data (magnified pictures) and the actual category names.

To combine this activity with the strategy of homework and practice, Mr. Brewer has his students visit www.museum.vic.gov.au/bugs/catcher/index.aspx to take advantage of the huge bug collection at the Museum Victoria in Australia. The website allows his students to conduct similar activities by playing an interactive game called *Bug Catcher*.

Data collection probeware is also very useful for identifying similarities and differences because its computer interface allows students to quickly create all sorts of graphical representations for comparison. An example of this is an experiment led by Mr. McGuire. After teaching his Algebra I class to calculate and graph the slope of a line, he uses a motion detector probe connected to a computer to help the students apply their knowledge, using the feedback from the computer graphing program tied to the motion detector.

The students are required to try and match their movements with graphical representations of position versus time. As they move, a line plots in real time, overlaying the plot they are trying to match. After some practice, they are to identify the similarities and differences in their movements compared to the graphical plot. This shows them how motion can be represented graphically in a very realistic and fun way.

### Figure 8.9

Classification Matrix of "Bugs" Featuring Observational Data

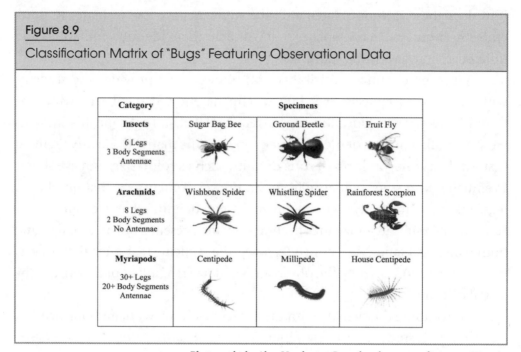

*Photographs by Alan Henderson. Reproduced courtesy of Museum Victoria.*

Figure 8.10 shows how one of Mr. McGuire's students needs to move to match the graphical plot. To get the graph to go up, she needs to move toward the detector and vice versa. Mr. McGuire also uses the strategy of generating and testing hypotheses by having students practice with the detector and then predict what the plot would be if they moved a certain way.

Nielson and Webb (2011) give examples of lessons using cell phones and other mobile devices as data collection tools in their publication *Teaching Generation Text: Using Cell Phones to Enhance Learning*. One section of their book focuses entirely on using mobile devices with the Classroom Instruction That Works strategies. For example, in one lesson, students use a voice recording app to create a "phonecast" comparing the literary characteristics of two novels they have read. In another example, students use a polling service to classify Olympic events into various categories, such as those that require a great deal of strength or those that require precision and accuracy. Nielson and Webb's ideas for using cell phones to help students compare and classify are especially exciting because they allow teachers and students to use relatively inexpensive and ubiquitous technology for higher-order thinking.

**Figure 8.10**

Graphing Motion Experiment Using Vernier Logger *Pro* and Microsoft Word

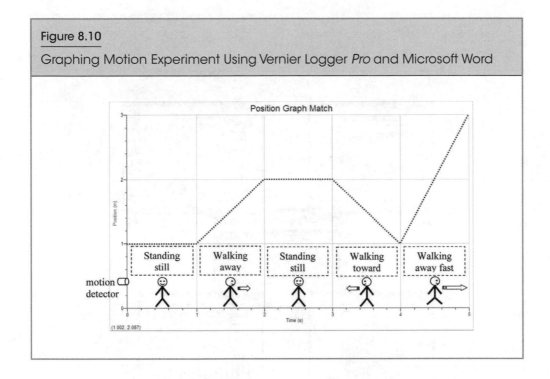

Some online tools are great for making data easy to compare and classify, too. For instance, students can use www.worldmapper.org or www.gapminder .org to compare global patterns, or www.schools.com/tools/career_outlook to compare education levels and careers.

Another great tool for collecting and analyzing data is InspireData, which teachers and students can use to compare and classify by analyzing and representing data using interactive graphs and charts. Features in Inspire-Data allow students to change variables and plot types to compare and create classifications. This encourages them to investigate data analytically, ask more questions, and apply their understanding to form better conclusions and think deeply about what the graphs and charts mean. In addition to the

100-plus subject-specific databases that come with InspireData, students and teachers can collect and enter data from multiple sources, including user-created e-surveys. Figure 8.11 shows examples of different types of charts created using the program.

**Figure 8.11**

Sample InspireData Plots

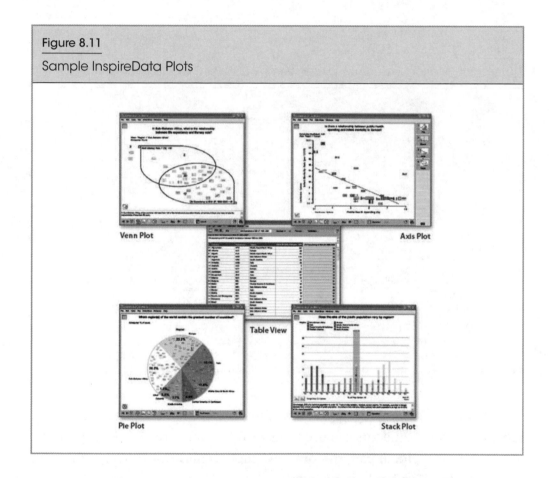

## ⏻ Organizing and Brainstorming Software

Kidspiration (for grades preK–5) and Inspiration (for intermediate and older students) are great tools to help you scaffold learning experiences for your students. By first ensuring that students are comfortable using graphic organizer models and templates in pairs, groups, or individually, you can more easily progress to letting them create their own graphic organizers.

One of the simplest but most effective ways to help students compare two or more items is to use the Venn Diagram template located in the Thinking Skills folder of Inspiration templates and in the More Activities folder of Kidspiration templates. For example, Mrs. Craig, a 3rd grade teacher, uses the template to have her students list the similarities and differences between foods in the United States and England (see Figure 8.12).

**Figure 8.12**

**Venn Diagram Created in Inspiration**

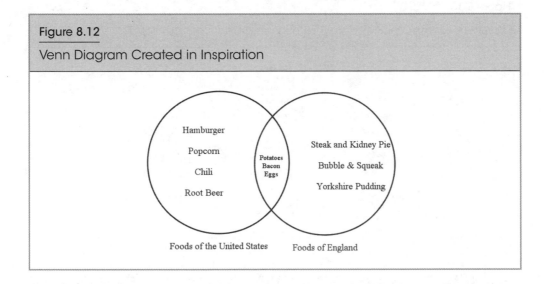

Another template similar to a Venn Diagram is the Comparison template, which is found in the Thinking Skills templates folder in Inspiration. The Book Comparison template in the Language Arts folder is also useful: It allows students to track and visualize information about two books, including similarities and differences in authors' lives and styles and in their books' themes, tone, mood, and messages. Figure 8.13 shows that high school students in one class used the Comparison template to compare the epic poem "Beowulf" with *Grendel*, a novel by John Gardner.

Younger students with minimal writing skills or who find it easiest to remember facts using nonlinguistic representations can also benefit from organizing and brainstorming software. Kidspiration and Inspiration have hundreds of graphics and symbols. If a desired graphic is not part of an existing symbol library, students can use the Symbol Maker tool in Kidspiration or create a custom Symbol Library using graphics from the Internet or photos taken with a digital camera. Students of all ages can also use their voices to record thoughts and ideas about similarities and differences. Figure 8.14 shows an example of a comparison graphic created by a 2nd grade student using the Comparison template found in the More Activities folder of Kidspiration.

**Figure 8.13**

**Literature Comparison Created with Inspiration's Comparison Template**

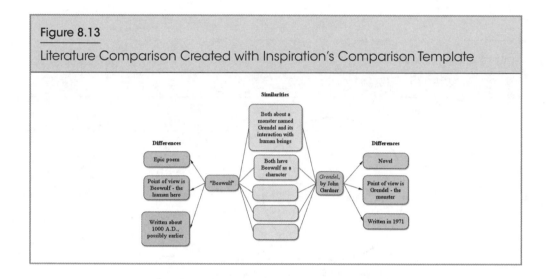

**Figure 8.14**

**Example Created Using Kidspiration's Comparison Template**

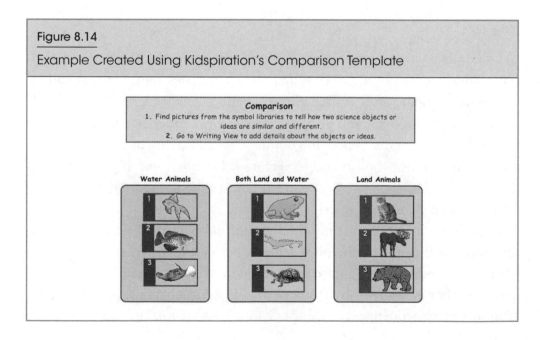

Organizing and brainstorming software works just as well for classifying as it does for comparing. Figure 8.15 shows an example using the Animal Classification template, found in the Science folder of Kidspiration. Students can search through graphics to find the animals that fit in each classification category. Teachers can expand this activity by asking students to use the writing feature of Kidspiration to brainstorm how the animals are alike and different. The more similarities and differences students can describe, the stronger their knowledge of animals becomes.

**Figure 8.15**

**Kidspiration's Animal Classification Template**

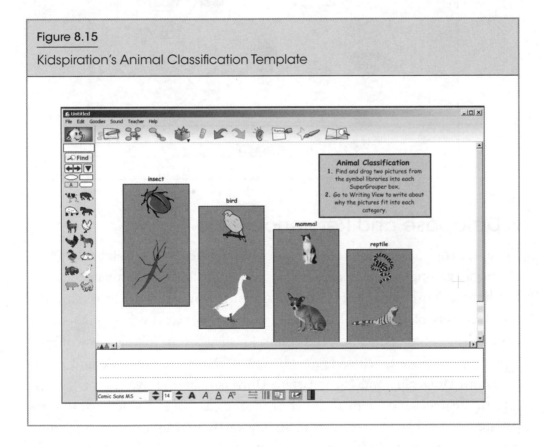

One final example, seen in Figure 8.16, shows a more advanced use of Kidspiration using the A Time in the Past template, located in the Social Studies folder. This template is particularly effective for classifying items and events in a historical context.

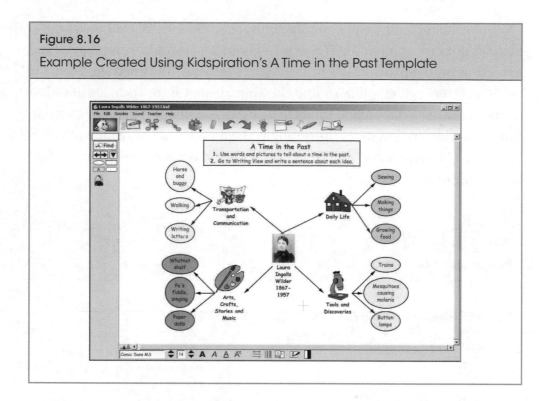

**Figure 8.16**

Example Created Using Kidspiration's A Time in the Past Template

## ⏻ Database and Reference Tools

Taylor is a sophomore and has begun looking at colleges. After taking the PSAT, she began getting college materials from over 40 colleges and universities. She has limited her choices to Stanford University, Northeastern University, and the University of Kansas but is looking for a quick, visual way to make some comparisons among the three. Her counselor suggests she go to www.wolfram-alpha.com to do a quick comparison. Taylor goes to the website and enters "Stanford University and Northeastern University and University of Kansas" into the search window. In a matter of seconds, she sees a side-by-side comparison of the three universities, including yearly tuition, campus size, number of in-state students versus out-of-state students, and more. Both Kansas and Stanford are classified "major research universities," while Northeastern is classified as simply a "research university." Taylor sees that Kansas has the largest student population of the three schools, while Stanford has the smallest. Northeastern had the highest number of part-time students, which makes

Taylor wonder about the quality of campus life—a big consideration for someone living away from home for the first time. Finally, the data present one piece of information that wasn't very apparent in the three schools' promotional materials: As Figure 8.17 shows, Kansas awarded a significantly higher number of bachelor's degrees, but fewer master's degrees and significantly fewer doctoral degrees, than Stanford. These data indicate to her that she might be better off going to Kansas for her bachelor's degree and then considering Stanford for post-graduate work.

**Figure 8.17**

## Comparison of Three Universities Using WolframAlpha

|  | Stanford University | Northeastern University | University of Kansas |
|---|---|---|---|
| one to two years |  | 1 |  |
| associate's |  | 62 |  |
| two to four years |  | 1 |  |
| bachelor's | 1778 | 3312 | 4411 |
| postbaccalaureate certificate |  | 38 |  |
| master's | 2004 | 1759 | 1481 |
| post-master's certificate | 8 | 27 | 10 |
| doctorate | 661 | 235 | 263 |
| first professional degree | 259 | 333 | 503 |

Source: *http://www.wolframalpha.com/input/?i=*
*Stanford+University+and+Northeastern+University+and+University+of+Kansas*

# 9

# Generating and Testing Hypotheses

Although we most often think of *generating and testing hypotheses* in the context of science concepts, this strategy is applicable to all content areas. When students generate and test hypotheses, they are engaging in complex mental processes, applying content knowledge like facts and vocabulary, and enhancing their overall understanding of the content.

Generating and testing hypotheses is particularly effective when compared to more "traditional" instructional activities, such as lectures and teacher-directed, step-by-step lessons. Studies by Hsu (2008), Rivet and Krajcik (2004), and Tarhan and Acar (2007) have all found that students who generate and test hypotheses by engaging in problem solving have a clearer understanding of lesson concepts. For example, in the Tarhan and Acar study, students in a chemistry class who learned through a lecture-based approach formed misconceptions about intermolecular forces, whereas those learning through problem solving did not.

We have two recommendations for classroom practice:

## RECOMMENDATIONS

• Engage students in a variety of structured tasks for generating and testing hypotheses.

• Ask students to explain their hypotheses or predictions and their conclusions.

The four processes that teachers can use to help students generate and test hypotheses are (1) systems analysis, (2) problem solving, (3) experimental inquiry, and (4) investigation.[1] The key features of each of these processes are described in Figure 9.1. To maximize students' learning, teachers should relate the learning embedded in tasks using these processes to students' previous knowledge, experience, or interests (Schroeder, Scott, Tolson, Huang, & Lee, 2007).

To ensure students' success with tasks involving each of these processes, teachers should first give students a model for the process and use familiar content to teach students the process's steps. Graphic organizers and teacher guidance help students to be successful in these types of higher-order thinking tasks.

Technology plays a vital role in generating and testing hypotheses because new developments in probeware and interactive applets allow students to spend more time *interpreting* the data rather than *gathering* the data—a process that can be tedious and error prone. In this section, we show how the following technologies significantly enhance the classroom practice of generating and testing hypotheses: *organizing and brainstorming software, data collection and analysis tools,* and *instructional interactives.*

## ⏻ Organizing and Brainstorming Software

Because generating and testing hypotheses are higher-level cognitive tasks, students often need some scaffolding at first to help them successfully attain higher levels of understanding. Graphic organizers are a good way to do this.

Kidspiration and Inspiration both have a variety of templates to help organize higher-level cognitive tasks in any content area, including Primary Source Exploration, Experiments, Lab Reports, Impact of an Innovation, and Root Cause Analysis. Figure 9.2 shows an example of a Root Cause Analysis template completed by a high school freshman. Note how she lists causes,

---

[1] Two other processes, decision making and invention, were included in the first edition of this book. In this edition, the basic aspects of decision making and invention have been incorporated into problem solving. For example, as students complete the steps of problem solving, they must determine which of the solutions is best. Invention requires determination of a solution to meet a specific need or make improvements. Finding a solution (the invention) that meets the standards for the invention is similar to overcoming the constraints in a problem.

### Figure 9.1

### Features of Structured Tasks for Generating and Testing Hypotheses

| Process | Definition/Questions | Steps in the Process |
|---|---|---|
| Systems Analysis | The process of describing how the parts of a system work together<br><br>How do the parts interact with the whole? What happens if I change one of the parts? | 1. Explain the purpose of the system, the parts of the system, and the function of each part.<br>2. Describe how the parts affect each other.<br>3. Identify a part of the system, describe a change in that part, and then hypothesize what would happen as a result of this change.<br>4. When possible, test your hypothesis by actually changing the part or by using a simulation to change the part. |
| Problem Solving | The process of overcoming limits or barriers that are in the way of reaching goals<br><br>What are the constraints or limiting conditions? Are they structured or unstructured? | 1. Identify the goal you are trying to accomplish.<br>2. Describe the barriers or constraints that are preventing you from achieving your goal—that are creating the problem.<br>3. Identify different solutions for overcoming the barriers or constraints and hypothesize which solution is likely to work.<br>4. Try your solution—either in reality or through a simulation.<br>5. Explain whether your hypothesis was correct. Determine if you want to test another hypothesis using a different solution. In some cases, this may be building or designing an invention. |
| Experimental Inquiry | The process of developing and testing explanations of things we observe<br><br>What was observed? How can I explain what I observed? | 1. Observe something of interest to you and describe what you observe.<br>2. Apply specific theories or rules to what you have observed.<br>3. Based on your explanation, generate a hypothesis to predict what would happen if you applied the theories or rules to what you observed or to a situation related to what you observed.<br>4. Set up an experiment or engage in an activity to test your hypothesis.<br>5. Explain the results of your experiment or activity. Decide if your hypothesis was correct and if you need to conduct additional experiments or activities or if you need to generate and test an alternative hypothesis. |
| Investigation | The process of suggesting and defending ways to clear up confusion about ideas or events<br><br>What are the opposing views on this event or idea? What data do I have to support or negate the views? | 1. Clearly identify the situation (i.e., concept to be defined, historical event to be explained, or hypothetical future event to be defined or explained).<br>2. Identify what is already known or agreed upon.<br>3. Based on what you understand about the situation, offer a hypothetical scenario.<br>4. Seek out and analyze evidence to determine if your hypothetical scenario is plausible. |

possible solutions, and possible problems with the solutions. The template helped her to organize her thoughts and consider many aspects that she may not have otherwise considered. This example falls under the process of problem solving.

**Figure 9.2**

**Root Cause Analysis Template in Inspiration**

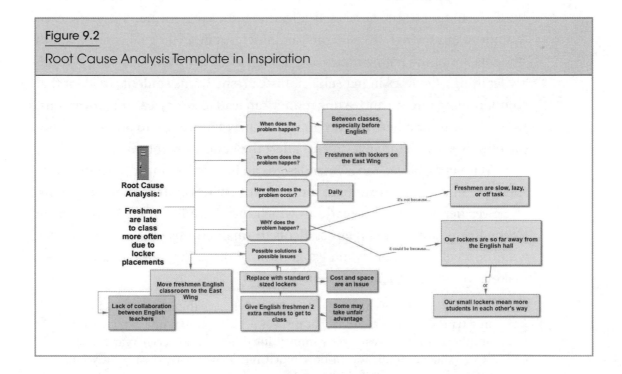

## ⏻ Data Collection and Analysis Tools

Spreadsheets to generate and test hypotheses are commonly used in science class, with students making informed predictions, collecting data, analyzing the data for patterns, and revising their original hypothesis or coming up with a new one. But what about spreadsheet uses in other subjects?

Making an educational spreadsheet can be time-consuming and requires technical know-how. Even though setting up a spreadsheet is a worthy technology skill for students to learn, content-area teachers don't want to use class time teaching students how to create spreadsheets; rather, they want to use spreadsheets to help students learn the content. Let's look at an example of a teacher-created interactive spreadsheet that achieves this purpose. We should note that by calling the spreadsheet *interactive*, we mean that the students will be able to manipulate it, consider graphical patterns, and test their predictions by receiving quick feedback on multiple scenarios.

To help students meet the district's economics benchmark in the social studies standards, Mrs. Omar sets a learning objective for her 5th grade class to understand savings, investments, and interest rates. Her goal is not to teach students about the mathematics or graphing skills involved; those are secondary learning outcomes in her subject. Instead, she wants students to learn that compounding interest and saving money can lead to strong earnings over time. Later, she will have her students apply this new knowledge to an understanding of how savings and investments affect the nation's economy.

With her goal set, Mrs. Omar designs an interactive spreadsheet in Microsoft Excel that will show students the results of savings and investment options. She gives her students a scenario in which they have inherited $10,000 from a long-lost relative. She assigns students to small groups to discuss what they would do with the money and explains three plans they should consider for making money from an investment:

> 1. Spend $9,000 of the money right away but save the remaining $1,000 in a typical savings account that earns 4 percent annual interest. Deposit another $1,000 of your own money into the account each year for 30 years. Make a prediction of how much money you would earn on your total investment of $30,000 over 30 years.

> 2. Invest the whole $10,000 in a "safe" fund from Standard & Poor's 500 mutual fund index that earns an average of 8 percent per year. No further investments are made, but no money can be taken out of the account for 30 years. Make a prediction of how much money you would earn on your one-time investment of $10,000 after 30 years.

> 3. Invest in a more unpredictable portfolio of diversified stocks from the Dow Jones Industrial Average, which has historically earned an average of 12 percent per year. Make a prediction of how much money you would earn on your one-time investment of $10,000 after 30 years.

After students have reviewed the three plans, Mrs. Omar distributes a laptop computer to each small group. She asks them to locate the class folder on the school's network drive and open the spreadsheet that she has created and saved for this activity. When the students open the spreadsheet, they see a template like the one in Figure 9.3.

## Figure 9.3
### Interactive Savings and Investment Spreadsheet Created in Microsoft Excel

| | Plan A | Plan B | Plan C | Plan A | Plan B | Plan C |
|---|---|---|---|---|---|---|
| Years | Spend $9,000 and save $1,000 a year for 30 years ($30,000) at 4% interest | Invest $10,000 once in the S&P 500 Index at 8% average annual return | Invest $10,000 once in the Dow Jones Industrial Average at 12% average annual return | Total Earned on Investments ($30,000) | Total Earned on Investments ($10,000) | Total Earned on Investments ($10,000) |
| 0 | $0 | $0 | $0 | | | |
| 1 | $0 | $0 | $0 | | | |
| 2 | $0 | $0 | $0 | | | |
| 3 | $0 | $0 | $0 | | | |
| 4 | $0 | $0 | $0 | | | |
| 5 | $0 | $0 | $0 | | | |
| ↕ | ↕ | ↕ | ↕ | | | |
| 26 | $0 | $0 | $0 | | | |
| 27 | $0 | $0 | $0 | | | |
| 28 | $0 | $0 | $0 | | | |
| 29 | $0 | $0 | $0 | | | |
| 30 | $0 | $0 | $0 | | | |
| Total Earned after Investment = | | | | $0 | $0 | $0 |
| Predicted Earnings (Total Account Value - Investment) = | | | | $ | $ | $ |

*What do I do with my $10,000 inheritance?*

Before the students begin manipulating data, Mrs. Omar gives them a brief explanation of investment risk and prompts them to discuss the plan options in their groups and fill in their predictions for all three plans, regardless of which plan they favor. Then she asks each student to choose a plan and quickly takes a visual poll of the class's preferences for later comparison. Next she tells them to fill in the amounts in the Year 0 row of the spreadsheet. They can choose the scenario values of $1,000, $10,000, and $10,000 respectively for Plans A, B, and C, or they can make up their own amounts. Because the spreadsheet is interactive, any value will produce results to compare to students' initial predictions. All they have to do is put numbers in the first row. The interactive formulation of the spreadsheet does the rest, filling in the table and mapping data on a chart, as shown in Figures 9.4 and 9.5.

**Figure 9.4**

**Interactive Savings and Investment Spreadsheet: Example Projections**

| | What do I do with my $10,000 inheritance? | | | | | |
|---|---|---|---|---|---|---|
| | Plan A | Plan B | Plan C | Plan A | Plan B | Plan C |
| Years | Spend $9,000 and save $1,000 a year for 30 years ($30,000) at 4% interest | Invest $10,000 once in the S&P 500 Index at 8% average annual return | Invest $10,000 once in the Dow Jones Industrial Average at 12% average annual return | Total Earned on Investments ($30,000) | Total Earned on Investments ($10,000) | Total Earned on Investments ($10,000) |
| 0 | $1,000 | $10,000 | $10,000 | | | |
| 1 | $2,040 | $10,800 | $11,200 | | | |
| 2 | $3,122 | $11,664 | $12,544 | | | |
| 3 | $4,246 | $12,597 | $14,049 | | | |
| 4 | $5,416 | $13,605 | $15,735 | | | |
| 5 | $6,633 | $14,693 | $17,623 | | | |
| 6 | $7,898 | $15,869 | $19,738 | | | |
| 7 | $9,214 | $17,138 | $22,107 | | | |
| 8 | $10,583 | $18,509 | $24,760 | | | |
| 9 | $12,006 | $19,990 | $27,731 | | | |
| 10 | $13,486 | $21,589 | $31,058 | | | |
| 11 | $15,026 | $23,316 | $34,785 | | | |
| 12 | $16,627 | $25,182 | $38,960 | | | |
| 13 | $18,292 | $27,196 | $43,635 | | | |
| 14 | $20,024 | $29,372 | $48,871 | | | |
| 15 | $21,825 | $31,722 | $54,736 | | | |
| 16 | $23,698 | $34,259 | $61,304 | | | |
| 17 | $25,645 | $37,000 | $68,660 | | | |
| 18 | $27,671 | $39,960 | $76,900 | | | |
| 19 | $29,778 | $43,157 | $86,128 | | | |
| 20 | $31,969 | $46,610 | $96,463 | | | |
| 21 | $34,248 | $50,338 | $108,038 | | | |
| 22 | $36,618 | $54,365 | $121,003 | | | |
| 23 | $39,083 | $58,715 | $135,523 | | | |
| 24 | $41,646 | $63,412 | $151,786 | | | |
| 25 | $44,312 | $68,485 | $170,001 | | | |
| 26 | $47,084 | $73,964 | $190,401 | | | |
| 27 | $49,968 | $79,881 | $213,249 | | | |
| 28 | $52,966 | $86,271 | $238,839 | | | |
| 29 | $56,085 | $93,173 | $267,499 | | | |
| 30 | $59,328 | $100,627 | $299,599 | | | |
| | Total Earned after Investment = | | | $29,328 | $90,627 | $289,599 |
| | Predicted Earnings (Total Account Value - Investment) = | | | $13,000 | $8,000 | $12,000 |

Using the teacher-created interactive spreadsheet, students can compare their predictions to actual results without spending an inordinate amount of time doing calculations and designing spreadsheets. They can enter many different monetary amounts and quickly see the results. This helps them see patterns, such as exponential growth. A mathematics teacher might decide to use the same lesson to focus on the compounding percentage calculations and exponential patterns. In either case, the teacher is using technology to maximize instructional time and meet learning objectives. This spreadsheet activity allows students to gain a deeper understanding of investment basics and requires them to use their critical thinking skills to predict outcomes. Students generate and test hypotheses in very little time and gain valuable experience that they can apply to future economic hypotheses.

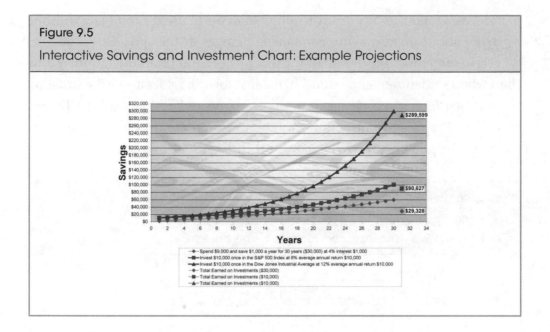

**Figure 9.5**

Interactive Savings and Investment Chart: Example Projections

How did Mrs. Omar create her interactive spreadsheet? She began by testing her own hypotheses to see what scenarios would work best. Then she put multiple formulas in the cells at the *fx* prompt that would calculate the different interest rates and totals, as seen in Figure 9.6.

She did not have to program a formula into each cell through row 32. Once she had programmed the first cells (B5, C5, and D5) she just highlighted the cell's formula by placing her mouse at the bottom right corner of the cell and dragging to highlight the column down to cell 34, as shown in Figure 9.7. This copies the format of the formula in all the cells with the correct column and row designation.

Next, she entered formulas (e.g., *fx*=B34>0, B34–30000,"$0") to show how much was earned on the total investments by taking the total earned in row 34 and subtracting the invested money (either $30,000 or $10,000) for each of the three plans (see Figure 9.8).

Finally, she inserted some numbers and created a line-graph chart. Then she highlighted the columns and chose **Edit > Clear > Contents**. She saved it as an Excel template by choosing **File > Save As > Save As Type > Template (*.xlt) > Save**. Because templates can only be saved as new files under a new name, Mrs. Omar was now ready to allow students to use the template without worrying about them making permanent changes to the spreadsheet design. Excel will remember the design of the spreadsheet and fill in the numbers and chart when students enter amounts in the first row. She does allow the students to save their own spreadsheets from the template and add any color schemes they like. (For more information on how to formulate cells and create templates, see http://office.microsoft.com and click on **Training > Excel**.)

**Figure 9.6**

Interactive Savings and Investment Spreadsheet Stage 1:
Cell Formula Programming for Compounding Interest

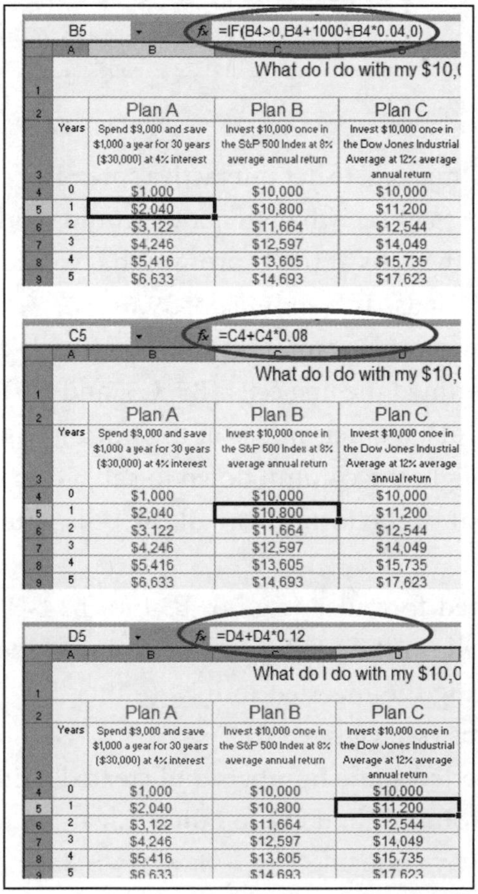


| Years | Plan A: Spend $9,000 and save $1,000 a year for 30 years ($30,000) at 4% interest | Plan B: Invest $10,000 once in the S&P 500 Index at 8% average annual return | Plan C: Invest $10,000 once in the Dow Jones Industrial Average at 12% average annual return |
|---|---|---|---|
| 0 | $1,000 | $10,000 | $10,000 |
| 1 | $2,040 | $10,800 | $11,200 |
| 2 | $3,122 | $11,664 | $12,544 |
| 3 | $4,246 | $12,597 | $14,049 |
| 4 | $5,416 | $13,605 | $15,735 |
| 5 | $6,633 | $14,693 | $17,623 |

## Figure 9.7

### Interactive Savings and Investment Spreadsheet Stage 2: Cell Formula Copy Programming for Compounding Interest

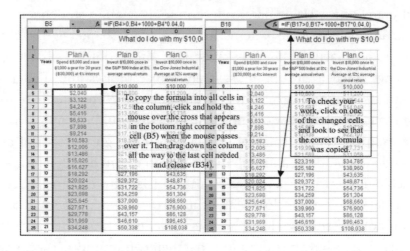

## Figure 9.8

### Interactive Savings and Investment Spreadsheet Stage 3: Cell Formula Programming for Totals Earned

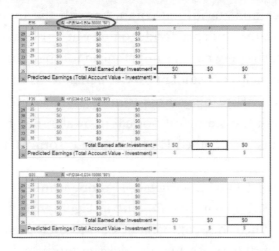

## Using Probes for Data Collection and Analysis

Collecting data usually answers some questions and generates new ones. Typically, students research a problem, form a hypothesis, and collect data to confirm, deny, or revise their last hypothesis. This cycle of inquiry can be repeated many times. Using data collection tools enables students to see the bigger picture and recognize patterns. As we noted in Chapter 5, digital probes and microscopes facilitate analysis, synthesis, and problem solving. By and large, science teachers are the most likely to use probes and digital microscopes, but resourceful teachers in all subjects can incorporate these tools to enhance the curriculum. For example, art students could use a light intensity probe to examine the interplay of light and color in great works of art, and history students could use a digital microscope to record detailed images from an archaeological excavation and gain further insight into an ancient culture.

Now let's look more closely at what we mean when we say that a data collection tool can enhance learning. The students in Mrs. Schwartz's middle school science class have heard rumors that their community gets acid rainfall. Is it true? Students would like to know. The students decide to conduct an experimental inquiry on acid rain as part of their studies in chemical reactions and meteorology. They find that "acid rain" is acidic rain, snow, fog, and dew. Distilled water has a neutral pH of 7. Liquids with a pH less than 7 are acidic, and those with a pH greater than 7 are basic. "Clean" or unpolluted rain has a moderately acidic pH of 5.6, because carbon dioxide and water in the air react together to form carbonic acid that combines with the moisture in the air. Based on these facts, the students decide to find out if their rain is more acidic than normal and focus on what this might mean for their local environment.

Mrs. Schwartz helps her students devise a plan to use a USB-connectable data probe to collect pH readings from various water sources in the community to compare with the 5.6 pH of normal rainwater. Before they begin collecting data, students predict the pH of the various sources. Figure 9.9 shows their predictions.

After collecting data with a digital pH probe from the various samples, students quickly create a chart like the one in Figure 9.10 using the Keynote app on their iPad. When they compare the data to their predictions, students surprisingly find that the pH of their rain is even more acidic than predicted.

**Figure 9.9**

Digital Probe Activity: Water pH Predictions

| Water Source | Predicted pH |
|---|---|
| Rain | 5.0 |
| Pond | 5.0 |
| River | 6.0 |
| Stream | 5.0 |
| Tap | 7.0 |

They also are puzzled by the differences among their various water sources. For instance, why was the pond water so much more acidic than the river water? And what does this mean for the life that depends on these waters? The data collection tool allows Mrs. Schwartz's students to gather and graph data quickly and accurately, leaving more time for analysis and synthesis. Their findings lead to further hypotheses and more inquiry.

Data collection tools are not always probes. The Internet is a huge data collection tool. To expand the inquiry to a larger scale, Mrs. Schwartz's students could share and compare their data online through collaborative project websites such as www.globalschoolnet.org or http://collaboratory.nunet.net. Sharing and comparing data from other localities gives students enough information to generate and test hypotheses concerning the nation and other parts of the world.

# ⏻ Instructional Interactives

Simulations and games allow students to apply their background knowledge to make predictions, receive immediate feedback, and see the outcomes of their hypotheses, often in virtual situations that would be impossible or financially unfeasible in real life. (A good example is Realityworks [www.reality works.com], which provides experiential learning in topics that can present a challenge to teach, such as career and technical education; health, family, and consumer sciences; and business.) Simulation software can also provide incredibly engaging learning environments, resulting in increased motivation and learning retention.

### Figure 9.10

## Water pH Comparison Chart Created Using Keynote on an iPad

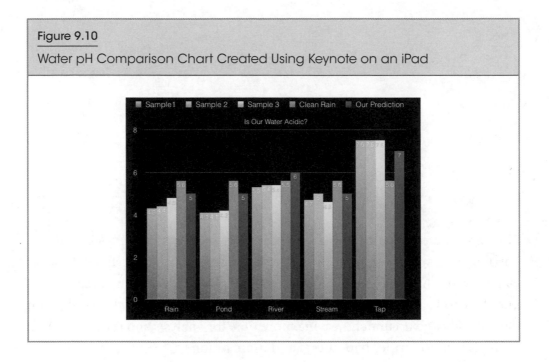

Consider the example of William Hiser, a high school business teacher who wanted his students to use the instructional strategy of generating and testing hypotheses by making informed financial forecasts and testing those forecasts in a meaningful business experience. He decided to use the Real-Career Business Finance Simulation from Realityworks (www.realityworks .com/businesssimulations/index.asp) with his students.

As you can see from Figure 9.11, Realityworks provides simulated data that help students make an informed hypothesis about the characteristics of their simulated product. Students choose levels of quality compared to market averages. The trade-off is that higher quality also means higher costs. Over time, students use the simulation program to manage a fictional medium-sized manufacturing company that is underperforming. The simulation helps students understand core financial concepts. Using two years of historical sales data, students work to set performance targets for the next three simulated years. Students then test their forecasts using monthly performance-to-forecast reports.

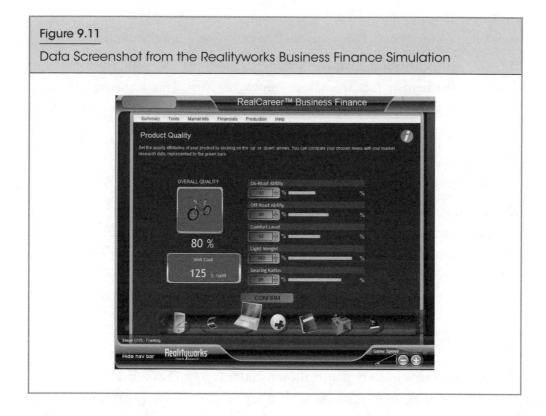

**Figure 9.11**

Data Screenshot from the Realityworks Business Finance Simulation

In the list of recommended resources below, we have included web-based simulations as well as a few software applications and iOS apps.

▶ Smog City
www.smogcity.com

This resource engages students in a systems analysis by allowing them to set parameters for weather, population, and emissions, then to see the effects on the ozone levels.

▶ NOVA Building Big
www.pbs.org/wgbh/buildingbig

This resource helps students learn about bridges, domes, skyscrapers, dams, and tunnels. In each activity, students apply what they have learned to problem solve a fictional city's needs by deciding which structure is best for each situation.

▶ Plimoth Plantation's You Are the Historian
www.plimoth.org/learn/thanksgiving-interactive-you-are-historian

This in-depth historical investigation helps students use primary sources in order to distinguish fact from lore about the first Thanksgiving. Students actively investigate sources from 1621 in order to make hypotheses about what actually happened.

▶ PrimaryAccess
www.primaryaccess.org

This website enables you to combine text, audio, and images into compelling personal narratives and digital stories using a simple moviemaking program. You can choose digital images from archives including the Library of Congress, upload your own images or audio, record audio online, save movies with unique web addresses, retrieve movies for editing, and share movies with others.

▶ Practicing with the Catapult
www.lcse.umn.edu/specs/labs/catapult/practice.html

This experimental inquiry game allows students to adjust a catapult's height, projectile velocity, launch angle, and other factors. The student must predict how the variables will affect the catapult's ability to land a hit on a building.

▶ Zoo Matchmaker
www.mnzoo.com/education/games/matchmaker/index.html

This resource from the Minnesota Zoo helps students learn about the decisions that zookeepers need to make in order to control diseases while keeping the genetic pool diverse.

▶ Windward!
http://broadband.ciconline.org/windward/default.aspx

This game helps students learn about weather and wind patterns across the world's oceans and then asks them to use that knowledge to navigate a ship around the world.

▶ Hurricane Strike!
http://meted.ucar.edu/hurrican/strike/index.htm

This simulation from the University Corporation for Atmospheric Research in Boulder, Colorado, takes students through tutorials about hurricanes and helps them apply what they've learned to make decisions as a hurricane approaches.

▶ ExploreLearning
www.explorelearning.com

Using the interactive manipulatives known as gizmos, students can generate and test hypotheses on a number of subjects: the genetic makeup of mice, balancing chemical equations, comparing and ordering fractions, and estimating population sizes, to name a few.

The following iPad apps also support the strategy of generating and testing hypotheses and are available from the Apple App Store.

▶ Isaac Newton's Gravity HD

Hosted by an animation of Sir Isaac Newton, this game is a physics puzzler with 50 stages. Students use various objects to preserve the momentum of a dropping ball.

▶ Angry Birds

One of the most popular iPad apps, Angry Birds provides an enjoyable and entertaining way for students (and their teachers) to apply the laws of physics.

▶ Star Chart

This app is a must-have for anyone teaching astronomy. Using GPS technology, Star Chart calculates the current location of all the stars and planets visible from Earth in real time and shows you precisely where they are—even in broad daylight. (This app is also available in the Android Marketplace.)

▶ Tiny Tower

This 8-bit–style game allows students to build floors on a tower to attract "bitizens." Students then manage, hire, evict, and so on.

# Conclusion: Putting It All Together

In this final chapter, we outline some of our best thinking on creating and teaching in technology-rich environments. The first section, Classroom Instruction, provides resources and advice for teachers incorporating technology into their instruction. The second section, School Leadership, provides resources for school and district leaders.

## ⏻ Classroom Instruction

As educators have learned from past experiences, using technology for technology's sake isn't a good use of instructional time or funding, and it most likely won't improve student achievement. It is important to first design a quality lesson plan and then select the most appropriate technologies to support that lesson. Good instruction starts with identifying the appropriate learning objectives, then identifying which strategies should be employed to teach the content and skills, and, finally, identifying how students will show their learning. Instructional technology is a powerful tool for learning, but its use should not be the goal of a lesson plan; it is, instead, a tool to make the lesson plan work.

When planning lessons, we should first consider what content standards students need to address before determining the technology standards and indicators that complement the content standards. Some districts have specific technology standards, but many are aligned to the National Educational Technology Standards for Students (NETS-S) developed by the International

Society for Technology in Education. The complete NETS-S document can be found online at www.iste.org/standards, where you can also find links to ISTE standards for teachers and administrators.

Another crucial step of lesson planning is determining how students will demonstrate their learning. For example, if the objective of the lesson is to have students do a presentation on a topic, educators should consider what the rubric would look like for the presentation: Will this be a cooperative project or individual work? Will the presentation involve a speech or student-created video? Are there any online resources that might help students meet learning goals? Answers to these questions begin to shape the lesson and suggest the technologies that will support it. Technology can and should allow students richness and variety when showing their learning.

## Assessing Students' Technology Literacy

The No Child Left Behind Act requires states to provide information on 8th grade students' technology literacy. However, assessing technology literacy requires more than simply a standardized test. There are many ways for students to show that they are technologically literate. We recommend that schools and districts develop a portfolio approach to assessing student technology literacy based on the most current version of the NETS-S. These standards are heavily weighted toward project-based learning and integration of technology with mainstream academic content. Through careful coordination, educators can build rubrics for technology literacy that can be assessed throughout the school year or by committee near the end of the school year. These could then be compiled to provide data on student, grade, and school levels of technology literacy.

## ⏻ School Leadership

School leaders face tough challenges, both in terms of budget and staff, in planning technology for their schools. Implementing large-scale technology initiatives requires careful thought and planning. Ideally, schools or districts will conduct a needs assessment or a technology audit prior to implementation. Such actions can often reveal surprising information about instruction and learning in the classroom.

Here's an example. Several years ago, leaders in one district were planning to roll out a one-to-one laptop initiative within the next year. The leaders' thinking was that they would start with the high schools, then eventually expand the initiative into the middle and elementary schools. The district leaders wanted information on the current level of technology use and what instruction looked like in the classrooms.

Their audit results surprised them. At the high school and lower elementary levels, instruction looked very traditional. Students spent most of their time receiving whole group instruction, followed by individual practice. The most common strategies used in the classroom were cues and questions, practice, and providing feedback. The evidence of learning was most often teacher-directed question/answer and worksheets.

At the upper elementary and middle school levels, however, an entirely different environment existed: Students were often observed working in pairs or small groups, and a wide variety of instructional strategies were being used. The evidence of learning included creative and collaborative projects that were often individualized for students.

What the audit revealed was that a one-to-one laptop initiative at the high school level would have likely resulted in very expensive technologies being used for routine tasks such as web-based research, word processing, and note taking. Technologies at the intermediate and middle school levels, however, had more potential to be used for dynamic communication, collaboration, and creative purposes. Given this information, the district decided to start the initiative at the middle school level while providing professional development to educators at the other levels focused on creating a project-based 21st century learning environment. Because of their careful planning, the district was able to provide the right professional development to the right audiences and avoid costly, time-consuming, and frustrating mistakes.

Although a technology audit has the advantage of having objective third parties gather information, other schools have independently gathered such data by simply conducting walkthroughs in their classrooms. What they often find is that teachers welcome this quick snapshot of which instructional strategies are being employed, how students are grouped, which technologies are being used, and how student learning is being assessed. When coupled with the right technologies, improvements in these areas can transform a learning environment into a vibrant, engaging experience for students.

## Top 12 Priorities for Planning Large Initiatives

In providing guidance for schools across the world on how to implement one-to-one initiatives, we have learned that careful planning is the key to success. Here are our top 12 priorities for schools considering similar initiatives.

1. Make sure you use resources to help you plan, such as the list of lessons from Maine's one-to-one initiative at http://mashable.com/2011/01/04/classroom-technology-education or the National Science Foundation–funded study of Henrico County Public Schools' one-to-one program at http://ubiqcomputing.org/FinalReport.pdf.

2. Decide whether your school will purchase all of the computers or allow a mixture of school- and student-owned computers. Although allowing student-owned computers will save you some money, it will require a technical services department with the capacity and skill to support multiple devices.

3. Decide upon a nucleus of cloud computing services and software tools that will be consistent across the school. This will help teachers spend their time teaching content rather software applications. Look for free quality services such as Google Apps for Education.

4. Integrate your school's curriculum with instructional technology applications and 21st century pedagogy by identifying research-based software, applications, and games that can support learning in core content areas. These need to be compatible with the operating system on the school's computers and supported by technical staff.

5. Conduct regular, specific, and mandatory professional development focused on integrating instructional technology.

6. Monitor and evaluate progress. Teachers will pay attention to what their leaders pay attention to. If leaders keep a close eye on the types and frequencies of instructional techniques, then data-driven decisions can be made that will focus the school, teams, and individuals on what is working and what needs to change.

7. Decide how much access students will have to the computer network. Internet filters are essential, but they should not inhibit real-time learning.

Trust the teachers as a staff to block or unblock resources under the oversight of the school or district's technical staff. Sanction misbehaving individuals, but do not punish all students for the actions of a few.

8. Create a long-term strategy for the obsolescence of software and hardware. It is critical to replace or update computers and software as they age. Your strategy should include developing a way to assign financial and technical resources. Sometimes long-term leases are more cost effective than hardware purchases.

9. Develop a plan to provide, repair, and replace additional equipment, such as interactive whiteboards, servers, data probes, batteries, microphones, printers, and other peripherals.

10. A good insurance plan goes a long way. Some computers will get broken, stolen, or pawned. Be proactive in dealing with this problem.

11. Plan for a robust wi-fi network. You must assume that all devices will be on the network at the same time. When you think you have a good estimate of the bandwidth needed, double it so it will last into the future.

12. Most important, have onsite technical support. A lack of support will be the biggest complaint of teachers and will negatively impact the learning program. This can include a mix of school staff and student volunteers.

Technology can transform teaching and learning. It is our hope that the Classroom Instruction That Works strategies, coupled with the right tools, can help educators and students create amazing, engaging, and relevant learning experiences.

# References

Adam, K. P. (2001). *Computerized scoring of essays for analytical writing assessments: Evaluating score validity.* Seattle, WA: National Council on Measurement in Education. (ERIC Document Reproduction Service No. ED 458 296).

Aleven, V., Ashley, K. D., Lynch, C., & Pinkwart, N. (2008). *Intelligent tutoring systems for ill-defined domains: Assessment and feedback in ill-defined domains.* Proceedings of a workshop held during the 9th International Conference on Intelligent Tutoring Systems. Montreal, Canada.

Anderson, J. R. (1995). *Learning and memory: An integrated approach.* New York: Wiley.

Bandura, A. (2000). Exercise of human agency through collective efficacy. *Current Directions in Psychological Science, 9*(3), 75–78.

Barley, Z., Lauer, P. A., Arens, S. A., Apthorp, H. S., Englert, K. S., Snow, D., & Akiba, M. (2002). *Helping at-risk students meet standards: A synthesis of evidence-based classroom practices.* Denver, CO: Mid-continent Research for Education and Learning.

Bouffard, T., Boisvert, J., Vezeau, C., & Larouche, C. (1995). The impact of goal orientation on self-regulation and performance among college students. *British Journal of Educational Psychology, 65*(3), 317–330.

Bransford, J., Brown, A., & Cocking, R. (2000). *How people learn: Brain, mind, experience, and school* (Expanded ed.). Washington, DC: National Academies Press.

Carpenter, S. K., Pashler, H., & Cepeda, J. (2009). Using tests to enhance 8th grade students' retention of U.S. history facts. *Applied Cognitive Psychology, 23,* 760–771.

Chambers, B., Cheung, A. C. K., Madden, N. A., Slavin, R. E., & Gifford, R. (2006). Achievement effects of embedded multimedia in a Success For All reading program. *Journal of Educational Psychology, 98*(1), 232–237.

Chen, Z. (1999). Schema induction in children's analogical problem solving. *Journal of Educational Psychology, 91*(4), 703–715.

Cholmsky, P. (2003). *Why gizmos work: Empirical evidence for the instructional effectiveness of ExploreLearning's interactive content.* Charlottesville, VA: ExploreLearning. Retrieved March 15, 2006, from http://www.explorelearning.com/View/downloads/WhyGizmosWork.pdf

Consortium of College and University Media Centers. (1996). *Fair use guidelines for educational multimedia.* Retrieved January 12, 2012, from http://www.adec.edu/admin/papers/fair10-17.html

Cooper, H., Robinson, J. C., & Patall, E. A. (2006). Does homework improve academic achievement? A synthesis of research, 1987–2003. *Review of Educational Research, 76*(1), 1–62.

Dean, C., Hubbell, E. R., Pitler, H., & Stone, B. J. (2012). *Classroom instruction that works* (2nd ed.). Alexandria, VA: ASCD.

Dodge, B., & March, T. (1995). *What Is a WebQuest?* Retrieved April 26, 2006, from http://webquest.sdsu.edu/overview.htm

Elliot, E. S., McGregor, H. A., & Gable, S. L. (1999). Achievement goals, study strategies, and exam performance: A mediational analysis. *Journal of Educational Psychology, 91,* 549–563.

Facebook. (n.d.). Statistics. Retrieved http://www.facebook.com/press/info.php?statistics

Fisch, K. (2006, August 15). Did you know? The Fischbowl. Retrieved September 15, 2011, from http://thefischbowl.blogspot.com/2006/08/did-you-know.html

Friedman, T. L. (2005). *The world is flat: A brief history of the twenty-first century.* New York: Farrar, Straus, and Giroux.

Fuchs, L. S., Fuchs, D., Finelli, R., Courey, S. J., Hamlett, C. L., Sones, E. M., & Hope, S. (2006). Teaching third graders about real-life mathematical problem solving: A randomized controlled study. *Elementary School Journal, 106,* 293–312.

Gee, J. P. (2009). Deep learning properties of good digital games: How far can they go? In (Eds.) U. Ritterfeld, M. Cody, & P. Vorderer, *Serious games: Mechanisms and effects.* London: Routledg.

Gentner, D., Loewenstein, J., & Thompson, L. (2003). Learning and transfer: A general role for analogical encoding. *Journal of Educational Psychology, 95,* 393–408.

Gerlach, J. M. (1994). Is this collaboration? In K. Bosworth & S. J. Hamilton (Eds.), *Collaborative Learning: Underlying Processes and Effective Techniques* (p. 59). San Francisco: Jossey-Bass.

Greene, B. A., Miller, R. B., Crowson, H. M., Duke, B. L., & Akey, K. L. (2004). Predicting high school students' cognitive engagement and achievement: Contributions of classroom perceptions and motivation. *Contemporary Educational Psychology, 29*(4), 462–482.

Hall, K. G., Domingues, D. A., & Cavazos, R. (1994). Contextual interference effects with skilled baseball players. *Perceptual and Motor Skills, 78,* 835–841.

Halverson, R. (2005). What can K–12 school leaders learn from video games and gaming? *Innovate 1*(6). Retrieved March 14, 2006, from http://www.innovateonline.info/index.php?view=article&id=81

Henderlong, J., & Lepper, M. R. (2002). The effects of praise on children's intrinsic motivation: A review and synthesis. *Psychological Bulletin, 128,* 774–795.

High schools plug into online writing program. (2003, November 1). *District Administrator 39*(11). Retrieved January 12, 2012, from http://findarticles.com/p/articles/mi_6938/is_11_39/ai_n28168501/

Hill, J., & Flynn, K. (2006). *Classroom instruction that works with English language learners.* Alexandria, VA: ASCD.

Holyoak, K. J. (2005). Analogy. In K. J. Holyoak and R. G. Morrison (Eds), *The Cambridge Handbook of Thinking and Reasoning* (pp. 117–142). Cambridge, United Kingdom: Cambridge University Press.

Hom, H. L., Jr., & Murphy, M. D. (1983). Low achiever's performance: The positive impact of a self-directed goal. *Personality and Social Psychology Bulletin, 11*, 275–285.

Hong, E., Milgram, R. M., & Rowell, L. L. (2004). Homework motivation and preference: A learner-centered homework approach. *Theory into Practice, 43*, 197–204.

Hsu, Y.-S. (2008). Learning about seasons in a technologically enhanced environment: The impact of teacher-guided and student-centered instructional approaches on the process of students' conceptual change. *Science Education, 92*(2), 320–344.

Johnson, D. W., & Johnson, R. T. (2003). Student motivation in co-operative groups. In R. M. Gillies & A. F. Ashman (Eds.), *Co-operative learning: The social and intellectual outcomes of learning in groups* (pp. 136-176). New York: Routledge Falmer.

Johnson, D. W., & Johnson, R. T. (2005). New developments in social interdependence theory. *Genetic, Social, and General Psychological Monographs, 131*(4), 285–358.

Kamins, M. L., & Dweck, C. S. (1999). Person versus process praise and criticism: Implications for contingent self-worth and coping. *Developmental Psychology, 35*, 835–847.

Karpicke, J. D., & Roediger, H. R. (2008). The critical importance of retrieval for learning. *Science, 319*, 966–968.

Kendeou, P., Bohn-Gettler, C., White, M. J., & van den Broek, P. (2008). Children's inference generation across different media. *Journal of Research in Reading, 31*(3), 259–272.

Klopfer, E. (July/August 2005). Playing to learn: state-of-the-art computer games go to school. *Access Learning.* Retrieved March 14, 2006, from http://www.ciconline.org/AboutCIC/Publications/Archives/HL_julaug05.htm

Kohn, A. (2006). *The homework myth: Why our kids get too much of a bad thing.* Cambridge, MA: Da Capo Press.

Kriz, W., & Eberle, T. (2004). *Bridging the gap: Transforming knowledge into action through gaming and simulation.* Proceedings of the 35th Conference of the International Simulation and Gaming Association (ISAGA). München, Germany.

Kulik, J. A., & Kulik, C. C. (1988). Timing of feedback and verbal learning. *Review of Educational Research, 58*, 79–97.

Lefrancois, G. R. (1997). *Psychology for teaching* (9th ed.). Belmont, CA: Wadsworth.

Li, R., & Liu, M. (2007). Understanding the effects of databases as cognitive tools in a problem-based multimedia learning environment. *Journal of Interactive Learning Research, 18*(3), 345–363.

Lobel, J. (2006). *Multiplayer computer gaming simulations facilitating cooperative learning.* Dublin, Ireland: IT in Education, Trinity College Dublin.

Lucas, G. (2005, November 17). [Podcast] George Lucas and the new world of learning. *Edutopia Radio Show.* Retrieved August 28, 2006, from http://www.edutopia.org/php/radio.php

Martorella, P. H. (1991). Knowledge and concept development in social studies. In J. P. Shaver (Ed.), *Handbook of research on social studies teaching and learning* (pp. 370–399). New York: McMillan.

Marzano, R. J. (1998). *A theory-based meta-analysis of research on instruction.* Aurora, CO: McREL. Retrieved February 7, 2006, from http://www.mcrel.org/instructionmetaanalysis

Marzano, R. J. & Pickering, D. J. (1997). *Dimensions of learning teacher's manual* (2nd ed.). Alexandria, VA: ASCD, and Denver, CO: McREL.

Marzano, R. J. & Pickering, D. J. (2007). Special topic: The case for and against homework. *Educational Leadership, 64*(6), p. 74–79.

Marzano, R. J., Pickering, D. J., & Pollock, J. E. (2001). *Classroom instruction that works: Research-based strategies for increasing student achievement.* Alexandria, VA: ASCD.

McDaniel, M. A., Roediger, H. L., III, & McDermott, K. B. (2007). Generalizing test-enhanced learning from the laboratory to the classroom. *Psychonomic Bulletin & Review, 14*(2), 200–206.

Medina, J. (2008). *Brain rules: 12 principles for surviving and thriving at work, home, and school.* Seattle, WA: Pear Press.

Minotti, J. L. (2005). Effects of learning-style-based homework prescriptions on the achievement and attitudes of middle school students. *NASSP Bulletin, 89,* 67–89.

Mize, C. D., & Gibbons, A. (2000). *More than inventory: Effective integration of instructional technology to support student learning in K-12 schools.* (ERIC Document Reproduction Service No. ED 444 563).

Moore-Partin, T. C., Robertson, R. E., Maggin, D. M., Oliver, R. M., & Wehby, J. H. (2010). Using teacher praise and opportunities to respond to appropriate student behavior. *Preventing School Failure, 54*(3), 172–178.

Morgan, R. L., Whorton, J. E., & Gunsalus, C. (2000). A comparison of short term and long term retention: Lecture combined with discussion versus cooperative learning. *Journal of Instructional Psychology, 27*(10), 53–58.

Newell, A., & Rosenbloom, P. S. (1981). Mechanisms of skill acquisition and the law of practice. In J. R. Anderson (Ed.), *Cognitive skills and their acquisition.* Hillsdale, NJ: Erlbaum.

Nielson, L., & Webb, W. (2011). *Teaching generation text: Using cell phones to enhance learning.* San Francisco: Jossey-Bass.

Page, M. S. (2002). Technology-enriched classrooms: Effects on students of low socioeconomic status. *Journal of Research on Technology in Education, 34*(4), 389–409.

Pashler, H., Rohrer, D., Cepeda, N. J., & Carpenter, S. K. (2007). Enhancing learning and retarding forgetting: Choices and consequences. *Psychonomic Bulletin and Review, 14*(2), 187–193.

Phan, H. P. (2009). Exploring students' reflective thinking practice, deep processing strategies, effort, and achievement goal orientations. *Educational Psychology, 29*(3), 297–313.

Pintrich, P. R., & Schunk, D. H. (2002). *Motivation in education: Theory, research and applications* (2nd ed.). Upper Saddle River, NJ: Merrill Prentice Hall.

Prensky, M. (2000). *Digital game-based learning.* New York: McGraw-Hill.

Reeves, T. (1998). *The impact of media and technology in schools.* Athens: University of Georgia. Research report for The Bertelsmann Foundation. Retrieved March 30, 2006, from http://www.athensacademy.org/instruct/media_tech/reeves0.html

Ringstaff, C., & Kelley, L. (2002). *The learning return on our education technology investment: A review of findings from research.* San Francisco: WestEd RTEC.

Rivet, A. E., & Krajcik, J. S. (2004). Achieving standards in urban systemic reform: An example of a sixth grade project-based science curriculum. *Journal of Research in Science Teaching, 41*(7), 669–692.

Rohrer, D., & Taylor, K. (2007). The shuffling of mathematics practice problems boosts learning. *Instructional Science, 35,* 481–498.

Rohrer, D., Taylor, K., & Sholar, B. (2010). Tests enhance the transfer of learning. *Journal of Experimental Psychology, 36*(1), 233–239.

Roseth, C. J., Johnson, D. W., & Johnson, R. T. (2008). Promoting early adolescents' achievement and peer relationships: The effects of cooperative, competitive, and individualistic goal structures. *Psychological Bulletin, 134*(2), 223–246.

Russell, J., & Sorge, D. (1999). Training facilitators to enhance technology integration. *Journal of Instruction Delivery Systems, 13*(4), 6.

Schacter, J. (1999). *The impact of education technology on student achievement: What the most current research has to say.* Santa Monica, CA: Milken Exchange on Education Technology.

Schacter, J., & Fagnano, C. (1999). Does computer technology improve student learning and achievement? How, when, and under what conditions? *Journal of Educational Computing Research, 20*(4), 329–343.

Schaffhauser, D. (2009, August). The vod couple. *T.H.E. Journal, 36*(7). Retrieved April 5, 2012, from http://thejournal.com/Articles/2009/08/09/Vodcasting.aspx?Page=1

Schroeder, C. M., Scott, T. P., Tolson, H., Huang, T.-Y., & Lee, Y.-H. (2007). A meta-analysis of national research: Effects of teaching strategies on student achievement in science in the United States. *Journal of Research in Science Teaching, 44*(10), 1436–1460.

Schunk, D. H. (2003). Self-efficacy for reading and writing: influence of modeling, goal setting, and self-evaluation. *Reading & Writing Quarterly, 19*, 159–172.

Siegle, D., & Foster, T. (2000, April). *Effects of laptop computers with multimedia and presentation software on student achievement.* Paper presented at the annual meeting of the American Education Research Association. New Orleans, Louisiana.

Simonson, B., Fairbanks, S., Briesch, A., Myers, D., & Sugai, G. (2008). Evidence-based practices in classroom management: Considerations for research to practice. *Education and Treatment of Children, 31*(3), 351–380.

So, W. M. W., & Kong, S. C. (2007). Approaches of inquiry learning with multimedia resources in primary classrooms. *Journal of Computers in Mathematics and Science Teaching, 28*(4), 329–354.

Squire, K. (2001). *Reframing the cultural space of computer and video games.* [Faculty working paper]. Retrieved March 14, 2006, from http://cms.mit.edu/games/education/research-vision.html

Surowiecki, J. (2004). *The wisdom of crowds: Why the many are smarter than the few and how collective wisdom shapes business, economies, societies, and nations.* New York: Doubleday.

Tarhan, L., & Acar, B. (2007). Problem-based learning in an eleventh grade chemistry class: "Factors affecting cell potential." *Research in Science and Technology Education, 25*(3), 351–369.

Urquhart, V., & McIver, M. (2005). *Teaching writing in the content areas.* Alexandria, VA: ASCD.

Vatterott, C. (2009). *Rethinking homework: Best practices that support diverse needs.* Alexandria, VA: ASCD.

Vogelstein, F. (2007, September). How Mark Zuckerberg turned Facebook into the world's hottest platform. *Wired.* Retrieved April 5, 2012, from http://www.wired.com/techbiz/startups/news/2007/09/ff_facebook

Vygotsky, L. S. (1978). *Mind in society: The development of higher psychological processes.* Cambridge, MA: Harvard University Press.

Waxman, H. C., Connell, M. L., & Gray, J. (2002). *A quantitative synthesis of recent research on the effects of teaching and learning with technology on student outcomes.* Naperville, IL: North Central Regional Educational Laboratory.

White, R. T., & Tisher, R. P. (1986). Research on natural sciences. In M. C. Wittrock (Ed.), *Handbook of research on teaching* (pp. 874–905). New York: McMillan.

Wong, H. K., & Wong, R. T. (1998). *How to be an effective teacher: The first days of school.* Mountain View, CA: Harry K. Wong Publications, Inc.

Woolfolk, A. (2004). *Educational psychology.* Boston: Pearson.

World at Work. (2009). Telework trendlines 2009. Available from http://www.worldatwork.org/waw/adimLink?id=31115

# Index

The letter *f* following a page number denotes a figure. Instructional Strategies are capitalized.

# About the Authors

**Howard Pitler** is a senior director at McREL. He conducts workshops and trainings for K–12 teachers and administrators on research-based instructional strategies, technology, and pedagogy; conducts technology audits for districts; and works with school and district leaders using Power Walkthrough classroom observation software. He holds an Ed.D. in Educational Administration from Wichita State University, an M.A. in Music Performance from Wichita State, and a B.A. in Music Education from Indiana State University. Howard is an Apple Distinguished Educator, a Smithsonian Laureate, and was a National Distinguished Principal. He has been published in several journals and is co-author of *Classroom Instruction That Works, 2nd Edition; Handbook for Classroom Instruction That Works, 2nd Edition;* and *Using Technology with Classroom Instruction That Works.*

**Elizabeth Ross Hubbell** is an educational technology consultant at McREL. She conducts workshops and training for K–12 teachers on research-based instructional strategies and technology integration, writes curriculum models for online classes, conducts technology audits for districts, and trains school and district leaders in using Power Walkthrough software. Prior to McREL,

Elizabeth served as a building-level curriculum director and elementary teacher, where she focused on combining 21st century learning environments with Montessori philosophies. She holds an M.A. in Information and Learning Technologies from the University of Colorado–Denver and a B.S. in Early Childhood/Elementary Education from the University of Georgia. Elizabeth was one of four national finalists in Technology & Learning's Ed Tech Leader of the Year 2003. She has been published in several journals, including *Principal, Montessori Life,* and *Learning & Leading with Technology* and is co-author of *Using Technology with Classroom Instruction That Works; The Future of Schooling: Educating America in 2020;* and *Classroom Instruction That Works, 2nd Edition.* Elizabeth has presented at a variety of national conferences, including ASCD, ISTE, and NSBA's T+L conference.

Matt Kuhn is a principal consultant in curriculum and instructional technology with McREL and a Google Certified Teacher. He conducts teacher professional development nationally in instructional technology, technology leadership, mathematics, and science. He has been published in several journals, including *Principal* and *Learning & Leading with Technology,* and is also a coauthor of *What We Know About Mathematics Teaching and Learning, 3rd Ed.* He has worked in U.S. national laboratory technology outreach and was a science and mathematics teacher in grades 6–12. He is also a former K–8 school principal. He has a B.S. in Aircraft Engineering, an M.A. in Science Education, and a Ph.D. in Educational Technology Administration from the University of Denver.

## ⏻ About McREL

Mid-continent Research for Education and Learning (McREL) is a nationally recognized, nonprofit education research and development organization, headquartered in Denver, Colorado, with offices in Honolulu, Hawai'i, and Omaha, Nebraska. Since 1966, McREL has helped translate research and professional wisdom about what works in education into practical guidance for educators. Our 120-plus staff members and affiliates include respected researchers, experienced consultants, and published writers who provide educators with research-based guidance, consultation, and professional development for improving student outcomes.

## Related ASCD Resources: Educational Technology

At the time of publication, the following ASCD resources were available (ASCD stock numbers appear in parentheses). For up-to-date information about ASCD resources, go to www.ascd.org. You can search the complete archives of *Educational Leadership* at http://www.ascd.org/el.

### ASCD EDge Group

Exchange ideas and connect with other educators interested in educational technology on the social networking site ASCD EDge™ at http://ascdedge.ascd.org/

### Print Products

*Brain-Based Teaching in the Digital Age* Marilee Sprenger (#110018)

*Curriculum 21: Essential Education for a Changing World* Heidi Hayes Jacobs (Ed.) (#109008)

*Teaching in the Information Age: Making Why and How We Teach Relevant to Students* Thomas R. Rosebrough and Ralph G. Leverett (#110078)

*Teaching 21st Century Skills* Sue Beers (ASCD Action Tool; #111021)

*Technology Fix: The Promise and Reality of Computers in Our Schools* William D. Pflaum (#104002)

**THE WHOLE CHILD** The Whole Child Initiative helps schools and communities create learning environments that allow students to be healthy, safe, engaged, supported, and challenged. To learn more about other books and resources that relate to the whole child, visit www.wholechildeducation.org.

For more information: send e-mail to member@ascd.org; call 1-800-933-2723 or 703-578-9600, press 2; send a fax to 703-575-5400; or write to Information Services, ASCD, 1703 N. Beauregard St., Alexandria, VA 22311-1714 USA.